I Blame
Dennis Hopper

I Blame
Dennis Hopper

AND OTHER STORIES FROM A LIFE
LIVED IN AND OUT OF THE MOVIES

Illeana Douglas

FLATIRON
BOOKS
NEW YORK

AUTHOR'S NOTE: The details of certain situations and locations have been changed, as have the names of some individuals, to protect their privacy. All photos in this book except those listed below with specific credit lines are courtesy of the author's personal collection. Any failure to credit the appropriate photographer is unintentional.

Photograph, page 129: Illeana Douglas with Robert De Niro © Phillip V. Caruso

Photographic insert: Illeana Douglas with Liza Minnelli: 2012 TCM Classic Film Festival Opening Night © Getty Images, Jordan Strauss; Illeana Douglas on the set of Search and Destroy © NBCUniversal; Illeana Douglas on the set of Picture Perfect © 20th Century Fox

www.flatironbooks.com

Designed by Steven Seighman

Library of Congress Cataloging-in-Publication Data

Douglas, Illeana.
    I blame Dennis Hopper : and other stories from a life lived in and out of the movies / Illeana Douglas.—First edition.
        pages cm
    ISBN 978-1-250-05291-9 (hardback)
    ISBN 978-1-250-05387-9 (e-book)
    1. Douglas, Illeana, 1965– 2. Douglas, Illeana, 1965—Anecdotes. 3. Actresses—United States—Biography. 4. Actresses—United States—Anecdotes. I. Title.
    PN2287.D5245A6 2015
    792.02'8092—dc23
    [B]
            2015022208

Our books may be purchased for promotional, educational, or business use. Please contact your local bookseller or the Macmillan Corporate and Premium Sales Department at 1-800-221-7945, extension 5442, or by e-mail at MacmillanSpecial Markets@macmillan.com.

First Edition: November 2015

10 9 8 7 6 5 4 3 2 1

For my mom—the most cinematic woman I know.

To my four grandparents. My grandfather Melvyn Douglas told me, "When you find someone you can learn from, hold on to them."

Contents

Prologue

Mike Nichols had just screened his masterpiece, *The Graduate*, in New York. Afterward, I was standing in line next to Glenn Gordon Caron, who had directed me in *Picture Perfect*, waiting to meet Mr. Nichols. I was holding one of his legendary comedy albums he had recorded with Elaine May, hoping to get him to sign it. Glenn whispered to me, "Only you could get away with that." I held out my album to Mr. Nichols, and he pointed at me and said, "You . . . you know what I like about you? You manage to be both *in* the movie and *outside it*, commenting to us in the audience." Then he signed my album: "With admiration, Mike Nichols."

Among the pantheon of movie gods I have traveled in, Mike Nichols was Zeus. I was getting the nod from Zeus. Mike Nichols was not just insightfully describing my on-screen persona. He was also describing my life, which has often played like a movie with me both *in* the movie and *outside it*, commenting to the audience, "Well, I remember how it began, but I have no idea how it's going to end." I pass this on not to impress you about me but to impress you about Mike Nichols. His words, and the advice he was about to give, had a profound influence on me.

He asked me, "Have you ever read De Tocqueville?" It sounded like a name that had come off the Nichols and May album I was holding, *Improvisations to Music*.

I shook my head and said no, I had not read De Tocqueville. I had never even heard of De Tocqueville.

"You should read it," he said thoughtfully. He sounded like a doctor prescribing a vital prescription. "In fact . . . " And he started to rattle off other books I should read.

I quickly grabbed the pen he had used to sign my record and wrote down the books he suggested. Anything by Alexis de Tocqueville, especially *Democracy in America*.

Vladimir Nabokov: *Speak, Memory*. Augusten Burroughs: *Running With Scissors* and *Dry*.

"Thank you," I said, not really sure what I was thanking him for but absolutely sure that I would be running to a bookstore the next day. You certainly don't disappoint the gods when they show you favor.

"Let me know what you think," he said. "Write me after you've read them."

"I will," I said, still unsure of why he had taken the time with me.

I had come there hoping just to meet Mike Nichols, to get his autograph. I was a fan of *his*. A picture of him directing *Catch-22*, along with those of other movie gods, had graced my bedroom wall when I was a kid. I was *his* admirer and champion. His quotes were pinned up on my office walls, including "The only safe thing is to take a chance. Play safe and you are dead."

And yet this god also seemed to be *my* admirer and champion. Why? What did he see in me that I could not yet see in myself? I never once told him that I had aspirations to write. I read the books he suggested, and he was astute—if not downright psychic—in having suggested them. Those books led me in the direction of this book, so thank you, Mike Nichols—thank you for giving me a through line to my life. In the pages that follow, I am both the narrator telling you about my experiences *in* the movies but also outside them; I'm a delighted fan sitting next to you on the couch exclaiming, "Aren't these people fascinating? Aren't movies the best?"

A word of warning. This is not a memoir with a wonderfully linear beginning, middle, and end. Sadly, it's not a tell-all, unless you consider being alone in a hotel room with Ethan Hawke and watching Paul Mazursky's movie *Blume in Love* a tell-all. It's also not a book about my career, which I hope explains the omissions of some of the films and television shows I've been in. That may sound surprisingly humble for an actor—don't worry, I make large, large costarring appearances—but I am always more comfortable talking about the actors and directors I have worked with and how their work has changed me.

Oh, this *is* a book about movies. How movies tell a story. In this case, mine. It's called *I Blame Dennis Hopper* because I think you will see from the first chapter that sometimes a movie or an actor can change your destiny. I believe that all of us have been changed by the experience of movies. Think of the first movie you saw. What effect did it have on you? Who took you to see it? These questions, and the answers you give, connect us in a vital and emotional way. You may not know some of the people I write about—such as Roddy McDowall and Rudy Vallée—yet their contributions are part of film history. These days, to look back at a classic movie is somehow considered to be old-fashioned. More and more we are asked to look forward without a glance back at the films and film stars that got us here.

The actor Rod Taylor recently died. He starred in such iconic films as Hitchcock's *The Birds* and George Pal's *The Time Machine*. I had an intense crush on Rod Taylor when I was a kid, and I thought I was the only one who was devastated when he died. But when I mentioned his passing to a friend, she said, "Well, a piece of my childhood just died." She was sobbing. "*Time Machine*," she cried, "and it wasn't even that good!"

"But it was good," I said. "It was good because you remembered it."

That's how movies change us: in ways we cannot even remember. Those images of movies stay in our brain; those fragments become shards in our memories. So when these gods die, it's as if a piece of our childhood dies with them. That's why it's important to be a living historian. To pass on stories of why these movies and movie gods matter. It's all a part of our collective memory, and we all have to take part in upholding it.

"Illeana, your life is like a movie." I hear that all the time—so much so that I finally accepted it. My life *is* like a movie! But so is yours. The greatest compliment I can give myself or anyone reading this is to say, You are the star of your own movie. You are surrounded by an amazing set of characters with a story that only you can tell. Now, you may not think it's the healthiest thing in the world to live your life as if it were a movie, but somehow it has worked for me, with Dennis Hopper and many other movie gods to blame for every glorious moment.

CHAPTER ONE

I Blame Dennis Hopper

We were poor, but we were unhappy.

I n 1969, my parents, like many others of their generation, saw
the counterculture movie *Easy Rider*. It's a road movie about
two alienated and rootless hippie bikers (Dennis Hopper and Peter
Fonda) traveling on their choppers through a broken America.
It depicted the rise of the hippie culture, celebrated drug use and
free love, and condemned the establishment. The tagline of the

film was "A man went looking for America. And couldn't find it anywhere," which is apparently how people felt in 1969 because it was the third-highest-grossing film of the year. *Easy Rider* was written by Dennis Hopper, Peter Fonda, and Terry Southern and was directed by Dennis Hopper. It became a cultural phenomenon, and many people who saw the film so identified with it that they sought to emulate the values of its two main characters, Captain America (Peter Fonda) and Billy (Dennis Hopper).

Little did I know that my life was about to change forever because of a movie, but that is exactly what happened.

My father seemed convinced that when Dennis Hopper's character said "This is what it's all about, man!" he was speaking directly to my father and telling *him* to change his life. Years later I met Dennis Hopper. I told him this story, basically blaming him for everything that had ever happened to me, and he grinned sheepishly and said, "Sorry."

You see, after my father saw Dennis Hopper in *Easy Rider*, he started, well, acting like Dennis Hopper in *Easy Rider*. He started to see "signs" as he drove home to suburbia in the endless rush hour traffic from a nine-to-five job. He heard the song "Nowhere Man" on the radio and said to my mother, "That's me, man! I'm a Nowhere Man!" He started saying "He knows what it's all about, man," meaning Dennis Hopper. And spouting such Dennis Hopper–esque philosophy as "I go to work every day, and you know what it means, man? It's just more garbage cans, man! I mean we started out with one garbage can and then we had two garbage cans, and now we're up to three garbage cans, man!" One day he grabbed my brother's orange plastic Hot Wheels set and shouted, "We don't promote plastic in this house. Not anymore!"

I blame Dennis Hopper for not having any cool toys growing up.

I didn't know we were rich until we became poor, but we became poor because of Dennis Hopper. At one point in *Easy Rider*, the two bikers visit a commune. My father decided to start a commune.

"This is what it's all about, man!" he said to my mom the day he left his job. He came up the driveway beeping the horn on the Buick convertible, which was usually his sign for "Kids, I've got some good news! We're going to live off the land! Have a garden, and animals! Support ourselves!" My mother looked worried. We had just moved into a large Colonial house in a wealthy community in Connecticut. My parents were achieving what my mother had always dreamed of: an upper-middle-class life in the country with estates on both sides of us. That life, which for many is the American Dream, came to an end because of Dennis Hopper and *Easy Rider*.

My father grew a mustache. Just like Dennis Hopper's. He bought a gigantic poster of Dennis Hopper and Peter Fonda riding their choppers and hung it in the middle of the living room. My father stared at the poster, that iconic image of two rebels, and I stared at my father. His mustache had filled in, and his sideburns and hair had grown longer. It was the first time I began to see a resemblance between my father and Dennis Hopper.

I blame Dennis Hopper for my never liking men with mustaches. Nope. Don't trust 'em.

The theme song to Easy Rider was "Born to Be Wild," by Steppenwolf. My father started playing the album incessantly. I don't remember any other songs on it. Were there any other songs on that album? For that matter, did Steppenwolf even have any other songs, ever? Some nights while my mother was trying to make dinner there would be fifty hippies in the other room, all looking like Dennis Hopper, alternately singing "Born to Be Wild" and shouting, "This is what it's all about, man!" When they got tired of singing and shouting they'd come in the kitchen and ask my mom, "Hey, is there any more spaghetti, man?"

I blame Dennis Hopper for making me hate the song "Born to be Wild" and for our always being out of pasta.

At first it was a challenge for my father even to find a hippie. You have to remember that in 1969 there was neither the Internet nor a hippie handbook to guide people led astray by Dennis Hopper. Eventually my father found one. His name was Tom. Tom the Hippie, I guess. I don't know if he had a last name. Tom was the first hippie I ever saw, and I was impressed—and what I mean by *impressed* is I was terrified of him. Tom had long hair, a mustache, aviator sunglasses, and a leather fringe jacket. He reeked of booze and smoke, rode a large chopper, and ended every sentence with *man*. Does that sound like Dennis Hopper to you? Well it should, because my father found a hippie who looked and acted exactly like Dennis Hopper in *Easy Rider*! To his credit, Tom the Hippie was an excellent hippie.

Now that my father had a friend—I'm not going to say that he had *his* Peter Fonda, because Tom the Hippie and my father were both Dennis Hopper—they started going to demonstrations and protests. Tom seemed to know the day and time of every peace rally in the area, and since neither of them worked, they went to a lot of them. They went to so many peace rallies and staged so many demonstrations that for a time I thought that that was my father's job. They took me with them once on one of their protests. I'm not sure what my father and Tom the Hippie were demonstrating when they went into a White Tower hamburger joint and started to chant "We're white, and we're in a tower. We're white, and we're in a tower." My father seemed to think this "message to the man" had great significance, but to me it signified only that we were called "dirty hippies" and asked to leave immediately and never come back.

I blame Dennis Hopper for my being afraid ever to set foot in a White Tower restaurant.

My mother seemed pretty accepting of Tom. I remember her admonishing him only once. She was in the kitchen cooking spaghetti, and Tom had dropped acid—something Dennis Hopper does a lot of in *Easy Rider*—and soon started tripping. He wandered into the kitchen and kept repeating to my mom, over and over again: "It's so beautiful, man; it's just so beautiful, man; so beautiful, man . . ."

Anyway, after about fifteen minutes of his twirling around the kitchen and saying everything was beautiful, my mother said rather sternly, "I don't need to take drugs to see it's beautiful, Tom. It's nature."

He was quiet for a time, taking that in, and then he started in again: "Yeah, nature, man. Nature is beautiful, man. Beautiful nature, man . . ."

Eventually Tom became less scary to me. I realized he wasn't going anywhere, so he became a kind of Crazy Uncle Tom the Hippie. He bought this old Dodge paneled van that didn't have any seats in the back, so he cut tree stumps to use as makeshift seats for us. My brother and I were sitting on our stumps, and Tom was driving along, smoking pot, with his Neil Young blasting, and as we rounded a corner, the stumps all tipped over and rolled to the back. The doors flew open, and my brother and I went rolling out of the van. The music was so loud that Tom drove another few hundred feet before he even noticed. I learned to balance on my stump, because riding with Tom was how I first learned about music. We would play Neil Young or the Beatles. Pretty soon a new hippie girlfriend named Annette came along for our rides.

Tom the Hippie had that same Dennis Hopper charm with the ladies. He had a string of girlfriends after Annette and even had an affair with a married housewife. This was definitely an opposites-attract kind of romance. She was wealthy and had hired Tom to do some construction on her house, to good and bad results, since he smoked pot every day before going to work. He often asked me to guard it for him, forgetting he had stashed it under her kitchen sink. The only time Tom got mad at me was when I flushed his precious "herb" down the toilet as a joke. I thought it was the kind of herbs my mom used in her cooking, and couldn't understand why Tom was so furious.

Meanwhile, my father started constructing something of his own. It was his very own commune, just a short walk from our own house at the bottom of the hill. He called it The Studio.

I blame Dennis Hopper for The Studio.

My father built it with his own two Dennis Hopper–strong hands. We didn't live in the commune, only my father did, but we could visit it or watch its progress or gradual demise any time we wanted. From the top of the hill you could look down at the pond and The Studio and see the large American flag hanging down the front.

The Studio itself was an impressive two stories, sitting atop an old barn foundation that had burned to the ground years ago.

The sleeping quarters were upstairs, accessed by ladder. The main floor featured a wood stove. The indoor plumbing amounted to a well pump with a handle that cranked water from the nearby pond. If you were inclined to bathe, there was an old claw-foot tub outside. You just had to carry about a hundred buckets of water from the pond to fill it. The roof was corrugated plastic, and plywood was slapped onto the front. When the chicken coop went up, my father threw a party to celebrate and invited all the neighbors. My mother described it as if it were fun. "We drank champagne and danced inside the chicken coop!" It was the last time we ever saw a bottle of champagne in our house.

I remember that the first goat that arrived was named Samson. He came from a petting zoo and had been given away because he was unable to mate. And no wonder: Whenever you went near him he would butt you within an inch of your life. We learned to stay away from him. My mother loved Samson and used to say that he was "just troubled or misunderstood." Like everything else, it all seemed out of my control, so I learned to play along as though our lives had become this fun, circuslike movie with "Dennis Hopper" now at its center.

Such as the time I came home with my mom from grocery shopping to find that a "happening" was happening in the middle of our living room. There were hippies holding hands and singing "This Land Is Your Land." My mom made her way through the throng to the kitchen to unpack the food, pretending that the happening wasn't happening.

My father got some help at The Studio from local college students. They built a garden, although I'm not sure they were supposed to be studying the pot plants that soon sprang up in the front yard. It seemed as if those students never left. The Studio was soon filled with college kids smoking pot; goats; nicer goats; and chickens laying eggs in their coops. Hippies spent the days making pottery. It was idyllic. They were going to change the world with those clay bowls, right?

And let me tell you, those hippies were like rabbits. They kept multiplying. Tom the Hippie had brought Annette, who brought Jane, who brought Michael, who brought Sasha. Every third person seemed to be called Sasha, whether a boy or a girl. Naturally, there was a lot of free love. But here's the thing about free love: It's expensive! As The Studio grew, so did the speed with which we slipped from being rich and privileged and comfortable to being poor and on food stamps. For my parents, this was a life choice. But I was becoming aware that *my* life choice was to still be rich and privileged.

My mom baked me a beautiful little girl's birthday cake covered with sunflowers. She made the mistake of bringing it down to The Studio, thinking that we could share the celebration with the hippies. Before I could even blow out the candles, a hippie on a motorcycle grabbed a handful of cake. Suddenly, all the hippies were grabbing cake, stuffing a child's birthday cake into their mouths, not even aware of their actions. More and more after that it seemed that my mom stayed up at the house.

I remember the day my mother first said we were poor. We were standing on the hill above The Studio. My mother was literally and metaphorically looking down at my father, who was frolicking with all the hippie girls. They all had these cool ponchos, and I really wanted a poncho of my own, but my mom said, "We can't afford it. We're poor now."

It was the first time I had ever heard her use that expression, and it didn't sound good.

"What?" I said. "I don't understand."

"We're poor now. We're poor." She repeated it over and over again, as if it were a news bulletin, and then she pulled her coat around her and slowly walked back to the house. I ran and found my older brother. He was busy watching the hippie girls who had started to undress to go skinny-dipping in the pond. Their ponchos and jeans hung on the branches of a nearby tree as if it were a dirty hippie Christmas tree.

I said, "Mom says we're poor!"

My brother looked up from the naked girls swimming and said, "No shit, Sherlock." As the child of Dennis Hopper, I was expected simply to accept our new hippie lifestyle with delight. Didn't I get to wear headbands and celebrate Earth Day? Roll little joints with my little fingers—separating the seeds in the lid of a shoebox to the delight of all the other hippies? My brother went back to watching the naked girls swimming. Their laughter echoed up the hill as I saw them splash around in the pond. I walked back to the house, and in my own act of rebellion, I poked holes in my father's *Easy Rider* poster. Right through Dennis Hopper's eyes.

Back when we were rich and socially accepted my mother had belonged to the garden club. Once a month all the ladies would meet at our house. They drank tea, ate little cakes, and talked about floral arrangements. When they saw my mother's new hippie lifestyle, they looked down their noses at it, so she quit their club. "They were a bunch of snobs anyway," she said at the time, but years later she confessed that she quit because she was embarrassed to have people see how we were living. We were living with Dennis Hopper and his merry band of hippies from *Easy Rider*! Who wouldn't have been embarrassed?

Here's how much damage one movie can cause: One day my father unscrewed every chandelier in the house and sold each of them at auction. He needed money to support The Studio. It was the early '70s, and he was living there permanently now.

My mother said, "I look up at the ceiling where my lights used to be and all I see are wires." The rain dripped through the wires into a bucket she had put on the dining room table.

Just as *Easy Rider* changed my father, our new economic circumstances changed my mother. She became an Italian Catholic drill sergeant. She took to standing outside the bathroom door while I took a bath or shower. "Time!" she'd yell if I'd run the water too long. I'd barely fill the tub before I'd hear, "That's too long! We can't afford hot water. We're poor now!" That became my mother's favorite expression. The thermostat stayed at 58, and we wore sweaters and hats to bed; in a letter I sent to my grandmother, I actually asked for a sleeping bag. My mother instructed me to save tin foil as if we were in World War II, carefully folding it out and putting it back in the drawer until it had been used so many times that it disintegrated in your hands. I wanted to try out for my school band, but a clarinet was "too expensive," so my mother got me a plastic recorder instead. *You* try learning "Eleanor Rigby" on a plastic recorder. You feel poor!

She traded our beloved Buick convertible for a used Volkswagen bug. The Buick—the last vestige of our old middle-class life—was gone. It was official: We were hippies. Poor, grimy, Volkswagen-bug hippies! One time I had a party to go to, and the VW—aka the poormobile—couldn't make it up the snowy hill, so I had to skip the party.

I blame Dennis Hopper for making me miss that party.

My mother started taking classes at night and got a teaching job to support us. I used to watch her drive down the driveway in the morning on the way to school, gray smoke billowing out of the poormobile. We got a tip from one of the hippies about free bread, so on Wednesdays we would drive to the Stop & Shop to get the day-old bread that was given away in a large brown bag. Sometimes there were doughnuts. I hid in the car when she got them, but they tasted pretty good back home. I think I became a vegetarian only because I didn't see very much meat as a child: "It's too expensive. We can't afford it! We're poor now! Have a doughnut!" What's funny is that my mother got food stamps, but her food choices always got her into trouble. My mother didn't understand why chicken wasn't on the government-approved list but Hamburger Helper was. She'd say, "I can buy Hamburger Helper, but I can't buy a fresh chicken? I can buy fish sticks but I can't buy a piece of fish?" Food stamps were for poor people. I'm sure they were happy with whatever they got, but it seemed to me that we had *chosen* to be poor. It was a difficult concept to understand, let alone explain to a beleaguered, underpaid sixteen-year-old cashier.

My mom could make four sandwiches out of a tiny can of Underwood Chicken Spread or tuna, stretching it with what seemed like a lot of celery. One day she was making me lunch, and instead of asking me if I wanted a peanut-butter-*and*-jelly sandwich for school she called up the stairs, "Peanut butter *or* jelly?"

My mother seemed to enjoy being poor. Maybe it finally gave her an identity. It was hard to compete with being married to Dennis Hopper, who was busy writing poetry and songs and assembling his band.

I blame Dennis Hopper for the band.

Of course there was a band! My father started a band called 40 Acres and a Mule. It consisted of two longhair guitarists and a longhair lead singer named Marvin. I remember that they played a lot of Stones covers, which made sense, because they were mostly stoned. They got some songs under their belt and somehow managed to get a few more bookings, so my father bought an old ambulance to drive the band and all their instruments from one gig to another. He and Tom the Hippie and the others painted it yellow, then covered it with flower decals and painted a giant American flag on the driver's side.

One day Tom abruptly decided to move on. By that time, hippies were coming and going at The Studio, but I had grown attached to Tom, as he had been a constant in my life, a father figure in a series of father figures who all looked like Dennis Hopper. And now he was leaving us. He was on his chopper wearing his dirty fringe jacket the last time I saw him. I still remember his toothy, mustached grin as he lighted up his last joint. Then he kick-started his chopper and rode down the driveway. We never saw him again. I am sorry to say that not long afterward, we heard that Tom the Hippie had died of a drug overdose. My father said that Tom had been a Vietnam vet and that he was probably suffering from shell shock. I don't blame Dennis Hopper for that, but I wish I could, because I'd do anything for one more crazy ride in the van with Tom the Hippie.

I want to mention that the goats had a great life at The Studio. My father had an old Comet, and he took the backseat out and replaced it with plywood so he could take the goats for rides around town. There was no real destination, but he was convinced that the goats didn't want to be penned in all the time. The goats did look pretty happy hanging their heads out the window, catching the wind just like dogs. It was quite a sight, and it started to draw attention around town.

One day while I was waiting for the school bus, this very sweet girl named Maggie Cooper asked me, "Isn't your dad the guy that drives around town with goats in his car?" I pointed over Maggie's shoulder and said, "Oh look, there's the bus! We don't want to be late for school!" I got onto the bus, and the bus driver gave me a dirty look, muttering under his breath that I lived in a nudist colony with hippies who were all smoking marijuana.

Damn you, Dennis Hopper!

At night, bundled in my new sleeping bag, sweaters, mittens, and a knit cap, I would curse you, Dennis Hopper! You took my father away from me. Instead of poring over brochures together and deciding which Ivy League school to go to, I spent evenings at a local bar watching 40 Acres and a Mule struggle through "You Can't Always Get What You Want." An element of danger crept into our lives when one of the hippies who claimed to be a member of Hells Angels moved in with us. Yes, I had dodged the rut of an upper-middle-class childhood for the sheer excitement of a childhood filled with goats, guns, and rock and roll! But eventually, my *Easy Rider* childhood came to an end. My father, like Tom the Hippie, decided to move on. He didn't leave on a chopper, though. He left in a Volkswagen. Not my mom's black one. This one was blue. He was driving it with his new girlfriend next to him and her two kids in the backseat. He left my mother a note asking her to take care of the goats.

I blame Dennis Hopper for making me hate Volkswagens.

The movie was over, and yet its effects continued. My mom was now a single mother on a teacher's salary. When I entered high school, I had little ambition. Going to college was out of the question. I knew that "We are poor and we can't afford it . . . " would be my mother's answer, so I thought about my options.

Well. There's a lot of drama associated with being poor. I could be dramatic! Also, *starving* and *actress* go very well in the same sentence. I decided I wanted to move to New York to become a poor starving dramatic actress! I got into acting school, and I found a cheap one-bedroom apartment. There were four other girls already living in it, but I moved in anyway. I couldn't afford to buy a bed so I slept on coats on the floor. It was freezing, of course, but I was used to wearing sweaters and mittens and hats at night, and that made me less homesick.

You never forget your first horrible cheap one-bedroom apartment—or your second or your third. But my first was in Brooklyn. Luckily, acting school kept me from spending a lot of time there. We didn't have any furniture, so a couple of us found a huge round cable holder down the street, then rolled it to our building, carried it up two flights of stairs, and moved it into the kitchen as a makeshift table. After a few days we realized that it must have been drenched in toxic chemicals, but we kept it because we couldn't figure out how to roll it back down the stairs. I was never sure if four girls were living there or six, because we all seemed to be on rotating schedules. You would know if someone new had moved in only if you saw a new bottle of shampoo in the bathroom. Just one girl had a job. She worked for a sheet company and contributed sheets to my coats on the floor. For that I will be forever grateful.

We couldn't afford to turn on the gas, so we cooked things in a coffee percolator: boiled eggs, hot dogs. Long, tall food worked best. Times were lean and I did some things I'm not proud of. The "sex for food" program was probably one of those things. "Sure, I'll go out with you. Is there food involved? There is? I find you very attractive all of a sudden. How do you feel about sleeping on coats?" I'm pretty sure I lived on popcorn for an entire year. I remember that we once ran out of toilet paper and that one of the girls brought home this industrial-size roll that she had stolen from the Actors' Equity lounge. It was like a gigantic wheel of Gouda cheese, only it was toilet paper! I repeatedly dropped it on my toe, and it became a great motivator to get a job. At Christmas I got myself a job at Saks Fifth Avenue department store. A store where I could not afford to shop. All I was supposed to do was hold and display an Estée Lauder Blockbuster makeup kit. Sounds easy enough, unless you're weak from hunger.

It was the twelfth day of Christmas, or something like, that I'm holding my Blockbuster, and it's a blockbuster, all right. It held fifty shades of eye shadow, multiple shades of coral lipsticks, powders, and blushes. This was the '80s. So they were playing the Philip Glass version of "Hark How the Bells." I hadn't had any breakfast—I'm still poor, remember—and I started to get very dizzy. I'm wobbling with my Blockbuster, and listening to the Philip Glass and people were coming toward me and moving away and coming toward me and moving away. In my mind they seemed like colorful fish . . . that I could eat. All while this monotonous Philip Glass version of "Hark How the Bells" is pumping out: Dum-da-da-dum-Dum-da-da-dum. Dum-da-da-Dum!

My break was coming up, and I only had a dollar, and I was debating whether I should spend 50 cents on a cup of coffee, which would curb my appetite, or get a hot chocolate for 75 cents, which would be as rich as a whole meal. I could skip lunch and have an apple for dinner or maybe an orange—these are the things you debate when you're poor. The electronic Christmas music was hypnotizing, and I started to daydream—and all of a sudden I heard this clatter as my Estée Lauder Blockbuster and I hit the ground. I had fainted from hunger on the floor of Saks Fifth Avenue. Just an hour before I had sprayed Kitty Carlisle Hart with perfume, making her laugh when I said, "Come on down, the Lauder's fine." Now I was lying on the ground watching coral lipsticks roll by me. I prayed that Kitty Carlisle Hart had seen me faint. She would rush to my side and say, "Why, this girl looks like she's hungry! When was the last time you had a decent meal? I was an actress once myself, my dear. Tell me everything!" Her butler would magically produce a thermos of hot chocolate, and as I drank, I would explain that although noble of birth, I now found myself in this situation of poverty. Kitty would invite me to live with her in her Park Avenue apartment. There I would live the rich and privileged life I was supposed to have lived. Over tea and biscuits we'd laugh about my poor hippie childhood and how Dennis Hopper had ruined everything. Instead, when I opened my eyes, I only saw my supervisor, Vicky, standing over me hissing, "What's the matter with you? Are you on drugs? Get up! You're going to the basement!"

I blame Dennis Hopper for what happened next.

Before Vicky fired me she sent me to the basement to wrap like a hundred Blockbusters for rich Estée Lauder customers like Barbara Walters. Bitter, still light-headed, and knowing that my time at Saks was about to abruptly end, I thought it would be funny to scrawl MERRY CHRISTMAS FROM A SAKS SATAN WORSHIPPER! inside all the pre-addressed cards. I want to apologize to anyone who got one. Mystery solved, Barbara Walters: It was I. All around me, poor employees who, like me, couldn't afford to shop at Saks Fifth Avenue were stealing items to give to their girlfriends or boyfriends as Christmas presents. Yes, it was pretty magical. I took a fifty-dollar Chloé perfume set. I didn't care that it was stolen. It made me feel special. I vowed to myself that one day I wouldn't have to steal expensive things to feel special. One day, when I was a rich and famous actress, people would give them to me in the form of gift baskets.

Oh! Here's the thing. Here's the thing I really blame Dennis Hopper for:

Even when I started making money, even when I had made it, I still felt poor. Like a poor, dirty, Dennis Hopper hippie. Right before *Cape Fear* came out, I was at my first big movie premiere in L.A., and at the after-party I stood at the buffet just stuffing my face with free food. The director of the film came up to me and asked, "Have you ever met James Woods?"

And I answered, "Free food! Did you see? There's free food!"

And he said, "I want you to tell Jimmy Woods that story you told me about Dennis Hopper. He'll love it. Let's go over before he leaves."

Now, I was very, very impressed with James Woods. One, because I loved his acting, and two, because he had once smiled and said hello to me at Hugo's on Santa Monica Boulevard. But I was starving, and there was free food.

I was faced with a dilemma: I had slathered a huge amount of goat cheese on a cracker and I didn't want to waste it, but I also wanted to meet James Woods. So I thought, OK, I'll go over to James Woods, I'll tell James Woods the Dennis Hopper story, and then I'll eat my cheese and cracker. Great plan. So the director, my cracker, and I walk over to James Woods, who is with a lovely young actress. The director sets me up; I tell James Woods the story. Everybody laughs. I'm a hit, and now I can eat my free food.

Right when James Woods starts in with a funny story of his

own I notice something is amiss. The goat cheese is missing from my cracker. I look around and see that my precious goat cheese has landed on James Woods's really expensive suede loafers. Landed, as a New Yorker would say, in a perfect schmear!

James Woods gets to the end of his story and everyone is laughing, and his lovely girlfriend is laughing, and he sees that I'm not laughing. In fact, he notices that not only am I not laughing but that I looked puzzled. I was puzzled, all right, because I was thinking, Why the hell did I have to take that cheese and cracker over to James Woods and how the hell am I going to get out of this? But James Woods thinks I'm puzzled because I don't understand his story. So he says, "Don't you get it?" and starts to tell me the *entire story* again. He gets to the punch line–which, for the record, was "Yes, officer, that man *is* in no condition to drive." And I start fake-laughing as if to say, "Oh, now I get it. Too drunk to drive . . . Ha-ha." And I just throw the cracker over my shoulder to get rid of it. James Woods is savoring the fact that I finally understand his joke, and he's looking around the room, and he's looking at his lovely girlfriend, and then he looks down at his shoe, and sees this huge schmear of goat cheese on his very expensive suede loafers and says, very James Woods–like, "Where the fuck did that come from?"

I shrug, like, Wow, weird, and cycle through a set of bad-acting facial expressions, and I can see James Woods beginning to think, reconstructing in his mind what could have caused this. I mean, this guy is smart. He went to MIT! He was re-creating the series of events that had led to the landing of goat cheese on his shoe. All the spindles of the lock in James Woods's enormous brain click into place, and he starts slowly turning his head toward me. The music is building in my brain. It was like a climax of a

Brian De Palma movie sequence. But before he can accuse me, I cut him off at the pass and decide to make a joke.

I said, "Maybe it came from the book depository!"

Everyone just stared at me. His young girlfriend was particularly confused. Maybe a Kennedy reference was too obscure for that moment. The director who had taken me over was looking at me like, Why would you do something like that, and to James Woods of all people?

I had no choice but to cop to it, because I was completely guilty. I said, "I mean, I think I did that. Because you know in my country when you admire someone, you just hurl goat cheese at them!"

You know that classic James Woods sort of half snarl, half smile? It is now burned into my memory bank. I continued to bury myself. "We actually met once before," I said. "At Hugo's?"

"Oh," he said, "did you spill breakfast on me?"

I blame Dennis Hopper for never being able to take advantage of the free buffet at a premiere again.

It was inevitable that with the impact that Dennis Hopper had had on making my life like a movie, I would return the favor by being in a movie with Dennis Hopper. It was called *Search and Destroy*—how appropriate. Once he was cast—Dennis Hopper playing my father-figure lover—I couldn't wait to meet him, tell him how he'd ruined my life, and ask for all the money I believed that he owed me. The movie was set in New York, and on the way to the set of this very low-budget film, the overworked, underpaid production assistant who was driving me in the production van fainted—just as I had at Saks—and smashed into the back of another car, causing a three-car pileup on Park Avenue South. If you're counting, this was my second van accident thanks to Dennis

Hopper, by the way. I hadn't been in the van long enough to even put on my seat belt, and my head slammed into the dashboard. That woke the assistant up! It turns out the production hadn't provided us with walkie-talkies—they were expensive, and the movie was poor—so, head throbbing, I staggered down Park Avenue South to the armory where we were shooting while the assistant stayed with the police. By the time I arrived on the set, I was dizzy as hell so I lay down on the marble floor of the lobby. With my eyes closed I explained to the first assistant director and the producer that we'd been in a car accident, and the producer asked me, "Are you going to be able to work today?"

I said, "I don't know. I mean my head really hurts."

Then I closed my eyes again to stop the spinning. Everyone was talking at once. I heard one of the producers trying to motivate me by saying "It's just a bump on the head, right? We have a hundred extras in there. I mean, I flew in the Israeli Army. With helicopters. This is nothing . . ."

I felt like I was going to sleep, and then one voice cut through the static in my brain.

The voice said, "Are you OK?"

I recognized that voice. It was my father. How did my father get here? Oh, my God, I thought, I'm dying and my Dennis Hopper–like life is flashing before my eyes! Then I realized, Wait, that *is* Dennis Hopper. The *real* Dennis Hopper. Dennis Hopper the iconic figure from *Easy Rider* who had changed my life and now had caused this poor bastard production assistant to have a three-car pileup.

I opened my eyes but could make out only his silhouette, bathed in white light, above me.

"Are you OK?" he repeated.

I said, "I'm fine, I just can't look at the light," and then I started to cry, and I could not stop crying.

And Dennis Hopper said, "Don't cry. You're going to be OK."

And I said, "No, I'm crying because my father saw *Easy Rider* when I was a kid and it changed his life and now we're in a movie together and it's a miracle!"

And Dennis Hopper knelt beside me, put his hand on my shoulder, and said, "Illeana, you've had a concussion. You know what that means? It means your brain moved inside your head. It's not supposed to do that."

He may have even said "man." I'm not sure. I was still crying, but I started laughing, too. Concussion aside, it *was* a miracle to meet the man who had changed my father's destiny, and thus my own. My father's image melded with that of the real Dennis Hopper standing over me, and in that moment, I felt like I was the child of Dennis Hopper. In that moment I felt like we were *all* the children of Dennis Hopper.

I looked up at Dennis Hopper, all bathed in white light, and I had a revelation. Dennis Hopper hadn't ruined my life. Dennis Hopper had saved my life. I ended up with the better life after all. As Dennis Hopper cradled my head, I reached up and touched his cheek and whispered, "This is what it's all about, man." I was hallucinating, of course. Just as Dennis had diagnosed, my brain had moved inside my head, and it's not supposed to do that. Still, it was a miracle. I thought about everything that had led me to this moment: Because my father had seen the movie *Easy Rider*, I did grow up poor, but if I had grown up rich, I probably wouldn't have become an actress. I would probably be working in advertising, which is what my guidance counselor advised me to do because she said I seemed "creative." I thought about the time when

I was a struggling and poor actress in New York. I had gone to the bank to withdraw my last twenty bucks, and I found a full bag of groceries that someone had left behind. It was filled with food I never could have afforded. That was a miracle.

I thought about the time I was walking to acting school, wondering where the next dollar would come from, and I found a *hundred*-dollar bill on the street where the prostitutes turned tricks. I looked down, and there it was. A crisp hundred-dollar bill. Just lying on the sidewalk. I wanted to do something special with the john's money, so I bought two tickets to *Dreamgirls* for my roommate and me. I still remember that night. How wonderful it felt to spend money. Dennis Hopper would do something like that— maybe not the *Dreamgirls* part but something with prostitutes.

I thought about how my mother could always get four sandwiches out of one can of tuna. Four sandwiches! I mean how did she do that? It was a miracle! I thought about The Studio, and how many of its positive ideals—the search for meaning in our lives; the need to feel free, really free, to express yourself as an artist; the ability not to judge others but to accept their life choices as a journey—they are all alive within me. (Though I'm not so sure about the goats.) It took courage for my father to shake things up, and *Easy Rider* gave him that courage. Sure, he completely screwed up my life, but I appreciate it now, and that is definitely a miracle!

Somewhere in our attic is the wrinkled poster of Dennis Hopper and Peter Fonda riding their choppers in *Easy Rider*. Dennis Hopper's eyes have been poked out. Peter Fonda's are still intact. I have had the honor of working with them both. People tell me I'm a bit of a rebel. It's true. I challenge the system. I question authority. Every day I tell myself, This is what it's all about, man. Don't blame me. Blame Dennis Hopper.

CHAPTER TWO

They Came from Within: Love and Romance at the Drive-In

Everything I learned about life, love, and men was from my ever-present position next to Grandpa. Here I'm waiting for him to be done so we could go for a spin in his '59 Mercedes convertible, seen in the background.

The first movie star who had an impact on my life was Dennis Hopper. The second was my grandfather. When I think of my grandfather Melvyn Douglas I don't first think of him as the acclaimed stage and screen actor. His amazing career spanned more than sixty years, through the studio system—with hits such as *Ninotchka* and *Mr. Blandings Builds His Dream House*—to his later diverse character roles onstage in *The Best Man,* for which he won a Tony Award, and in films such as *The Candidate, I Never Sang For My Father, Hud,* and *Being There.* For the latter two, he won Academy Awards.

Instead, I think of the quiet moments over breakfast. There I had him all to myself. I could watch him as if I were watching a movie. I recall the mornings sitting across from him while he ate his buttered toast and marmalade—looking every inch the movie star in his Sulka robe and pajamas—before I knew that he actually *was* a movie star. Every summer we would drive to my grandparents' summerhouse on a lake in Vermont. There, other cousins, uncles, nieces and nephews, a slew of visiting friends, and sometimes dignitaries such as Gloria Steinem and the actress and now dear friend Diane Baker would join us. I was shy around my family, but for some reason I lit up for my grandfather. I would entertain him with my little adventures, most of them involving animals I had rescued. There was the cat that was hit by a car, the mallard duck I kept in the dining room. I had found a red-tailed hawk, for instance, that I had managed to train to eat chicken off my head. This feat had landed me my first television appearance on a local program called *The Ranger Andy Show.* My grandfather's bemused expression at my account of Aquarius the hawk was my first encouragement that I was a born actress, even if no one else thought so.

But he could be intimidating. When I was a child, he and my grandmother gave a dinner party for the playwrights Sam and Bella Spewack. I asked if I could sit at the grown-ups' table rather than in the kitchen with the staff, and my grandfather said, "When you're interesting you can sit at the grown-ups' table." I vowed

to become interesting! It was hard to understand that my grandfather was both my grandfather and a movie star. In his apartment on Riverside Drive in New York City, I would trace my
hand over—and over and over—the many photographs of his
life in films. He kept his many awards in a closet in his bedroom.
I remember once secretly taking them all out and photographing
them. There was no doubt in my mind that I was going to be an
actress, but he seemed to wince every time I mentioned it. I would
be mumbling some rambling anecdote or describing my future
career as an actress when he would interrupt and lecture me rather
sternly. "Illeana," he would say, "If you want to be an actress you
had better learn to *enunciate*." He would then wait for me to say,
in a clear, loud voice, "Yes!" before I could continue. My grandfather abhorred the use of the word *yea* in conversation. I'm often
told that I have a very unusual way of saying *yes*. It comes out as
"Yeah. Yes! Yas!" The first two of the three words combine my
forgetting to say *yes*; the third awkwardly combines the previous
two to form a new word: *Yas!*

Of course, I was saddened that my grandfather didn't live long
enough to see me become a working actress who enunciates and
says *Yes!* But, that's what dreams are for. The last page of my journal from 1994 reads: "Last night I had an amazing dream. It was
like I fell through twilight. I dreamed I saw Grandpa. He was
on a movie set about to shoot a scene. I knew in my mind that he
wasn't alive anymore, that somehow I had managed to go back
in time. I wasn't supposed to be there, but I had to tell him that
I was coming from the future, so I decided I would sneak up to
him before anyone saw me. He turned around, and I whispered
to him, you don't know me, but I am your granddaughter all

grown up. It's me, Illeana. I'm an actress now, and I've made it. He smiled with that twinkle he always had in his eyes, happy that his legacy would continue. We looked around. No one had seen us. It would be our secret."

But let's go to the past again: the magical summer of drive-ins, fast cars, and movie stars. The summer after my parents saw *Easy Rider*, my family was on our annual vacation to visit my grandparents at their Vermont country house, called Cliff Mull. We arrived in our poormobile—aka the Volkswagen—dirty and barefoot, in full hippie attire, with my father looking very much like Dennis Hopper. We had even managed to fit our mutt Gunther in the car. The first night Gunther chased my aunt's beloved cat across the dinner table and was banned from the house after that. Poor Gunther. Even our pets were outsiders.

Cliff Mull was a beautiful yellow turn-of-the-century house on a lake that always reminded me of something out of a Chekhov story. It was surrounded by gardens and stone walkways. I would hold my grandmother's hand, and we would pick flowers or imitate the birds. I could spend hours watching my grandfather play Scrabble or gin rummy, running to refill his glass with scotch when he needed me to. I liked being his helper. It gave me a chance to go to the kitchen, where I could always find some fresh cherries or local strawberries. Everyone else always stayed down by the lake, boating or water-skiing, but I hadn't learned how to swim and was afraid of the water, so I was content to stay with my grandparents. One afternoon, I heard a commotion of footsteps and voices coming up from the lake.

After a day of swimming and lounging around the dock someone must have decided it would be a great idea to go to the local drive-in to see a movie. All of a sudden there were contingents of

families and friends and cousins running down stairs and loading kids into backseats of cars and driving away. Before I knew
what was happening and before I could get anyone's attention,
everyone was gone and I was alone in the driveway. I didn't know
what a drive-in was, but everyone seemed pretty excited by it,
and I certainly didn't like the idea of being left behind. Being the
youngest, I always seemed to be brushed aside or forgotten by the
older kids, and I started to cry after watching the parade of cars
pass me by. My grandfather scooped me up in his arms and assured
me that I was certainly not being left behind. I would be going
with *him* to the drive-in.

"We don't want to be with that noisy crowd anyway, do we,
Peaches?" he said, which was his nickname for me. "We're going
in style."

At the time, my grandfather had an absolutely stunning 1959
Mercedes-Benz 220S convertible sports car. It was steel gray with
gorgeous red leather interior and bright, shiny chrome bumpers.
It haunts me, it was so perfect. I'm not much for cars, but I have
never been in a car as beautiful as my memory of what that Mercedes looked and felt like, especially when Melvyn Douglas—the
movie star—was at the wheel.

We climbed in, and I sat next to him in the front seat—a privilege I rarely had in my own family, so it felt very grown-up.
He gave me a smile with that familiar twinkle in his eye, and we
were off, flying eighty miles per hour toward the drive-in. No
one wore seat belts in those days, and these were winding country
roads. My grandfather liked to drive really fast, but he was a
terrible driver. Later I figured out that I was riding with him less
out of privilege and more by default—because other friends and
relatives were simply too scared. Maybe that's why everyone had

piled so quickly into my grandmother's "safe" Volvo station wagon and taken off before he had come out of the house.

My grandfather drove that Mercedes with utter exuberance and a complete lack of fear. I can't say the same for his passengers over the years, who in a typical outing would share many nervous glances and the slamming of imaginary brakes. We had our share of near misses during those summers in Vermont. We scared a lot of deer, and took out more than a few mailboxes on our way to get ice cream or pick something up in town. My grandfather would announce that he was on his way to pick up a prescription or to go to an antiques fair, but there were never any takers to accompany him. But for me, any excuse to climb into that Mercedes and sit next to him at the wheel . . . well, it was as close to heaven as you could want to be. We were always backing into things or over things. Magically, the car never seemed to dent, as if movie stars were somehow exempt from something as mundane as a fender bender. Eventually I just got used to the sound of squealing brakes or the horrified looks of passersby as they leaped out of the way, shouting, "Melvyn Douglas is on the loose again!"

The night of the drive-in, we raced down Route 5, making an extremely sharp and illegal left turn past the red light and turned at the large neon sign next to a dirt field that read FAIRLEE DRIVE-IN. It was dark by the time we got there, and we couldn't spot any cars that were familiar, so my grandfather started speeding through row after row as we got closer and closer to the screen. We finally spotted the Volvo up toward the front. He backed the car down the row to turn around but went right over a curb. Then he spun the car around in a cloud of dust, drove back over the same curb, and continued at the same speed toward the front.

He didn't even acknowledge it was happening. It was fantastic. To this day I call that move "the Melvyn Douglas." We pulled up next to the others and waved. Car, driver, and passenger intact. The story was forever told by anyone who was there that night to witness it.

What I first remember about the drive-in was looking out the window and seeing the movie being projected in the sky. The screen was surrounded by stars. The movie was *Romeo and Juliet*. What I remember most about *Romeo and Juliet* was the whispering sound of lovers. The wonderful echoed sound combined with the gigantic images that played against that starry Vermont sky. The sound seemed to come right from the sky, like voices from the heavens. It was the first time I saw kissing in a movie, and I spent the rest of the summer apparently trying to kiss my cousin, who was about five years older than I was. Nobody could understand why I had this sudden precociousness for kissing boys. Well, I saw it in *Romeo and Juliet*! Olivia Hussey as Juliet was never more beautiful and romantic and, well, kissable.

I also remember the end, when the lovers couldn't be together and they both killed themselves. The unfairness of their deaths stayed within me somehow. Doomed love would be something I would experience myself at another drive-in many years later. It was also the first time I saw nudity on screen, and although it was only a bare bottom, it was something the boys talked about a lot the next day. I realized I had seen something that I wasn't supposed to see. It forever linked in my mind the forbidden and adult nature of drive-ins. You didn't see *Bambi* or *Mary Poppins* at the drive-in. You saw naked people kissing, and then they ended up dead. Of course I also remember the score. The music haunted me, and whenever I hear it I am instantly brought back to that summer night sitting next to my grandfather in his Mercedes as we watched *Romeo and Juliet*. Our dangerous and memorable ride had brought us here, and now I was watching my first movie.

By the time I was going to the Middletown Drive-In, our local spot, with my friends and boyfriends in Connecticut, it was featuring only "Dusk Till Dawn" horror flicks. But before that, they had actually played some great movies. There my parents saw Andy Warhol's *Trash*, *Midnight Cowboy*, and *King of Hearts*—one of their favorites. During our hippie days, my mother would dress us in our pajamas, and we'd get to go to the Middletown Drive-In in the back of one of the hippies' trucks. It was a great way to watch films. You'd fall asleep during one film only to wake up to another—as if it were one long continuous movie. I remember seeing just an amazing array of movies and genres that way. *Serpico* and *Scarecrow*; *The Sugarland Express* with *Dirty Mary, Crazy Larry*; *Freebie and the Bean* on a double bill with *Blazing Saddles*. *Nashville* paired with *M*A*S*H*, which was the *second* time I saw nudity. Nudity = drive-in. I woke up and my brothers were screaming and pointing at the screen. It was the first time I saw breasts in a movie. In *M*A*S*H*, Sally Kellerman was "Hot Lips" O'Houlihan, naked as a jaybird in the shower. Sally Kellerman, who I knew first because of her breasts, later became my friend after we met doing a staged reading of a Paul Mazursky play.

As I got older, and without my parents or brothers around, the nudity at the drive-in was usually happening in the front seat, unfortunately *while* I was trying to watch the movie. I was in the backseat with a girlfriend watching *Bang the Drum Slowly*, which was paired with *Report to the Commissioner*. A Michael Moriarty double bill, I guess. *Bang the Drum Slowly* was riveting. It had an actor I had never seen before named Robert De Niro, and in the film he's dying. My friend and I were watching the movie—perhaps the saddest ever made—and meanwhile her sister is in the front seat, oblivious. She's making out with her date, and getting pretty hot and heavy, and we're holding back tears in the back! Two completely different cinematic experiences. Finally we had to get out of the car so we wouldn't disturb them with our sniffles. We watched the rest of the movie on the hood of the car, careful *not* to turn around until the car stopped moving. Let me tell you, they missed one good movie. That De Niro fellow. He went places.

By the time I got to high school, the Middletown Drive-In was associated not only with sex but with all sorts of teenage misbehavior. Some of it was sort of innocent, like the tradition of sneaking in extra people in the trunk of the car.

The admission was only 99 cents, so the practice was more about getting away with something than it was about the money. But hey, we were poor, so I didn't mind nearly suffocating to save a buck. I became friends with an older girl named Molly. Molly's mom had this champagne-colored Pontiac Grand Prix. It was a massive car with a huge trunk, and if she only knew how we misused it. I can't tell you how it drove, because I rarely got to sit in it, but I can assure you, the trunk of a Pontiac Grand Prix can fit three small teenage girls.

A typical Friday night went like this: Molly would pick everyone up. There would be about seven or eight girls stuffed into the car. When we got close to the drive-in, Molly would pull over and decide who would have to get into the trunk. I usually volunteered, because I knew she would pick me anyway. I was younger and not in any way cool, so I had no clout to stand up and say "You know, just once I'd like to ride *in* the car like a passenger, not in the trunk like a corpse." I was also not one of the upper-crust girls who had beautiful hair and clothing and would never dare do something as demeaning as get in a trunk and sneak into the drive-in to save 99 cents! Besides, it was date night, and they had to look their best because there were going to be boys there. That was the main reason anyone went to the drive-in.

I became known as a fearless trunker, which was far from the truth. The scary part of sneaking in through the trunk was not so much worrying about being caught. It was knowing that we were right over the fuel tank whenever we hit a bump. Rolled up in a ball inside the trunk, you could hear everyone in the car laughing and talking and you'd keep thinking about that fuel tank. The car would slow down at the drive-in entrance and Molly would yell, "We're here! Don't say anything!"

Yeah, as if it were easy to carry on a conversation from the trunk of a car!

You'd feel the bumpity-bump as the car drove in and then over to the farthest end of the drive-in before you were let out. Sometimes it was still dusk, and you'd have to wait for it to get dark before anyone would let you out. By that point, it was hard to breathe, and you were convinced they had left you inside as a joke—which did happen to me, a lot, and it's still not funny! What *is* funny is that in all the years we snuck in, no one ever asked to open the trunk of anyone's car.

Maybe they just accepted it as petty drive-in theft. Punks and stowaways. It was always a relief to see Molly's smiling face as she popped open the trunk and let me out. Maybe there'd be a small impression of the spare tire on my face, but that would fade as the night went on.

By the time I'd be released, the first movie would have started, but as I've said, folks didn't really go there for the cinematic experience; it was more an act of teenage lust.

Once outside the trunk, the girls would give each other a quick once-over. We would put even more makeup on our already made-up faces, apply more sticky lip gloss, and head to the burger stand to check out who was there. The burger stand was basically a screened-in outhouse that smelled of rancid grease. Inside, the fluorescent lighting made you look like one of the zombies that were often playing on the screen. You'd stand in line to get your French fries, the paper soaked with grease. You'd match it with an equally greasy burger and a watered-down Coke, and you had your perfect *un*happy meal. It was better to eat outside, because inside it was too hard not to notice the dead, greasy flies stuck in the flypaper catchers dangling from the ceiling—last changed probably in the 1950s. The Middletown Drive-In had the best fries I have ever eaten. I have searched and almost caught that memorable smell whenever I am near a carnival or state fair. That wonderful nostalgic smell and taste of youth. Top it off with a blue or purple snow cone and there you have it. Snapshot. I remember talking to a boy I liked and thinking it was going really well. I went to the bathroom, which was conveniently located inside, right next to where they fried everything. I looked in the mirror, and my entire mouth was circled bright blue. As if the clown Emmett Kelly had just eaten a Smurf and wiped it on his mouth. The boy was gone by the time I got it off my face. Another time, I was chatting up a boy about a movie when a fly got stuck in my lip gloss. He was getting it off my mouth and got a handful of pink-colored goop with the live, coated fly still attached. I had hoped that my expertise and knowledge about films would draw boys to me like flies at the drive-in. It never happened.

The Middletown Drive-In was a good place to smoke without getting caught, drink without getting caught, meet up with boys and make out in cars without getting caught. It was *not* a place to watch movies, yet I was there actually to watch the movies. Maybe I couldn't shake my earlier magical experiences of drive-in movies.

Even when the movies started to be geared more toward horror flicks. I still wanted to watch them. I'd say, "The movie is starting; let's go watch the movie," and finally, pitifully, "Isn't anyone going to watch the movie?" But no one was interested. There was nothing worse than seeing a great scary movie, such as *The Reincarnation of Peter Proud* or *When a Stranger Calls*, and having no one to talk to about it. There were times I would find myself alone in a car absorbed in a movie, and realize it was dawn. I'd watched *five movies in a row*, and my friends were God-knows-where.

Once, I was in Molly's car watching a scary movie by myself, and it turned into a scary movie in real life. It was very late. At the drive-in, there were no clocks, just a string of movies, so you lost track of time. My guess is that it was probably somewhere between dusk and dawn.

I had just got through watching *Carrie*. It was gruesome. Great scary ending. And again there was a lot of nudity in it. Nudity = drive-in! I couldn't believe that my friends had missed this movie! Next up was *Alice, Sweet Alice* with a young Brooke Shields. Pretty good—I kept watching, thinking, Surely someone is going to show up soon. Eventually, the next movie started, and it was *Burnt Offerings*. The movie began innocently enough, not half as scary as *Carrie*. Lots of creepy zooms. A sinister chauffeur. And who is in the upstairs window? It was almost cheesy, so I kept watching. All of a sudden there was a scene with water. Now, I was always kind of afraid of the water. I never wanted to go swimming. I had one fear as a child. It was completely irrational, but I was terrified of someone holding me under the water and drowning me. I would not go swimming with my brothers, because I was so afraid. My mother would be trying to give me a bath and I would scream, "She's drowning me!" Maybe it was a past-life thing, I don't know, but that was my crazy fear. In *Burnt Offerings* there is a scene in which Oliver Reed becomes possessed by this demon living through the house. The demon feeds off the life force of all of the house's inhabitants. At one point in the movie, Oliver Reed starts holding his son under water, trying to drown him. That was my fear, and now I am seeing it in a movie. Bette Davis is screaming at him to stop, but Oliver Reed just keeps holding the kid under water, and he can't control himself. He's gone insane. He's trying to kill his son. The kid is splashing around fighting for his life.

I thought I was going to be sick. I jumped out of the car and just started running. I was scared to death; I just wanted to go home. I started frantically looking in cars for someone I knew. I couldn't find anyone, and I could hear *Burnt Offerings* playing as I made my way through the cars, that horrible voice of Oliver Reed following me.

At one end of the drive-in, near some pine trees, there were some swings. "I'll meet you at the swings" was code because the swings were a kind of lovers' lane. When it was late, you hoped that the person driving you home wasn't at the swings, but I headed over there anyway looking for Molly or any other familiar face. I was at the swings seeing if I recognized anyone when I suddenly noticed the strangest thing. Just past where the swings met the forest I saw an empty wooden chair, like an old saloon chair. Next to it was a large popcorn box and some food wrappers. It seemed really creepy all of a sudden to see this completely empty chair in the middle of the trees—ominously lighted from *Burnt Offerings*. Who was sitting there? Was it a man? Was it a bear? Did whoever it was carry a chair through the forest in the dark, then climb over a fence, just to see a free movie? I mean, who would do something like that? Obviously someone just like me, but . . .

I was still staring at the empty chair in the forest when a car pulled up beside me. It was a wood-paneled station wagon. A lot of my friends' parents had station wagons, so at first I thought it might be one of them looking for one of their kids, which happened all the time. It wasn't. It was a slightly older guy. I can't really describe him, but I will always remember his voice, because he sounded sort of like the character actor Dabney Coleman. It was a voice with authority, completely trusting and calm. He said, "You look lost. You OK? You need help?"

"No," I said, "I'm just looking for my friends . . ."

"Oh, you by yourself?" he asked.

"Yeah," I said.

There was nothing unusual about his asking me if I was alone. Of course he would want to be helpful. You met all sorts of interesting people at the drive-in. The light from *Burnt Offerings* was illuminating that weird empty chair, and again I was wondering, Where had all my friends gone?

I was wearing a pink tube top. For a second I thought I caught the guy glance at my chest, but that was impossible. I thought that

I was just being self-conscious because I was a little busty. Maybe it was because he was a grown-up, or maybe because I was still shaken up by the movie, but for some reason, I kept talking to him. He was talking about *Burnt Offerings*, saying he didn't like it, so he was leaving. "Just trash," he said, "I'm heading out. You need a lift?" I didn't answer him, because I was still staring, fascinated by the empty chair in the forest, when he reached across the seat, and offered me—I'm not kidding—a large supply of his candy. "Would you look at this?" he said. "I bought all this candy, and now it's going to go to waste."

I have replayed the next moment many times in my mind, and it never fails to give me the shivers. He was holding out his cardboard tray with all the candy in it, and I started to lean in to the car to get a better look at what was there. In that second while I contemplated whether or not I was going to take his candy, he grabbed my forearm and tried to pull me into the car. It happened so quickly. Just about three seconds of sheer terror, but just as quickly I was able to pull free and get away. I will never forget the slap of his hand on my forearm as he tried to pull me into the car—or the angry sound his arm made as it slammed against the car door as I broke free and started running. I did not look back. I was sure he was right behind me, getting ready to drag me back to his car. I ran toward the familiar light of the burger stand. To my relief I finally saw one of my friends and tearfully told her what had happened. Everyone was pretty shaken up. I mean the drive-in was a dive, but things like that just didn't happen. It had always been a pretty safe place. Word spread and a posse of grown-ups set out looking for the wood-paneled station wagon, but no one could find it. About a week later, the State Police came to our house to interview me because another girl my age had described seeing the same paneled station wagon following her at the drive-in. Whoever it was, they never caught him, and life went on. Dusk till dawn.

But I wondered. Was he the guy in the empty chair? I imagined his sitting near the swings watching kids as they made out, then preying on innocent young girls—girls who were probably a little too young to be wearing tube tops. The drive–in was never the same for me after that. I would see that empty chair now and again, alone in the forest. I never once saw a person sitting in it, though.

By the late '70s and early '80s the movies at the drive-in were pretty much all cheap and sleazy stuff. Who knew the grainy images I was subjected to would later be heralded by Quentin Tarantino as grindhouse classics! Those dark movies fit with some equally gruesome dates. I think I saw every horror "classic" that is bandied about at the drive-in while on a date of some kind. *It's Alive. Basket Case. Squirm. Sssssss. Sisters. I Spit on Your Grave.* One stands out, because I had recurring nightmares about it. The plot revolves around a leech-like parasite that infects you and makes you want to have sex with everyone while red goop comes out of your mouth. Two scenes are seared into my memory. In one, a leech swims inside a girl who may or may not be masturbating while she is taking a bath. The other one is an orgy scene in which a sex-crazed father offers his daughter to another man by saying, "This is my daughter Vanessa. You'll like Vanessa. I do," and then starts having sex with her first!

I was in a car with a boy and he took that as a cue to do the same. I made him drive me home immediately. For years, I remembered it as the most disturbing movie I ever saw, and for years—because we didn't have Internet back then—I didn't even know the name of it! One night, many years later, I was with Martin Scorsese and Brian De Palma describing this absolutely vile film I had been subjected to as a child at the drive-in. I was getting to the orgy and the red goop, and they started to scream *"THEY CAME FROM WITHIN*!!*"* They were absolutely delighted that I had seen it, extolling it for several minutes as "a classic," and went on to tell me it was the "commercial" debut of director David Cronenberg, whom I had just met on the set of *To Die For.* For those of you who love red goop, leeches, and incestuous orgy scenes, the movie is also known as *Shivers.* It is my deepest regret that I didn't know that he had directed *They Came From Within* at the time, because I would have had just one question for him: "Mr. Cronenberg, why?"

The last movie I ever saw at the drive-in was *Motel Hell,* in 1980. Like my first drive-in movie, *Romeo and Juliet,* it also was centered on a short-lived, doomed romance. I had met a boy named Henry in history class. He was a little older than I, from a wealthy family, but he thought I was funny and he asked me out on a few dates. Soon enough we were going steady. I was thrilled, until he asked me to the drive-in. We had never done anything more than kiss, and I was a little nervous about what "going to the drive-in" with a boy meant. I reluctantly agreed to go, convincing myself that he was a nice boy from a good family and certainly wouldn't expect anything more from me beyond watching a good R-rated thriller! We were watching *Motel Hell,* and it was, again, sometime between dusk and dawn, and surprise, surprise, Henry suddenly wanted to do more than just watch the movie. I was very disappointed, because I'm a big Rory

Calhoun fan, and I love movies about making meat products out of human beings. But there I was, trying to make some sense of the plot, and Henry kept trying to put his hand down my pants.

I kept squirming and saying "C'mon, I want to watch the movie," which, when the movie is *Motel Hell*, is kind of lame, but it's all I had. He kept trying. Back then, the teenage girl's version of "I have a headache" was to tell a guy you have your period, so I said, "Henry, I'm sorry, I have my period," and that put an end to it. He looked bored after that and started talking about his blue Corvette. I had to stop watching the movie and pretend I was interested in his blue Corvette. Basically, Henry ruined *Motel Hell* for me.

In the weeks before our drive-in date, Henry had kept telling me about the new car his dad was buying him, which was the aforementioned Corvette. Back then it seemed fairly interesting. He showed me countless pictures of it, describing it in loving detail. At the drive-in, when he made me stop watching *Motel Hell*, he said, "Pretty soon I won't have to be driving my parents' car. I'll have my blue Corvette." It was the symbol of his being a wealthy kid. His father could simply order him a Corvette. We left the drive-in way before dawn, and he talked about his stupid Corvette the entire drive home. A week or so later Henry called me, very excited to tell me that his blue Corvette had arrived, and, true to his word, he asked if I wanted to go for a spin. I was thrilled. My mother was making dinner, and I threw on my denim jacket and told her that Henry was taking me for a drive in his brand-new car. Even my mother had heard about this stupid blue Corvette. We were all waiting for it. My mom—bless her heart—was then driving another poormobile, a burnt-orange Chevy Chevette.

Henry pulled up in the car, he honked the horn, and it was a beauty. Baby blue. Lots of chrome. Not my kind of car—I don't really like Corvettes—but I could appreciate the artistry. He finally finished stroking and petting the car, I jumped in, and we headed down the driveway and out onto the road. He was driving really slowly, like 20 miles an hour, and I shouted, "C'mon, let's put the pedal to the metal!"

"I don't want a wreck," he said. "She's brand new."

All of a sudden, I felt really gauche.

"Sure," I said.

Henry looked really handsome driving his car like a senior citizen down the road. He was beaming, and I started thinking about what had happened—or rather, what had not happened—at the drive-in. Maybe I was a little uptight? I mean, I didn't want to lose a nice boy like Henry. I should probably let him get to second base in his new Corvette. I looked at Henry and smiled, moving closer to him.

Henry was driving, staring at the road, going ever so slowly, when he said, "What do you think of Gerry Haines?" I was completely thrown. She was the kind of girl I used to see Henry with before we started dating. She was kind of horsey-looking, wealthy, a complete snob, and a bully.

A week before, she had pushed me against my locker and said, "You look like a frog. Ribbit. Ribbit." Then she gave me this smug look and said, "Your family's poor, and you're ugly, and you're not half good enough to date Henry. You'll see." It gave me a sick feeling in the pit of my stomach. We had driven maybe a hundred feet and he gushed, "She's beautiful, isn't she?"

"Yes," I said. "It's a great ride."

"Not the car, doofus. Gerry Haines!"

Then he blurted out, "I'm in love with Gerry Haines, and I

want to break up with you." Henry seemed to feel better after he got that off his chest. He even accelerated to a cool thirty-five miles per hour. I was speechless, and we drove in silence until we got to the end of the street—where, instead of heading out to the highway, Henry started to turn the car around. He turned it around so carefully, so slowly, like a really good driver. Not at all like those crazy dangerous rides I had taken with my grandfather. But this drive was much scarier, because I realized he was driving me home. My romance had been doomed, just as Gerry had predicted. My ride was over. Henry dropped me off in front of my house and said, "We'll still be friends." Of course, he never spoke to me again.

Was my fascination with doomed love planted in me the night I saw *Romeo and Juliet* at the Fairlee Drive-In? Or maybe, as in *They Came From Within*, it had snuck up inside me while I was taking a bath and planted itself like a leech. Maybe I would always be chasing that same doomed love. Faster and faster, never arriving, but never driving fast enough to get away from it. Drive-ins are no longer here, but that's what dreams are for. I can always remember my grandfather's swinging open the door of his '59 Mercedes that summer night in Vermont and saying, "Hop in, Peaches. Let's go for a ride."

CHAPTER THREE

Camelot

My first attempt at a head shot, age fifteen.
Obviously I hadn't realized that the MGM
studio system had collapsed. Still, it launched
my career as a cocktail waitress.

D on't let it be forgot / That there was once a spot / For one
brief shining moment that was known / As Camelot." Those
are the famous words King Arthur utters to an idealistic young
boy about the magical kingdom of Camelot.

My entrance into show business could not have been further

from the magic of the Alan Jay Lerner and Frederick Loewe musical *Camelot* except that it was brief, it lasted for a moment, and it was called Camelot.

I got my start at the Camelot Dinner Theatre, in Connecticut. Don't remember it, you say? That would be accurate. It lasted about six months. The Camelot was the kind of joint you performed in on your last stop *out* of show business on the way to the graveyard. Donald O'Connor was there for a week—died a week later. Richard Kiley toured in the musical *Man of La Mancha* for fifty years—he played the Camelot and never did the show again. The Camelot spared no one. One night a man actually died *in* the audience. In the middle of *You're a Good Man, Charlie Brown,* we heard a crash, followed by a scream of "My husband, my husband!" Snoopy and the chorus slowly stopped singing "Happiness," the lights came up, and I saw a man literally killed by show business–his head facedown in mashed potatoes and prime rib. His wife cried while the firemen slowly shook their heads and wheeled him away in a stretcher. They say the show must go on, but it's kind of hard to get the audience back after a thing like that. The highlight of the Camelot for me was meeting Rudy Vallée, and learning the value of a good tape recorder, but I will get to that. The Camelot became the first sign of many that I was being singled out for larger life lessons, that maybe my life was destined to be a really, really good movie with twists and turns that made you wonder if the heroine would ever really make it. And if she did, would there be music playing in the background?

One day, I was riding my ten-speed home from high school when I saw a sign: COMING SOON. THE CAMELOT DINNER THE-ATRE. I nearly skidded off the road.

My grandfather got his break in the late '20s when he auditioned for theater god David Belasco. He headed to Broadway at the Belasco Theatre. I was stuck in the boondocks without a theater or impresario in sight to give me a chance. The Camelot Dinner Theatre would be my entrée onto the boards!

The next day, dolled up to an inch of my life and carrying a homemade head shot of myself, complete with hat, pretending to be a successful actress who had somehow managed to end up in the sticks, I met with a guy named Phil who seemed to be in charge. He sat me down for an interview, and I immediately started trying to charm him. Mildly flirting with a man twice one's age to get a job was not yet considered politically incorrect. It worked, and he genuinely seemed to take an interest in me. Clearly he had picked up on my earnestness about a career in show business. He was my David Belasco.

This is what I would later learn about Phil: Phil had no theatre background. Phil was a manager of sorts, looking to try something new. Phil, I would learn, was a pimp. Being a pimp meant that Phil's occupation left him with a lot of spare cash. Dirty money needs to be run through a legitimate business. So Phil's idea was simple: Why not open a dinner theater? Cleanse your money and put on a pretty good show while you're at it!

Phil, as I later learned, ran "by the hour" motels out on the Berlin Turnpike. This was code for *brothels*. That's how prostitution worked in Connecticut. You drove out to the Berlin Turnpike and got a room or you had sex in the middle of the woods with deer watching you. It's true. The first time I made out with a boy was in the middle of a forest. Ever since, the scent of pine needles has turned me on. Bring in a raccoon to watch me, and we could make serious dough.

Phil had a partner at the Camelot, and they had worked together before. Her name was Rosie (not her real name—her real name was probably inmate #6660027, but let's stick with Rosie).

Phil's partner Rosie was—again, as the gossip went—a former prostitute and Phil's number-one girl. She was a hooker with a heart of gold who apparently loved the smell of greasepaint. It turns out that Rosie's dream, much like Rose's dream from *Gypsy* and much like my dream, too, was to be in show business! Now, my dream had not included working for a pimp and an ex-hooker who wanted to be out of "the business" and into "show business," but beggars can't be choosers.

Phil was your classic movie villain, with slicked-back hair and a thin mustache. Beady brown eyes. Reeking of Brut cologne. He usually wore some sort of horrible brown polyester suit, his gut bulging through a pistachio shirt with a tie that was much too short. Phil was hard to look at, and he was a little scary, but for some reason he took to me. Maybe it's because I didn't flinch the first time he showed me his gun. "This is a dangerous business," he said one night. Then he opened his jacket revealing a pistol in a shoulder holster. It was only a dinner theater, but I didn't argue. I just nodded.

"You ever see a gun before, kid?" he said, patting his piece.

"Sure," I said. "Like on *Burke's Law*."

Phil cracked up. "You're too much, kid."

I hadn't meant to be funny. *Burke's Law* was a television show from the '60s (and revived in the '90s) about a millionaire chief of police who rode around in a chauffeur-driven Rolls-Royce catching bad guys. Phil thought this dated reference was meant to be "ironic." Most of my TV viewing took place during extended stays with my Italian grandparents in Queens, watching the shows that they liked. I thought that *was* TV. Twenty-year-old reruns of *The Jack Benny Program*, *You Bet Your Life*, *The Phil Silvers Show*, *The Untouchables*. But my favorite was *Burke's Law*, with its gangsters and dames and all the men who wore guns under their jackets.

"You're a good kid," Phil said, putting away his gun.

I told Phil at that first interview that I wanted to audition for the upcoming musical, but he explained that all the shows were being cast out of New York. I was crestfallen. Phil said that I might be able to be in the chorus, but anyone who was in the chorus would not be paid: "That was a freebie." I would be paid only if I worked as a waitress, a busboy, or a cocktail hostess. I could be in the chorus "after I paid my dues." Seemed pretty harsh, but this was show business, so I went along. Out of all the options, cocktail waitress seemed the most glamorous. And I had certainly seen my parents make drinks often enough. Luckily for me, Phil gave it away when he said, "But you have to be eighteen to carry booze. How old are you?"

"I'm eighteen, Phil," I said with a straight face.

Phil laughed. "Sure, kid." Then he paused. "You're sixteen, right?"

I got the feeling that Phil said "You're sixteen, right?" a lot in his line of work.

"Yeah, Phil. I'm sixteen."

He stared at my homemade head shot. It was a very vampy pose. Backlit as if I were a film siren. Phil looked me up and down again and made his decision.

"Good," he said. "We'll tell everyone you're eighteen. I need someone with good boobs to carry booze. Let's go meet Rosie. She runs the day-to-day." Then he winked at me—a wink that promised, "Someday, if you're lucky, I will take you out back and grope you while you pretend you want me to stop."

I found out two very important things that day. One, I had good boobs. No one had ever said that to me, although I thought I did. And two, keep your mouth shut during an interview. I was only fourteen and should have in no way been hired to carry booze.

Phil brought me back to meet Rosie. She was tall and thin and closely resembled the actress Susan Hayward. Her face looked like a gun moll out of film noir. One side of her face drooped slightly, and I later found out this malady was called Bell's palsy. It marred her once-beautiful features. She was smoking a cigarette and stood up briefly to take a look at me. "OK, Phil" is all she said. Phil seemed to think that I had made a good impression. He walked me out the door and said, "You start on Thursday." I waited until he got inside to get on my bike, knowing that leaving on my ten-speed Peugeot might betray my age.

All week I rode past as the kingdom of Camelot seemed to come together. Outside a sign went up that said "Opening Night. *Godspell.*"

I told my mother that I had got a job at the newly opened Camelot Dinner Theatre. This former abandoned building was in a sketchy area on the outskirts of town near an old Greyhound bus terminal. It had last been a biker bar, closed by the police after too many fights. Angry, drunk bikers still showed up to do wheelies in the parking lot. At first she was concerned, but once I said, "Mom, they're giving me free food, and I will no longer need to be here for dinner," she softened and gave me her blessing.

Part of my job meant I got a free meal, but only if I got there at five o'clock, an hour before I began my shift as a cocktail waitress. My first night, I sat at the bar with some of the staff and ate chicken cordon bleu, corn, green beans, and a roll while the orchestra was tuning up and the actors were getting ready for the show. I was in heaven. Until I actually had to go to work, and then it turned into a bit of a nightmare. Opening nights are never easy.

Godspell was going on. The singers sang, "Pre-pare ye, the way of the Lord!" I started to take drink orders. That's when everyone learned I had no skills as a cocktail waitress. Someone asked for a VO and Seven and I actually brought them a V8 and Seven. By week's end I was no better, although I had finally learned what went into a rusty nail. Man, that was a popular drink. Glenlivet and Drambuie and a twist of lemon. I was so awful that every night I told people it was my first night working. That excuse combined with my low-cut blouse actually got me great tips—and I was learning all the songs to *Godspell*. And waiting for my big break: to be in the chorus. In a week, *Godspell* was over and now I had to learn all the songs to *No, No, Nanette*. Even though I was a horrible cocktail waitress, I loved my job, because I could interact with the audience—I could brag, "You think this is good? You should have seen *Godspell*!" And then proceed to sing every song I had learned to the helpless customers who just wanted a rusty nail.

Two weeks in, Rosie called me to the back. At the Camelot, you saw Rosie for two reasons. You got your paycheck, or you were fired for stealing. I thought I was getting my first paycheck, so

I bounced back there full of excitement and to ask Phil about auditioning for *Damn Yankees*, which was coming in week three. He avoided eye contact as Rosie informed me that I was being switched from "cocktail hostess" to simply "hostess."

"You'll just walk people to their tables," she said in such a way as to emphasize my stupidity. Then she handed me a diagram that she had drawn with round tables on it numbered from one to twenty. "Can you handle it?"

I took the paper and nodded. Phil still wouldn't look at me and fiddled absentmindedly with the gun under his jacket.

"Good," Rosie said. "Memorize it."

I tried to explain that I was not really a cocktail waitress. I was an actress.

Rosie lit a cigarette and said, "Yeah. That's what they all say."

"She's a good kid, Rosie," Phil said. "She keeps her mouth shut."

That was true. I never once told Phil my real age nor repeated the torrid and now recurring gossip that he and Rosie were common criminals laundering money through the kingdom of Camelot. Phil as a creepy King Arthur and Rosie as a bitter, past-her-prime Guinevere. Phil confided in me because I guess he assumed I understood things like this. He said that Rosie had been his number-one girl. "She could have been a madam if she'd wanted to, but she wanted to go legit." He said it with pride. As if they were just a normal couple now running a theater. Like the Lunts, not a couple of crooks. "That's showbiz," Phil said when he saw me hostessing the next night.

Sometimes I'd be hanging around and I'd hear Rosie and Phil fighting just like other couples about how to run the business. By week four, bills started to pile up. No one was getting paid. Phil had been happier back at his motels on the Berlin Turnpike, and he stopped coming to work. Rosie rarely left the office. I'm not sure that she ever saw a show. It was a shame because *Damn Yankees* was probably the biggest triumph. No one died. Although someone did fall off the stage during "Shoeless Joe from Hannibal, Mo" while backing up and singing, "Look out, Look out, Look out, Look out." Yup—right off the stage.

"Food costs," I heard Phil scream one day. Phil now thought that we on the staff should have to pay for our meals or have the price taken out of our salary. At this point no one was really getting a salary, so free food was an incentive for workers to show up. The Camelot started to go downhill.

Not for me. I never stopped believing in Camelot even when I was demoted to hostess. Every night the audience filed in, and as I led them to their seats and said "Thank you for coming to the Camelot and please enjoy the show!" I could feel their excitement. Not so much after the show, but I was usually backstage by the time they filed out complaining about the food, or their seats, or whatever calamity had occurred that night.

My hostess duties took half an hour. I led folks to their seats and was then free to go backstage and watch the show. This turned out to be great because now I had more free time to spend with the actors. Most of them lived in an apartment above the Greyhound terminal next to the theater. From them I learned that the Camelot Dinner Theatre was not where you wanted to be. One dancer told me, "You want to be booked in a show in Vegas— preferably wearing feathers and dancing behind Liza Minnelli." All the chorus boys felt that way. They would gossip and fuss with me, teaching me how to put on makeup and false eyelashes. As gay men they all had one story in common, and that story always seemed to involve the actor Paul Lynde. He was gay? I couldn't believe it! There was one actor I met who was very serious. He was studying with Lee Strasberg at the Actors Studio in New York. He told me, "If you want to be a serious actor, you go to New York and study with Lee at the Studio." Then he offered to give me a massage. What did having a massage have to do with being an actor? I thought. When I declined, he told me, "If you want to be an actress you shouldn't be so uptight." Hmmm. Maybe that's why I never liked The Method.

To save money, the Camelot started to book just one performer. That's when you got someone like Donald O'Connor telling stories about Gene Kelly and tap dancing, or *An Evening with Kaye Ballard.* Then Rudy Vallée came to the Camelot. And just like Lee Marvin would a few years later, Rudy saw something in me, some hidden talent that I could not see in myself.

I was backstage avoiding the audience during Rudy Vallée's opening night, and he thought I was someone important, so he handed me his raccoon coat to hold while he did his quick change. I assumed this task with authority, never letting him know that I really had no skills in that department, either. But it went well. I held his coat while he went and got his ukulele. I gave him back the coat and he went onstage—to great success. Rudy Vallée was pretty old at the time, so his act was simple. It consisted of telling a few corny jokes about being a ladies' man. He was—in 1920. Rudy Vallée invented a style of singing called crooning, which Bing Crosby later popularized. So Rudy would croon his many hits—again from the 1920s and early 1930s. "Life Is Just a Bowl of Cherries," "Brother, Can You Spare a Dime?" He even played a little on his saxophone. It was impressive. He ended the evening by strumming a ukulele while wearing that raccoon coat. The coat was a nod to his days at Yale as a Connecticut Yankee. Then, in a spotlight, he sang "I'm Just a Vagabond Lover," and people cheered. The cumulative effect of the show paid off in the simplicity of the ending. It was mesmerizing.

The next night, I made sure to be stationed in the same place backstage, but I caught his eye before the show. "I'll be ready with your coat, sir," I volunteered, and he smiled at me. This became a nightly routine that I never tired of. Rudy Vallée would hand me his coat, and while he got his ukulele and was getting ready for "I'm Just a Vagabond Lover," I would say something stupid, such as "It's going great. They really love you."

The crowd—most of them women in their sixties—really did love him. I loved him. And he loved being loved. He had been in show business for more than sixty years. He was the only act at the Camelot that made you feel as if you were at the opening night of a Broadway show. He gave it all he had. Each night he got better, and that's what I told him every night when he left the stage: "Sir, that was amazing!"

"Do you think so?"

"Think so? I know so!" And he would laugh and head back to his dressing room to freshen up and get ready to sign autographs for the adoring elderly women in the front of the house.

He was only there for a week, and on his last night, he handed me his raccoon coat for the final time. He went out and, as usual, knocked 'em dead. My only interaction with him had been to hand him his coat and tell him how great I thought he was, but I seemed to make an impression on him. I told him that I was really going to miss him, and I meant it.

That night, after his last performance, he invited me back to his dressing room. I didn't know what to expect. I had certainly heard stories from my grandfather of older men making passes at young girls. I knocked on the door and went in. He told me to take a seat on a nearby couch. He was alone, sitting at his dressing table drenched in sweat. Now, out of the stage lights, his heavy pancake makeup and overly rouged cheeks made him look macabre, like a marionette. It was like a scene from that movie *Limelight* with Charlie Chaplin. I got a little nervous all of a sudden. Was Rudy Vallée–Vagabond Lover going to pounce on me?

Finally he turned around and smiled at me. "I want you to listen to something," he said. "I think you'll appreciate this."

He took out a small, cheap GE cassette tape recorder and pressed PLAY. We both sat there in his dressing room listening to the tape, which played a whooshing sound, then was quiet, then whooshed again. I had no idea what I was listening to, but he seemed to be enjoying it. He leaned back and smiled. Full of pride. "Do you know what that is?" he asked.

I listened again very hard but all I heard was a rushing, whooshing sound. I finally said, "Is it the ocean?"

He spun around from the mirror and raised his hand in the air with a flourish.

"It's my applause," he said.

"Oh, yes," I said. "Yes, now I hear it."

Rudy Vallée smiled at me with complete satisfaction. "I tape it every night," he said. "I knew *you* would appreciate that."

And I did. It is one of my most touching and vivid memories of show business. Rudy was a real trouper. A trouper who went out there night after night to give the performance of his life. Drenched in sweat, in the middle of the boondocks. It didn't matter. A show is a show is a show. All that was left of it were the echoes of the applause. If you could somehow keep that sound, that joy, to remind you of why you were put on the planet. To entertain people. To make them happy just for a little while. I listened to Rudy Vallée's applause and then quietly excused myself.

Not long after that, we showed up for work and Phil and Rosie had skipped town. The office was cleaned out. The safe was empty. There was helpless panic felt by the staff, which quickly turned to anger. I felt betrayed. How could they do this to the Camelot? Audience members began showing up for that night's performance of *Mame* and refused to be turned away. We explained to them that there would be no show, but they wouldn't believe it. I watched people sitting in their seats, waiting for a show to start. As if the lights would go up through their sheer will. In the back, waiters and cooks were loading their cars with steaks and booze—they hadn't been paid for weeks. Actors were making calls about their next gigs.

There was no show that night. There was never a show again. There was never a theater in that location again. Six glorious months and Rudy Vallée. It was over.

The Camelot closed, and the building was abandoned. All that was left from the magic of the Camelot were ghostly echoes of the applause.

CHAPTER FOUR

In the Key of Liza

This is what happens when a child sees *Cabaret* too many times.

After the Camelot Dinner Theatre closed, I was pretty down. Even though I never got paid to act, I thought of myself as a professional actor. I knew that if I had continued to work at the Camelot, eventually I would have been in one of the shows if not starring in my own one-woman production!

Incidentally, that's the kind of delusion you need when you're starting out. After all the excitement of hanging out with real actors at the Camelot, the prospect of simply returning to school and acting as if I wanted to learn anything but a time step was unbearable. I filled the void with movies. There was a small TV studio in my high school, so I proposed doing my own movie-review show. And—God help everyone else—the TV instructor agreed. It became a great way of forcing my mom to take me to the movies: I now had "reviews" to deliver.

There was one problem. We never had a newspaper in our house. Something pretty important had better be happening if my mom was going to break down and spend fifty cents on a newspaper. We were poor, and she considered it a needless expense.

"Who needs a paper? The news isn't going to change a week later."

My mother actually said that.

The problem was, I needed the movie section to see what was playing so I could write my reviews and, more important, so I could stay on television. In what became a kind of crazy ritual, I would ride my bike to our neighbors' house to get their old paper. I'd ride up to their house, and they would throw the paper at me. Then I'd ride away, paper in hand, like a paperboy in reverse. I was recycling, and I didn't even know it! I'd get back to my house, grab the movie section, and take it up to my room while my mom read the rest so she could find out what the hell happened last week.

Let me tell you about my room: By this time I was obsessed with movies. I was reading about movies, thinking about movies, making lists of my favorite movies. I was trying to *live* in a movie. Our Colonial house was very old, and I persuaded my mom to let me paint my room entirely black and white and silver, which I felt was a correct depiction of cinema. Everything had to be black and white. The bed was black and white. I had black shelves lined with silver wallpaper, and black and white pictures on the wall. My grandfather had given me this wonderful book by Arlene Croce, *The Fred Astaire & Ginger Rogers Book*, and I used it as a manual for turning my room into an Art Deco set.

So I was nuts about movies, and every week I'd look in the newspaper to find out which one I'd become obsessed with next. Once I had the movie picked out, I had a bigger problem: persuading my mother to drive me, because again, "gas costs money" and "we are poor," and all the theaters were at least ten to twenty miles away. Unless the film had Alan Bates in it. If Alan Bates was in the movie, it could have been forty miles away and my mom would swoon and just start driving. Hey, I saw some great movies that way. *An Unmarried Woman*, *The Rose*, *Far From the Madding Crowd*, *Whistle Down the Wind*—I could do the entire Alan Bates film canon, but I will spare you a detailed retelling of the wrestling scene from *Women in Love*.

My mom took advantage of this by devising a clever "chores for movies" exchange. Every day I would have to wash dishes, vacuum, or clean the basement while she would *consider* taking me to a movie. Then, on Saturday morning, she would make her final decision. If there was one misstep—if I was sullen (constantly), if I argued with her (always), if I fought with my brothers (let's not go there)—it was off, and I would not get to do my movie reviews. I would be further disappointed because—although I would never have admitted this to my mom—I liked going to the movies with her, and I think she liked seeing a wide array of movies with me, too.

One Saturday morning everything was going great. The house was freshly cleaned, it was painted, and I had just finished re-shingling the roof! I had my movie picked out from the paper, and then . . . disaster.

My parents were divorced, and we did not see a lot of my father, so when he showed up there was always a lot of . . . let's call it tension.

I heard the arguing begin. Slowly, as it always did, then gradually, one remark would build upon another until a full-blown fight had broken out. The movie started at two, and I was trying to interrupt to get my mother's attention. One o'clock hit, then half past. By 1:45, I was pleading, "I'm going to miss the movie!" but no one was listening.

It was now past two o'clock. The movie had started. That sick feeling came over me. I've missed the movie. *These people* have made me miss the movie. Somewhere other people are watching the movie, and I'm not there. As if it would never play again. As if nothing would ever be right again. I felt completely betrayed by my parents, who were in their own world, just as I was in my own world. I trudged back up to my black-and-white room and threw myself onto my bed. I think all movie lovers have some sort of void or sadness in them that movies fill. When I was deprived of a movie, I felt heartsick. My parents were still fighting, and to block them out, and also to stop myself from obsessing about what might be happening in the movie I was currently missing, I picked up the newspaper and began to skim through it. Something interesting caught my eye, and I'm not sure what would have happened to me acting-wise if I hadn't stumbled upon that random newspaper article that one morning. That single article in the week-old discarded paper started my career for real.

The story was about the Hartford Stage Company. It was holding auditions for a new program called the Hartford Stage Youth Theatre. It was looking for exceptional youth, ages fourteen to eighteen, with some theater and acting skills. Those accepted would receive $100 a week, receive training in all aspects of theater, and perform on the main stage in a musical at the end of the summer.

My heart raced. Somehow I knew that this program and the training it offered were going to be my ticket out of the rut I had found myself in post-Camelot. But there was a catch. The whole enterprise was being underwritten by a large insurance company in Hartford to help "underprivileged youths from high-risk backgrounds who live in the inner city." I read the story again trying to figure out how I could become an underprivileged youth from a high-risk background who lived in the inner city. And I needed to do it quickly because they were accepting applications and this paper was already a week old.

I thought of myself as an actor, so I started my act. The first thing was that even to be considered I had to pretend that I lived in the inner city. I called a family friend who was living in Hartford and asked her if I could use her family's house as my mailing address because it seemed inner-city-ish. Somehow she agreed. I filled out the application, careful to mail it back from her address. The questions were pretty standard: What plays have you done? What kind of singer are you? Then it got tougher: Please describe your ethnicity—"Caucasian" was the last one listed—and your high-risk background. Hmmm . . . moral dilemma? Can I say I'm black? After all, some Italians are descendants of the Moors. No, couldn't get away with it. Although I didn't technically live in Hartford, I did feel certain that I belonged in this theater group. I came from a high-risk background, and we were poor. So, I justified what I was doing. Small little lies for a bigger cause: my musical comedy career! My application came back, and my mother handed me the phone. My "parents," Mr. and Mrs. Murray, told me that I had been accepted and that my audition would be in a few weeks. I was to be prepared to dance and have one song that showed off my voice.

I had no formal training—well, that's not exactly true. I had stood in front of the television and watched Fred Astaire dance . . . a lot. I also loved Ruby Keeler . . . a lot. And . . . there was Liza Minnelli. I did my best to sound like Liza Minnelli, who was my favorite performer. If someone had asked me at age fifteen who I wanted to be when I grew up, I would have said, "I want to be Liza Minnelli." She could sing; she could dance; she was sexy in an offbeat way. I wanted to be Liza Minnelli in *Cabaret*—putting the plot of the movie aside—wearing the bowler hat and the stockings and belting "Maybe This Time," just as she had. My love affair with Liza was solidified when my grandfather took me to see her onstage in *Chicago*. She replaced Gwen Verdon, and I was lucky enough to see her in her prime in that great show. I also wanted to be her in *New York, New York*, which, putting the plot aside *again*, is like an old MGM musical—with domestic abuse—but I loved it. So I not only admired Liza Minnelli; I thought I could do a good enough impression of her to actually get myself into the Hartford Stage Company's inner-city youth group.

The audition was approaching, and I couldn't decide between

two songs. Liza Minnelli's version of "The Man I Love," which I learned off of the *New York, New York* soundtrack album, which was completely inappropriate, or "Maybe This Time," which I had learned off the *Cabaret* album, which was also completely inappropriate—but I thought I could "act" it. I decided on "Maybe This Time," because I felt it depicted both my desire and my desperation to be a performer. Stop reading and play the song right now. You'll see what I mean. I was fifteen and delusional and living in a bedroom that was a movie set . . . so there's also that.

I'm not sure what would have happened if there had been a power outage in our house, or if the needle had broken on the record player. For weeks I practiced, again and again. I had mastered every nuance of Liza Minnelli's singing "Maybe This Time." I would put the record on, and there in my black-and-white-and-silver room, I would belt out the lyrics with such sincerity that I would actually reduce myself to tears. The song had that much meaning for me. It was my anthem: "It's got to happen / Happen sometime / Maybe this time I'll win."

I could actually see the folks at the Hartford Stage Company as I sang. They would stand up and cheer. Then, while I collected myself, I would imagine how humble I would be when they told me, "You have the part . . . you have *any* part . . . you can have *all* the parts you want! We have never seen anything like you, kid. You're the next Liza Minnelli!" The only thing that ruined it was my mother's yelling up, "Dinner is ready; have you fed the dog yet? And could you please stop playing that record?"

The day of the audition came, and Liza—I mean I—was very nervous. I listened to the record one last time. My mom was getting the car keys, and then . . . disaster. As we were getting ready to go, my father showed up. His girlfriend had dropped him off at our house to pick up some antique plates that he and my mom had been fighting over. So, now, for reasons that are still unclear to me, my mother agreed to give him the plates, and then give him a ride back to his girlfriend's house with the plates, before my big audition.

I couldn't believe this was happening. My mother was in the kitchen stacking plates for my father and his new girlfriend, and I was going to miss the audition. And the consequences were a little larger than just missing a movie. I suggested that my father stay behind with his plates and that maybe his girlfriend could come pick him up, but those thoughts—which I articulated very clearly—were ignored, and the three of us got into the car. My mother, trying to keep the peace or just gain mileage on her car, decided it would be easier to drive me forty-five minutes to the audition, then drive my father back thirty minutes to his girl-friend's house, then turn around and drive back the forty-five minutes to pick me up when I was finished.

I don't want to ruin the surprise, but no sooner had we got into the car than the arguing began. "It's your fault . . . No it's your fault!" It's always been very important in our family to as-sign blame. Once we straighten out whose fault something is, we can move on. The fight escalated to pretty bad pretty quickly. The drive to the audition was like a moving Edward Albee play, my parents hurling insults at each other like a "best of" from every terrible fight they had ever had. I was in the backseat just trying to block them out, by silently singing, "Maybe this time . . ."

I kept on going.

"Everybody loves a winner, so nobody loved me / 'Lady Peace-ful,' 'Lady Happy,' that's what I long to be . . ." I did this for forty-five minutes. It was not easy, but it kept me from screaming "What is the matter with you people? Your daughter is trying to do something with her life. Can we stop talking about plates?"

People ask me about movie acting. It's all concentration. Concentration in the midst of chaos. Maybe that's where I learned it—with my eyes closed, trying to keep a tune and lyrics in my head when it seemed that everything in the universe was pitted against me. All I heard in my mind was, I know this song; I love singing this song; I know this is going to be great. We pulled up in front of the theater, and I felt as if I had emerged from a blackout. I got out of the backseat, and my father cheerfully said, "Good luck," as if we had been on a nice family drive in the country. The way he said it made me think he wanted me to fail. And all of a sudden I felt like I was going to fail. I quickly started to hum to myself, "Maybe this time . . . "

I didn't look back at my parents. I thought, All I have to do is to keep walking. Do not turn around. They will be gone by the time you get inside.

I signed in, and it was pretty intimidating. There were hundreds of kids—mainly black and Hispanic—warming up, stretching, vocalizing, sounding and looking pretty experienced. My first instinct was to run away, but I knew my mother was already on her way to my father's girlfriend's house, so that was no longer an option. I tried to find my inner strength, but the trip had worn me down, and I felt exhausted and defeated before I had even begun.

I got my number and waited. First up was dancing. If you didn't pass the dancing, you wouldn't even get to the singing. For the first round, we were given some choreography, and I was completely lost. One dancer, a tall slim black kid, was a standout, clearly the best in the group. He was a ballet dancer and had already been in some professional productions. In an act of mercy I appreciate to this day, he pulled me aside and taught me all the steps until I had the dance down cold. With his help I made all the dancing cuts and was part of the remaining fifty kids. His name was Michael, further proof that he was an angel. My name was called for the next round, which was singing, and I smiled at my new friend.

I entered the room, and there was a long table with a lot of folks sitting behind it. The director introduced himself. He asked me a few questions about my training, and I mentioned the Camelot, hoping that he had heard of it. He hadn't.

"What will you be singing?" he asked.

Secret weapon. I grandly handed my music to the piano player and then stepped to the center of the room and said, "Maybe This Time."

There was some very pleasant smiling and nodding at my choice, and then everyone sat back to listen.

Now, the application had stated that we were supposed to bring our sheet music for the accompanist to play, but no one had actually ever *played* the sheet music of "Maybe This Time" for me. I had assumed that the sheet music was the same as the record. The piano player started to play, and he was about an octave higher than the record from which I had learned the song. I'm singing, and he's playing something much higher than what I'm singing. I gave him a sideways look of panic, and he started banging out the higher notes louder as if I was signaling to him that what was wrong was that I couldn't *hear* him. I tried to follow him, going up and down the scale of "Maybe This Time" searching for the right notes. It was pitiful. He stopped abruptly and said very pointedly, "You are singing in the wrong key."

And I turned right around and stared defiantly at him and said, "I'm singing in the *right* key. I'm singing in the key of Liza, and *you're* in the wrong key!"

My first—and thankfully huge—showbiz laugh brought the house down. But I have to say, I wasn't joking. I hadn't known that there *was* any other way to sing that song than in the key of Liza.

The director sat up straight in his chair—clearly I had his attention—and started exchanging looks with everyone behind the table as if to say, "The kid's got moxie, but now what?" The music director hopped up and said, "I have an idea." He walked across the room and asked the piano player to get up and exchanged places with him. Then he asked me to sing the first line of the song, which I did.

He smiled at me and said, "You're in C, by the way."

I was terrified but I didn't show it. I just nodded, like, Yeah, key of Liza, like I told you!

Then he said, "I'll tell you what. Why don't you just sing, and I will follow you."

That sounded good to me!

I can't explain what that music director saw in me, probably blind terror, but his faith in me gave me confidence. I had been given a second chance, and I wasn't going to blow it. I started to sing, and I could feel everyone in the room pulling for me to succeed. Suddenly, all the pent-up emotion from the drive with my parents, the feelings of how much I really needed to get into this company, how much I couldn't fail, started to kick in. Fueled by all this, the song built, and my emotions built with it, and I sang "Maybe This Time" to within an inch of its life.

Well, at least as good as I had learned it on the record. I'm not sure if they were applauding for me, or for Liza Minnelli, but by the end of the song I had the entire group behind that table clapping and cheering for me. Just as I had fantasized back in my black-and-white-and-silver room.

I came out of the rehearsal hall, and my new friend Michael was waiting for me, asking me, "How did you do? You were in there forever!" I was grinning from ear to ear.

"Pretty good," I said humbly. "I did pretty good." He just started laughing. "You were so worried," he said. Three weeks later we would be rehearsing the musical *Two Gentlemen of Verona* together. I had made it into the company and was living with my pretend inner-city family, the Murrays.

Beautiful, tall, and slim Michael was the best dancer in the company, and we remained friends until I moved to New York a few years later. Sadly, he was fired during the third summer of the program for arriving ten minutes late for rehearsal. It was a very tough lesson, but I learned a lot about discipline from that moment.

I was quiet on the ride home from the audition, trying not to worry about what would have happened if I hadn't got through "Maybe This Time" but also thinking, I am an actor. For real now, not just in my black-and-white-and-silver room. I knew, in that strange way you just know, that I was becoming a professional performer.

I've always stumbled toward success. I'm like a marathon runner who trips on the finishing line but manages to skid across in spite of herself. I called my grandfather to tell him I had my first professional gig. He couldn't have been happier for me.

I was in the Hartford Stage Youth Theatre for three summers, starring in *Two Gentlemen of Verona* and two other musicals, *On the Town* and *The Boys from Syracuse*. It was a racially integrated company, way ahead of its time. Arts funding at its best. It was there that I learned everything about the theater. The first thing being, of course, what sheet music was! But I also learned the joy, the discipline, the hard work of performing. It was also my first taste of how a brand—in this case, an insurance company—could support the arts, as we were completely subsidized. I used this positive experience when I pitched a branded entertainment series to IKEA called *Easy to Assemble* many years later.

In 2012, I was working with Turner Classic Movies at its annual TCM Classic Film Festival. The opening-night film was *Cabaret*. It was, of course, amazing to see it on the big screen and to have all the stars, including Liza Minnelli, in attendance. At the after-party one of the TCM hosts, my good friend Ben Mankiewicz, came up to me and said, "Liza Minnelli would like to meet you."

I thought he was teasing me.

But he assured me that no, he wasn't. "She asked to meet you," he said.

She was of course so very gracious and kind. I mean she's Liza! We spoke about *Cabaret* and some of her other films that I had admired. While we were talking, someone came up and snapped our picture. It was only later, after looking at the photograph of us together, that I realized the impact that she had had on my life. Without Liza Minnelli, I would have never made it through that audition, and that's a fact. We look up to movie stars. We believe in them, because they are larger than life, and it makes us believe in ourselves when no one else does. At least that's how

I felt, all alone in my room singing "Maybe This Time." Who knows what would have happened if I had sung it in the "right" key? What's the "right" key, anyway? Without mistakes you never learn anything, and this was a happy mistake. Always be yourself and always sing in the key of Liza!

CHAPTER FIVE

Chance Encounters

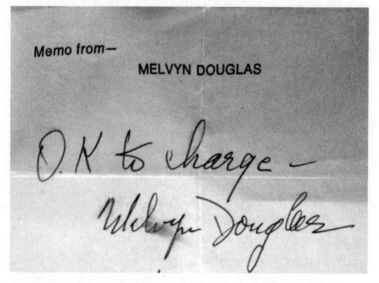

From *Easy Rider* to easy living! An Oscar winner's version of food stamps.

Always ride a unicycle. Because it's hard, and not everyone can do it."

That's what Peter Sellers had said to me on the set of *Being There*. What did it mean? Or have I always known what it meant but was afraid to face it?

I have always looked for signs in my career. When you have no money, you live on dreams and magic signs that foretell where you're going, signs that promise you something to eat when you get there. When those dreams and magical signs actually come true, it keeps you going through the rough spots. Here's a prime example.

The first movie I remember seeing with my Italian grandmother (my mom's mom) was *Paint Your Wagon*. My grandmother was not in show business, but she should have been. The closest Annie got was being a stand-in for the silent film star Theda Bara at Astoria Studios in Queens, New York City, which is where she grew up, one of ten children whose parents had come to America through Ellis Island. My grandmother and I shared a passion for going to the movies, something that began that magical night she took me to her favorite movie palace, Radio City. She had been a tap dancer, and her dream was to become one of the Radio City Rockettes—a dream cut short when she got pregnant at sixteen and got married. Annie was a pistol. She would say things such as "Fix your hair, so we can get free beer" or "Your father isn't so bad. He has his good faults." All of my comedic timing comes from her. The infamous reference to Miami I made to Lorraine Bracco in the movie *Goodfellas*—"It's like I died and woke up in Jew Heaven"—was her line, a reference to her brief stay in a retirement village in Florida. Annie visited me on many sets, asking Jennifer Aniston on *Picture Perfect*, "Are you the hair-and-makeup girl?" She danced until 3 A.M. at the after-party for the premier of *Stir of Echoes*, and made many lasagnas for Martin Scorsese. She even fulfilled her dream of being on TV with Regis Philbin when she appeared on *Live! with Regis and Kathie Lee*. "Now I can die," she said. Luckily for me, she lived for many more years after that.

All that I remember about seeing *Paint Your Wagon* with my grandmother is Lee Marvin's face, fifty feet high, singing

"Wand'rin' Star." Still, in that moment, I fell instantly and hopelessly in love. I could actually feel my heart ache when Jean Seberg chose Clint Eastwood over him. It was the first time that I remember feeling an emotion, and that emotion was love. Now, maybe a psychiatrist could explain why I chose Lee Marvin as the object of my desire, and not young and handsome Clint Eastwood. But those first movie images of Lee Marvin became implanted in my brain and were interwoven with romantic notions I carried for years to come.

We had a four o'clock movie on TV in those days, and it seemed to play *Cat Ballou* or *The Dirty Dozen* in constant rotation just for me. I would sit in front of the TV and imagine kissing my precious Lee Marvin. *The Dirty Dozen* is a war movie, but I've seen it so many times I could be called upon to be an expert on the film—from a purely romantic point of view. *The Big Red One*, directed by Sam Fuller, was another film that starred Lee Marvin, which I made my grandmother take me to again and again. Years later, I met Sam Fuller, and he was so impressed that I could speak so eloquently about the effect this WWII film had on me. (Secret weapon, Sam: it starred Lee Marvin.)

Cut to early one morning in New York, in 1982. I was walking up Madison Avenue on my way to acting school. When my grandfather was alive, he had hoped that I would be living with him and going to Juilliard. Yeah, me too. But he passed away in 1981. I certainly didn't have the funds to go to Juilliard, but I desperately wanted to move to New York, so I regrouped and found an affordable acting school I could attend. I will kindly just say that this acting school . . . was no Juilliard. But it did take me to New York City, give me lifelong friends and memories, and, thankfully, it eventually led me to another acting school.

It was the end of a school year that had been memorable for all the wrong reasons. I was—contrary to my own opinion of myself—not considered to have much of a future as a thespian. This made no sense to me, since back in Connecticut, post–Hartford Stage Youth Theatre, I had been getting paid to act in various amateur productions, in the chorus of such classics as *Gypsy*. And, well, *Gypsy*! (It was a popular show at the time in amateur theater.) I had also worked at the Camelot Dinner Theatre personally assisting Rudy Vallée! Still, the teachers at my acting school were not impressed.

One teacher said to me, "Some people *are* sexy, but it's like you're Lucille Ball trying to *be* sexy."

I actually landed in a "remedial" acting class taught by the tough headmistress of the school. When I first auditioned for the school, after hearing my monologue, she had said, "And . . . have you thought about what you will do if you *don't* make it into the school?" In remedial class, we were supposed to go around the room and validate *why* we thought we had ended up there. I thought it was meant to break our spirits, so when she got to me I said indignantly, "I have no idea why I'm here!" She insisted that I had a bad attitude toward learning The Method, which was Lee Strasberg's Actors Studio technique. It emphasized sense memory and place more than meaning of the text. She went on to mock a scene I had done as Lady Macbeth, saying, "Illeana, after you walked through the imaginary wall of your castle, I didn't believe a word you said."

The Method seemed contrary to everything I had learned working at the Camelot. There was never any time at the Camelot to think, Why are you doing *Godspell*? You were there to entertain an audience who had paid $19.95 for dinner and a show! In my opinion, I had learned more per week watching bus-and-truck tours break down and put up a show at the Camelot than I ever would by practicing The Method. I learned more about acting watching Rudy Vallée perform in his eighties, sweat dripping down his face for a crowd of strangers and still getting solid laughs with pretty creaky material. When he sang "For I'm just a vagabond lover / In search of a sweetheart it seems / And I know that someday I'll discover her / The girl of my vagabond dreams," he had that audience in the palm of his hand. Nothing in my memory was as solitary and beautiful as that. It was the essence of everything I wanted to be able to do. Still want to do. In a word: pathos. But that was long ago and not much help when dealing with imaginary walls or pantomimed steaming-hot coffee cups.

But back to that morning in 1982. After a rocky year, I was going to be performing what they called "final scenes" for the faculty. Their reaction would determine whether or not I would be "asked back" for another year. I was pretty nervous, and I asked the universe for some sign that I would have a chance.

I was walking up Madison Avenue toward my destiny when suddenly, I couldn't believe my eyes. There, taking a morning stroll, without a single person aware of who he was, was my lanky, silver-haired movie star from *Paint Your Wagon*. There was my childhood sweetheart. My first love. There was Lee Marvin! This wasn't a sign; it was a billboard!

I know what you're thinking. Poor Lee Marvin. Minding his own business, in town to promote his film *Death Hunt*, taking a nice little early morning walk, probably hungover, and now all of my hopes and dreams rested on his shoulders. Broad shoulders. (Sigh.) I could barely breathe as I stepped into his path. "Mr. Marvin," I said. "I'm sorry to interrupt you . . ."

The next part came out in an emotional jumble, but the odds of ever seeing Lee Marvin again were scarce, so I wanted to get everything in. "You were in the first movie I ever saw with my grandmother, *Paint Your Wagon* at Radio City Music Hall . . ." Then I went on to list his credits—you know, in case he forgot—all the movies I had seen him in, the number of times I'd seen him in them, how much they had meant to me. *The Dirty Dozen*, *The Big Red One*, *Pocket Money*, which I had seen on TV. *Pocket Money* was a very obscure reference; was he possibly impressed?

In the same breath, I continued, "And I'm an actor, and I'm on my way to do my final scene, and I asked the universe for a sign, and here you are, and it's meant to be, and I am going to be an actress, and is there any advice . . . " I was about to keep going when Lee Marvin—bless his heart—gently held up his hand to stop me. He smiled his wry Lee Marvin smile, and in that velvety, gravelly voice, he said, "Young lady, if you have half as much energy on the stage as you do off—you ought to do very well."

Then he asked me my name. Lee Marvin had come off the movie screen and appeared to me, and he was now asking me my name. "Illeana," I said.

He leaned down and kissed me on the cheek. "Good luck, Illeana." All those years I had practiced kissing him into my pillow, and now he was finally kissing me back.

And then he continued walking. I watched his back disappear up Madison Avenue. No one recognized him. No one turned to look. Just me. I touched my cheek. You know how people say "I will never wash that cheek again?" That's how it felt. Lee Marvin had kissed my cheek, and I was sure he had passed his movie magic onto me. Some of that magic faded when half of my classmates reacted by saying "So what, who cares" or "Who's Lee Marvin?" But I was on cloud nine. I did my final scenes assured that Lee Marvin's "Good Luck, Illeana" was not only a sign; it was an omen. I was bouncing off the walls. Final scenes indeed! I was a shoe-in to be asked back.

After the performance the headmistress came up to me and shook my hand. Clearly she was impressed, I thought. Her opinion of me had changed. I waited for her compliments. "Goodbye, Illeana," she said. What? That didn't sound good. Where was Lee Marvin when I needed him? He could have punched her out. Or at least explained to her about my marvelous offstage energy! Two weeks later I got a letter informing me I was not being "asked back."

Where is the sign? Is that what you're asking? Well . . . I was pretty angry about not being asked back. I was convinced that they were wrong, and that Lee Marvin and I were right. So, I decided to prove it. I applied to another acting school called The Neighborhood Playhouse. It was there that I found the teachers—Sanford Meisner, Richard Pinter, and Phil Gushie—who were right for me. At the end of that first year, I was once again required to do my "final" scenes. There was no Lee Marvin in sight this time. But right before I went onstage, my teacher Richard Pinter said he wanted to talk to me. "Remember everything you used to do before you got here? Everything you learned doing musical and dinner theater?" he asked. "Do it now." I smiled. I knew exactly what he meant. I was a serious actor now, and I hadn't thought about the Camelot Dinner Theatre or musicals in a while—and even though I hadn't actually ever been on its stage, when Richard Pinter told me to remember the Camelot, I knew that he understood me. That was the sign I needed.

But back to Peter Sellers and riding unicycles—and how that became another influential sign in my life. I had just about forgotten his words of wisdom, when, twenty-five years later, Peter Sellers himself reminded me of our exchange. But I'll get to that.

My grandfather invited me to watch him at work—on the set of *Being There*. It was the first time I had seen my grandfather on the set of a movie. I knew he was important. I knew he made movies. But most of the time he was just Grandpa, and I was his only granddaughter. He had been amused when I told him "I'm going to be an actress. Like Ruby Keeler." She was the adorable tap-dancing star of many Busby Berkeley musicals. I was almost fourteen now and wanted to be a real actress, not just Ruby Keeler, so inviting me to the set of *Being There* was his way of acknowledging that he knew I wanted to follow in his footsteps. We shared a special bond, and the bond was simple. He took an interest in me when no one else did. I think he knew it, and for that I will be forever grateful. *Being There* permanently shifted my view of movies from outsider to insider. Before, I had been on the outside looking *in* at a movie. Now I was going behind the curtain, inside the movie looking *out*. I would never be the same.

When I was growing up, my grandparents' rambling apartment, at 77th Street and Riverside Drive in New York City, with its servants and maids, was a stark contrast to life at The Studio with its goats and hippies. The guest room had a double bed and a view of Frank Sinatra's yacht on the Hudson River. There was also a friendly doorman to hail you a cab or help you with your groceries. Your fingers never even came close to a door of any kind. It was always opened for you. We dressed for dinner. My grandfather would ring a bell and food would be served. Ring another bell and it would be taken away. I couldn't believe people lived this way . . . and that I didn't!

Staying with my grandfather, I learned the concept of ordering food for delivery. I would watch in amazement as he would call a place named Zabar's—which sounded magical—and tell them what he wanted: eggs, bread, coffee, etc., and then a man would deliver it! Sometimes my grandfather would give me a piece of paper with just his signature on it, and I would walk around the corner to Zabar's, show someone there the piece of paper, and a nice man would help me get whatever I'd asked for.

"What else for you?"

"Um . . . Häagen-Dazs?"

"What else?"

I loved this guy! He'd pinch my cheek, and there would be no bill. They'd just put it on the account: Melvyn Douglas. When I was a starving actress I would wander into Zabar's for a bagel and a coffee, and let me tell you, I did not get the same treatment. I remember overhearing my grandfather on the phone after one of my shopping trips, ordering from Zabar's.

"Yes, and also some Häagen-Dazs vanilla ice cream . . . for my granddaughter, yes." And he would wink at me, because he had become addicted to it, too, thanks to my having sneaked it into the basket. I especially loved going to Zabar's when we'd go together. My grandfather and I would walk down the aisles while folks nudged each other and whispered, "That's Melvyn Douglas." Everyone was so friendly. So helpful! The same thing happened at the candy store. Always free samples of chocolate-covered cherries for Melvyn Douglas and his granddaughter. He would take me to a Broadway show and afterward we would eat at a showbiz restaurant called Sardi's. Everyone was so friendly. So helpful! Actors stopped by the table to say hello. Waiters were constantly making sure everything was all right, bringing more and more food that was "on the house." I could never finish anything, because the portions were huge. Years later, the first time I had some money in my pocket, I invited someone to go to Sardi's, promising them huge portions. The meal came and everything was regular size, and I was so disappointed. I wanted "Melvyn Douglas size."

As I got older, my grandfather started telling me more about the movies he was going to be shooting. He would act out the entire story, playing all the parts. I remember him acting out the movie *The Tenant,* and the way he told it was actually scarier than the film. He described something that happened on the set that was equally chilling. He was shooting a climactic scene with Roman Polanski—the tenant—after Polanski tries to commit suicide by jumping out a window. It required Polanski to be covered in stage blood. After each take, Polanski would ask for more blood. After numerous takes Polanski and the set were covered in blood, but he was still dissatisfied, and kept insisting they needed more. My grandfather described an eerie feeling that descended upon the set, as Polanski, drenched in blood, kept insisting there still wasn't enough. He said, "You see, in poor Roman's mind there would probably never be 'enough blood' to match the horror of what he had once witnessed." Which was, of course, the bloody scene of his wife Sharon Tate's murder. And the way my grandfather told me that story, with such helpless empathy, has stayed with me all these years.

We were in the apartment on Riverside Drive when he handed me a paperback book and said that it was going to be his next movie. The book was *Being There*, by Jerzy Kosiński. He said, "And if it's done right, it could be something quite interesting." He told me that Peter Sellers was going to play Chance the Gardener. My eyes lit up. Peter Sellers? From *The Pink Panther*? By this time, my room at home was a collage of movie posters, magazine covers, and pictures of my favorite actors and actresses. Peter Sellers was one of those smiling faces who watched over me. My poster from *The Return of the Pink Panther* was next to a pink *People* magazine cover on which he appeared. This was next to Peter Sellers on a cover of *Fate Magazine: True Stories of the Strange and Unknown*, which had an article discussing his interest in ESP and psychics.

I was excited to see my grandfather work, but I was over the moon to meet Peter Sellers. He was a movie star! Inspector Clouseau! I loved watching movies—I wanted to be in the movies—but as I've said, I was still on the outside, watching movies as an audience member. I still didn't understand that there was a director, and a crew, and a whole lot of folks behind the scenes who actually *made* a movie. For me, it was still all pictures and posters on my wall, movie stars such as Peter Sellers, and the characters they played, such as Inspector Clouseau. Now my grandfather was going to make me an insider, and that, I realized, was even more fun.

Some of the scenes in *Being There* were shot at a mansion called Biltmore House, in Asheville, North Carolina. My grandfather was staying at a hotel nearby, aptly called the Grand Bohemian. People always ask me, Did your grandfather ever give you advice? And the answer is Yes, he did. Here's the most important thing he taught me. We were at the Grand Bohemian and once again he was ordering food for delivery.

He said, "Illeana, you want to be an actress, I want you to remember one fact. Wherever you are, whatever country you are in, if you don't know what to order from room service, always get the club sandwich. It will always be good."

I can't tell you how many times I have arrived at a hotel late at night—whether it's in Toronto or Madrid or Shreveport, Louisiana—skimmed through the menu, and thought, Grandpa's right. Order the club sandwich! Best advice I've ever got, and I'm passing it on to you, courtesy of Melvyn Douglas.

We got up at dawn, and someone drove us to what looked to my young eyes like the grandest, most magical castle I had ever seen. Once again, everyone was so friendly! So helpful! My grandfather had said, "Films result from the collective efforts of many human beings." I was beginning to understand what he meant. My grandfather had a bit of a cold, so someone immediately brought him some tea. A man with long white hair and a crazy beard smiled at me and said to a woman holding a large notebook, "Mel's granddaughter is on set; can we please find a place for her to sit?" This man with the long white hair and crazy beard seemed to be in charge, because when he spoke things happened very quickly. Immediately a director's chair was found for me and then placed next to the woman with the large notebook. She smiled at me and asked, "You're Mel's granddaughter?"

I nodded, feeling shy all of a sudden.

"Have you ever been on a movie set before?"

"No," I said. "It's a lot of people."

"It *is* a lot of people," said the man with the long white hair and the crazy beard.

Of course, years later I would realize that the man with the long white hair and the crazy beard was the director Hal Ashby.

All I was interested in was seeing Inspector Clouseau. I never would have dreamed that years later Hal Ashby—with his movies such as *Shampoo, Coming Home,* and *Harold and Maude*— would become one of my all-time-favorite directors.

The woman with the notebook spoke to some other women who came over and began fussing over me.

"This is Mel's granddaughter!"

"Oh, isn't that nice!"

"Everyone *loves* your grandfather!"

"Are you going to be an actress?"

The man with the long white hair and a crazy beard called for quiet, and all the hustle and bustle suddenly stopped. "Peter's here," I heard him say.

Inspector Clouseau! I could barely look up.

At first I didn't even recognize that it was Peter Sellers. Without his Clouseau mustache he looked completely different, not at all like the pictures on my bedroom wall. He was much older, with grayish white hair, and almost bald. They started to rehearse the scene where Peter Sellers as Chance the Gardener is introduced by my grandfather to the president, played by Jack Warden. I couldn't really hear anything, but I watched as Hal Ashby demonstrated to Peter Sellers how he wanted him to shake Jack Warden's hand. There seemed to be some banter about the handshake, and then I saw Peter Sellers bent over laughing, and then the actors, including my grandfather, all started to laugh, too. I couldn't even hear anything, and I truly thought, This is the most exciting thing I have ever seen.

While they rehearsed, a tall man with glasses walked all around them. He looked very serious. He was squinting a lot and adjusting the lights. He would stare at the actors and then stare at the lights. What I remember is how even though it was a rainy day, he was able to create these beautiful columns of light that looked like they were coming through the window. He didn't talk to anyone, and he kept to himself. I would later learn that this was the director of photography, Caleb Deschanel. I had the privilege of working with him years later on the movie *Message in a Bottle*. During that filming, he brought his daughter Zooey on set and said to me, "Can you please talk her out of being an actress?"

"No way," I said.

As they prepared to shoot the *Being There* scene, more and more crew came out of the shadows and gathered around the actors. The women who were talking to me were hair-and-makeup ladies. They hovered over Peter Sellers. He had a hairpiece that had to be adjusted so that the camera wouldn't pick it up. One woman held up a small mirror for him to inspect. Another woman powdered and patted my grandfather's and Jack Warden's faces. Another man inspected their clothes, brushing off lint and adjusting their ties until they looked perfect. Another man was hiding microphones under the table. I was riveted by the number of people it all required. I loved the sense that everyone had a job to do; yet they were all focused on doing it together. As my grandfather had said: the collective efforts of human beings. To me, it felt like this was a secret place away from the world, where everybody was happy in his or her work.

"Mel, Peter, Jack. Can we put one in the can?" asked Hal Ashby. Then he called, "Action." My heart skipped a beat. I was on a movie set watching my grandfather film a scene from a movie. The cameras moved in on their dollies, and the crew focused toward the light as the actors brought the scene to life. Every moment was orchestrated by a "Yes. Yes. Perfect. Brilliant. Oh, that's not good" from Hal Ashby. When the scene was over, he called "Cut" and everyone applauded or started to laugh. He jumped out of his chair to go talk to the actors, and then they did the whole thing again. What I remember was that each time they filmed, he would watch the scene completely enthralled, smiling or nodding his head like a proud parent. My grandfather was very happy with his work in the film. "He's a good director," he said to me on the car ride home. At the time, I didn't understand what that meant. Now I do.

My grandfather could be quite the raconteur, and between scenes he and Jack Warden and Peter Sellers—they had all been in the service—began swapping war stories. I later learned that my grandfather and Peter Sellers had actually met years before when they were both stationed in Burma during World War II. That may have been the main reason my grandfather got the part. Peter Sellers had purchased the rights to the book *Being There* and was trying to get it made. In the 1970s he was walking on the beach in the Malibu Colony and met Hal Ashby. The director had someone else in mind for my grandfather's part, but Peter Sellers was a man who believed in signs and omens. He insisted that having been in the service with my grandfather would add depth to their relationship on-screen. The role of Benjamin Rand had to be played by Melvyn Douglas. Their connection is reflected in the movie.

On the set of *Message in a Bottle*, Caleb Deschanel told me that they were filming a scene in *Being There* in which Sellers and my grandfather walked down a long marble hallway. As they walked side by side, almost touching, their steps became the same until they were walking as one. He pointed out to Ashby that their reflections could be seen on the black marble floor.

Ashby said, "Peter Sellers and Melvyn Douglas are achieving such clarity, such simplicity, it looks like they are walking on water." He paused and said, "In fact, Gardener *will* walk on water."

That walk gave him the idea for changing the ending of the film. Instead of Chance walking into the woods—which was the original ending—it would end with Chance walking on water.

By the end of the day I was over my shyness, and I only had one thing on my mind. "Grandpa," I said, "can I meet Peter Sellers?"

"Oh, Peter," my grandfather said to him, clearing his throat. "I think you have a fan here. My granddaughter loves," and he took a pause . . . "Inspector Clouseau." He said it with a French accent.

This prompted Peter Sellers, and he immediately went into character as the bumbling Inspector Clouseau. I was in heaven. He began to interrogate me as the suspect of a mass baguette-stealing crime. Everyone was laughing, but then he got sort of serious and asked me, "Can you ride a unicycle?"

And I laughed and said, "No . . . "

And he said, "Oh, you must. You must learn to ride a unicycle, because it's hard and not everyone can do it."

The set of *Being There* was a sacred experience. Making a movie—like riding a unicycle—is hard, and not everyone can do it. Whenever I step on a set I try to remember the temple of art that Hal Ashby, Peter Sellers, Jack Warden, and many others, including my grandfather, created for me that day. It made me want to be in those dancing columns of light, where all those eyes were focused, away from the shadows.

When *Being There* was over, my grandfather was given a wrap gift of a Sony television set that had been used in the film and something else. My grandfather showed me this thing, called a Sony Walkman, and said, "This is going to change everything. You can listen to music on it."

When he was nominated for an Academy Award for his performance he wanted me to attend with him, but my grandmother was sick, and he didn't want to leave her.

I screamed when they called out his name as the winner.

"You won! Grandpa!"

"Yes, I beat out a child and a horse." He was referring to Justin Henry in *Kramer vs. Kramer* and Mickey Rooney in *The Black Stallion*.

I spent even more time with him on the set of *Ghost Story*. I gathered things were not going well on the set. Although my grandfather never complained, I could see how he winced when yellow pages—meaning new lines to be learned—would arrive late at night at our suite at the Gideon Putnam Hotel, in Saratoga Springs, New York.

My grandmother had passed away, and he was talking about my moving in with him to pursue my acting career.

"I think it's a good idea," he said. "I don't want to live alone, and I'll be able to protect you from men such as myself in show business." Of course, he had a twinkle in his eye.

My grandfather died within a year of filming *Ghost Story*. He had caught pneumonia filming numerous scenes in the snow. At his memorial service they played clips from his movies on the same television set that had been his wrap gift from the set of *Being There*. Then they played the actual movie *Being There*. I couldn't look at it. I could not watch my grandfather die again.

It was years before I could see the movie *Being There*. It held such a special place in my heart. But the movie began to follow me in strange, almost mystical ways. It started when my grandfather bequeathed me the Academy Award he had won for playing Benjamin Rand. His Oscar has traveled with me from cheap apartment, to cheap apartment, to a nicer apartment, to a house, to another house, across country, and back again. At the time he won this Oscar—his second; the first was for *Hud,* in 1963—he was seventy-nine years old. Makes me think I have something to look forward to.

In 1995, I was being fitted for a wig for *Grace of My Heart* when out of the blue the wigmaker showed me a plaster bust he had once made of Peter Sellers. "We made all his hairpieces for *Being There!*" I said, "That's weird because I actually saw Peter Sellers wearing that hairpiece." After I told him who my grandfather was he gave me the bust! It's in my house, and people always ask me, "Why do you have Peter Sellers's death masque?" I have to convince them that it was a gift, but somewhere inside of me I feel it's Peter Sellers having a laugh at my expense.

In 1998, I was at a thrift shop in Los Angeles looking at a vintage Gucci wallet when the owner said, "Oh, you like that wallet. You have good taste. It belonged to Peter Sellers." Of course it became my lucky wallet, something I have to have on every set to ensure good comedy.

When I was first looking to rent a house in the Malibu Colony in 1999, I thought I had found a beauty. It was a blue-and-white gingerbread Victorian with little turrets and diamond-shaped eaves in the bedrooms. I asked the owner if anyone famous had ever lived there, and he said, "Not really . . . There was some crazy director, never paid his rent on time, Hal somebody."

"Hal Ashby?" I asked in disbelief.

"Yeah. Hal Ashby. He actually died in this house. He had cancer, and he believed in pyramid power or some crazy thing like that. He used to sit under the eaves of the loft of one of the bedrooms. He thought the pyramid energy would cure him." I realized that this must have been the same house where Peter Sellers once talked to Hal Ashby about casting my grandfather.

It felt as if I had been mysteriously led there. On the spot I said, "I'll take it."

At night, I used to go way up on this ladder and sit under the eaves of the house. I would listen to the ocean and try to feel pyramid power like Hal Ashby. It made me feel as if somehow I was communicating with him.

Over the years, in one way or another, I met practically everyone ever associated with *Being There*. Every time I'd meet someone new who had worked on the film, I'd hear a story I had never heard before. Whenever these things happened, I would shrug it off as coincidence until one day in 2001. I was in New York after a big life change. I was feeling a little down, and I decided to go see a psychic. Men go to prostitutes for comfort. Women go to psychics! Anyway, I get there and it turns out she's not a psychic. She's a medium. She contacts the dead. Oh. OK. What the hell, I've paid my money. I ask her to try to contact my grandfather. So she's contacting my grandfather and during the session she starts to tell me that there's a man *with* my grandfather and that he's riding a unicycle! I was so taken aback that I asked, "Is it Peter Sellers?"

She said, "Yes." Then she said that he was showing her a pink photo of a man drawing a tic-tac-toe board. She was describing the *People* magazine cover of him that had once been on my bedroom wall! Now, you can believe in these things or not, but how could she have known that? She started to impart a lot of information to me. That he—Peter Sellers—and my grandfather were together, that Peter Sellers was my guardian angel! Who was I to argue that Peter Sellers was my guardian angel? The *Fate* magazine cover I also had on my bedroom wall had boasted the headline SPIRITS GUIDE PETER SELLERS' SUCCESS! Then the medium said, "He wants you to know that he's holding an umbrella over you, and he wants you to know that he always has that umbrella over you." In the last shot of *Being There*, Chance the Gardener is walking on water holding a large black umbrella. I'm listening to this, taking it in stride, then all of a sudden she says, "Oh. He wants to watch the movie *Being There* with you." Okay. This may sound like the craziest thing, but I was not about to turn down the chance to watch the movie *Being There* with a commentary from "the other side" by Peter Sellers. I hadn't seen the movie in years. It was still very difficult for me to see that movie. But I booked another appointment with the medium. We made popcorn, and then we—me, the medium, Peter Sellers, my grandfather, and I can't verify who else from the spirit world might have been in the audience—all watched *Being There*. The medium would listen to Peter and laugh, and then tell me what he had said to her. It was great to see the movie again and also to hear what appeared to be Peter Sellers's genuinely funny and insightful commentary. It was like being with an interpreter at the UN.

For instance, during the Shirley MacLaine masturbation scene Peter apparently told the medium that the filming of this scene had been difficult for him, because he was such a ladies' man and he and Shirley MacLaine had chemistry. "That was real acting, because it would be impossible for me to ever turn a lady down," the medium said, passing along what Peter had told her.

It was all a little crazy, but all in good fun, right? A couple of days later I was back at my house in Connecticut. I went down to the basement to get something, and there, leaning against the wall, was a unicycle. Its seat was gleaming white with silver sparkles. I did not own, or ever think of owning, a unicycle. I ran upstairs and said to my brother, "There's a unicycle in the basement! Where did it come from?" And he said, "I found it at the dump. Someone just left it there. I think I'm going to learn how to ride it." I looked up to heaven—or wherever Mr. Sellers was—and started to laugh. Message received, P. S.

To this day, whenever I see a unicycle, I know Peter Sellers is sending me a message, reminding me with that knowing smile, "Always ride a unicycle. Because it's difficult, and not everyone can do it."

"Life is a state of mind." That's the last line from the movie *Being There*. You can believe that or you can not believe it. I choose to believe in chance encounters.

CHAPTER SIX

Me Doing Dreyfuss Doing Tracy

The Goodbye Girl meets Duddy Kravitz. Me imitating Richard Dreyfuss in acting school. The play was *Uncommon Woman and Others.* The actor—me—was shameless.

Lately, when I am working on a movie, I ask the young actors around me the same question. Do you know who Spencer Tracy is? The answer, sadly, is that no, they do not know who Spencer Tracy is. Acting is a craft. One actor watches another actor and admires and copies his technique, and so on and so on. This is how our art form continues and is passed on. If we don't know who Spencer Tracy is then we cannot fully appreciate Richard Dreyfuss or, dare I say, Illeana Douglas.

The 1970s were the decade when watching movies helped form and change me into the actor I would later become. I went from wanting to see a movie, any movie, to seeking out my favorite actors and watching their performances in the movies they made. What's funny is that most of the movies I liked and wanted to see again and again had one common denominator: They all starred Richard Dreyfuss. And in many ways—some I am only still beginning to understand—my appreciation of him has led me to appreciate the deeply personal connections and identifications that can lead any of us to become a movie-lover.

I could run my own Richard Dreyfuss film festival; I've seen his entire body of work. I've watched as his performances became less driving and comedic and more thoughtful and introspective. I've consciously emulated him, and I've worked opposite him, doing my best *not* to emulate him. I've written about him; I have interviewed him. I wore him down until he was basically forced finally to participate in a friendship with me so that I wouldn't seem like a stalker. Luckily for me, Richard has accepted my obsession with great humor, because it's rooted in my admiration of him as an actor. He was the first actor I studied, and tried to be like, like a painter copying a master until he has a technique of his own. I recently discovered that Richard and I have that in common.

I was getting ready for an interview I was going to be doing with Richard for Turner Classic Movies, but by that point I had interviewed him so many times I was actually running out of questions. "Richard . . . what's the name of the shark in *Jaws*?" (His name was Bruce, by the way.) We started talking about acting and our respective training. We decided that the theme of this particular conversation—which would be our fifth—should address how the styles of movie acting have changed over the years, from Paul Muni to Marlon Brando. Richard said to me, "Nobody knows that I was pretending to be Spencer Tracy."

And I laughed and said, "Wait, I was pretending to be you, so I was doing you, and you were doing Tracy? I was doing Dreyfuss doing Tracy!" That's why we need to know who Spencer Tracy is. So you can watch Richard Dreyfuss and have some context about an actor who influenced him. And then you can watch me and have some context about an actor who influenced me and even saved my ass at times.

I was in my first acting school—the one I did not get asked back to—and I was cast in the play *Uncommon Women and Others*, playing a very brazen and confident law student. I had no idea what I was doing and I thought, Screw it, I'm just going to be Richard Dreyfuss. I'm going to throw out everything I'm doing, because it's not working, and I'm going to play this part pretending to be Richard Dreyfuss. I started doing his cadence, his walk. I even dressed like him. We got to the dress rehearsal, and the director said, "I'm not sure what you were doing, but it's really working. Keep it up."

And I did!

The next night, the director was even more impressed. "Illeana, you were just terrific! I just love what you are doing! What *are* you doing?"

"Um, *Jaws*?"

It may have started with *Jaws* (1975). I never could have guessed that summer that when my mother dropped me off at the movie theater with my friends to watch *Jaws* (I think for me it was at least five times that summer), we would become part of the generation that created repeat movie viewing and the summer blockbuster. Um . . . OK . . . Mr. Spielberg might have had something to do with it, but we helped. There was an innocent authenticity about the success of *Jaws* that was not driven simply by marketing. It was good, old-fashioned word of mouth about the shared experience of a movie that had affected us. Affected us? Wait. That sounds like a grown-up talking, and this was not a movie that I watched with grown-ups. Do you know what 600 kids all screaming sounds like? I probably got early hearing loss from being so freaked out at *Jaws*. My mom picked us up afterward on the sidewalk and all we talked about was seeing *Jaws*, again and again, and again. My mom made a lot of trips to the movie theater that summer. We became an army. One buzzed kid after another looking for that same adrenaline rush that *Jaws* gave us. And the second or third time you saw it, you felt superior, because you knew *when* everyone was going to scream. Something else took a hold of me in the dark, and it wasn't just that irksome shark. It was the more irksome Richard Dreyfuss, whose energetic performance leaped off the screen then as now, because I never tire of seeing him. Studying him. It's a performance that I blatantly ripped off. Of course, now that I know I was doing Dreyfuss doing Tracy, I don't feel as bad.

In *Jaws*, Richard Dreyfuss plays a marine biologist, Matt Hooper, who warns that "a great white shark" is still lurking in the water off an island called Amity, near Nantucket. One of the things that I first noticed about his performance is that you can actually watch him think on-screen. In fact, he's one of the best on-screen thinkers I've ever seen. An example of this occurs in the scene in which Hooper gets in the faces of Sheriff Brody (Roy Scheider) and the mayor (Murray Hamilton) at the dock after they have strung up a tiger shark. Brody thinks they've caught the murdering great white, and Hooper is trying to convince them that it's the wrong shark. First of all, Hooper just appears. I mean he's a complete stranger, and he starts ranting and lecturing them in front of the entire town without a hair of doubt that he's right. He's listening to their explanation, and I love watching his eyes as he is taking in information from the other characters. He's getting ready to explode. He can barely wait for Brody to finish his sentence. You can see his thoughts scrolling across his forehead like ticker tape. They read: I know I'm right, and as soon as you finish talking, I will convince you that I'm right. It's so much fun to watch him verbally assault someone with facts, with knowledge. Hooper was never afraid to be smart even if he came off as a smart-ass. The camera stays on Dreyfuss, which I love, because Dreyfuss looks physically exhausted by the end of his telling them off and pointing out how stupid they are. He's like a deflated balloon. Then, later that night, Hooper goes to Brody's house to apologize. What I love about this entire sequence is that after browbeating and humiliating Brody, Hooper thinks nothing of visiting Brody that very same night and bringing over a bottle of wine and quietly continuing to plead his case. Brilliant. I don't know who was more aggressive: Hooper or the shark! Was he annoying, as he was sometimes described in reviews? Maybe. But more important, was he right?

The second time I saw Richard Dreyfuss in a movie was

American Graffiti (1973) at the Middletown Drive-In. The movie had just been rereleased and was the bottom of a bill that included *The Gumball Rally* and *Dirty Mary, Crazy Larry*.

I was in the backseat watching the movie with someone older and cooler than I in the front seat. Her name was Susan. I knew my place. My place was to be her funny, compliant friend. If she needed a Coke, I would gladly run and get her a Coke. If she was sad about a recent breakup and needed me to make her laugh, I would make a joke. And I was not embarrassed. There were other kids on rungs farther down the social ladder from me who would have dreamed of getting a Coke for Susan. She was the most popular girl in school, for God's sake, and she liked me. But I knew my place.

In *American Graffiti* Richard Dreyfuss plays Curt, who is kind of a backseat friend to Ron Howard. Curt's a little younger, not cool enough to sit in the front seat. One night while driving around, Curt spots what he calls his "dream girl," played by Suzanne Somers, who mouths "I love you" to him from a passing white convertible. No one else in the car sees this but him, and Curt wants to go look for her. His pals think he's nuts and start to make fun of him. He has no power to look for her himself because he's stuck in the backseat. Curt is short, chubby, and not the best-looking guy in the crowd, but I'll never forget his face as he internalizes his buddies' mocking. He takes it, and he just smiles to himself, because he knows that he *will* see her again. And he knows something else. He knows he is going somewhere the other guys in the car are not. It's that same brilliant on-screen thinking that I saw in *Jaws*. Watching *American Graffiti* that first time, I felt like I was reading thoughts that were so private that even I shouldn't be seeing them. He feels superior to the guys in the front seat, so he'll just be patient, because they are wrong. Curt's unwavering belief in himself touched me deeply. At the end of the movie, as he boards the plane to leave the small town— and leave his buddies behind—he does see his dream girl again. I always thought that in that movie Richard Dreyfuss paved the way for a new type of comic romantic lead. The funny, smart, schlubby guy who gets the girl despite all the odds. Who proves that even the not-best-looking guys deserve their dream girls. And even though I was not Curt, and not Richard Dreyfuss, for the first time, I saw myself in a movie, which is one of the greatest gifts a movie can give us. To see ourselves in those forty-foot images.

I, too, was a backseat friend. I was always younger than my friends, a borderline outcast, not considered very pretty, but I got by, sitting in the backseat, supporting anything the girls who sat in the front seat said. I was funny and could make smart-aleck comments for their amusement. I was a real sensitive kid with pent-up, sensitive thoughts that were often out of place with my surroundings. Sometimes we would be riding around, and I would look out the window and see something beautiful, such as a full moon, or something sad, such as the town drunk sleeping in the snow, or I'd hear a sad song that reminded me of a boy I liked, but I knew I could never share things like that. I would be laughed out of the car. Watching *American Graffiti*, I realized that I was a phony. I wasn't going to do anything about it. I wasn't going to change anything, but it made me self-aware.

When you're a kid, you look for the character in the movie you can relate to, and Richard Dreyfuss always seemed like a big kid to me. A big kid with a difference: He was the one who had a keen sense of right and wrong, of morality and injustice. He seemed like a friend you could hide behind while he questioned authority—and he questioned authority a lot. It was Richard Dreyfuss who once made a professor apologize for having criticized Marlon Brando's performance in *Julius Caesar*. Years later, when I asked Richard if this was true or just a rumor, he said with some lingering indignation, "That is correct!" He was confident, even a little cocky, but his confidence seemed to come from having accepted who he was. I didn't know who I was, but I knew I wanted to be like him. Outspoken. Confident. He knew where he was going.

There's another milestone I owe to Richard Dreyfuss. It's the '70s cult classic I was never supposed to see but did anyway. It's an obscure film called *Inserts* (1975). I didn't know anything about *Inserts* except that it starred Richard Dreyfuss, so I asked my grandmother to take me to see it. We bought our tickets, got our popcorn, and the screen comes up and it's rated X! My Italian grandmother, who was very old-fashioned, was horrified. "Hey, what the hell is this?" she said in her thick accent. "What kinda of a movie you taking me to?"

She grabbed me by the arm and was dragging me up the aisle, but I begged her to let me stay, insisting it must be a comedy. After all, it had Richard Dreyfuss in it. We stayed. For the record, *Inserts* is *not* a comedy.

Inserts is about a washed-up film director, a former boy wonder, forced to make pornographic films. So thanks to Richard Dreyfuss, I saw my first X-rated film. Profoundly disturbing little movie by the way. My grandmother never forgave me.

I didn't really understand the film, but I saw the difference in his performance from *Jaws* and *American Graffiti*. It may sound like I'm kidding, but I'm not. What I understood for the first time was that the person you see on-screen is not that person, but an actor creating a character. I developed an understanding of the *craft* of acting from watching *Inserts*, because I couldn't believe that this lively funny actor whom I wanted to emulate could also do something as dark and gut-wrenching on-screen.

And then came *The Goodbye Girl* (1977). When you talk about the qualities you want to see in a romantic comedy, *The Goodbye Girl* has them all. It is the epitome of a feel-good movie: It has humor and heart and at its center it has a tour de force comedic performance by Richard Dreyfuss. He is not your typical romantic lead, but he is so charming and funny and confident that you just fall for him. I fell for him. Big time. Who didn't? Richard Dreyfuss manages to make both the mother, Paula (played by Marsha Mason), and her precocious twelve-year-old daughter, Lucy (Quinn Cummings), fall for him. He was that funny prince, that nice guy that all girls are looking for. He shows up, and he comes through. He had something in that movie that a typically handsome guy doesn't have: confidence that his inner self is as attractive as his outer self.

Dreyfuss does an interesting thing as Elliot in *The Goodbye Girl*. He chases the girl by not chasing the girl. There's a terrific scene where he is eating spaghetti with Lucy. He's being very cute and charming with her because he knows that *she* has a crush on him. All the while, he is also interacting with Paula. He also knows that *she* has a crush on him, too, but she's scared because she has had a bad history with men. Paula's acting like she's not interested in him, but he senses she is watching him, so he starts watching her back, all the while interacting with Lucy. He's innocently eating spaghetti with a twelve-year-old, but he's flirting through her to get to her mom. Remember what I said about the on-screen thinking. As the romance progresses, Paula is washing off her white "kabuki" makeup, as he calls it. She starts nervously pulling on her robe, getting all hot and bothered, because he's thinking sexy thoughts about her. You can see it on his face. What I love about the scene is that he's not overtly sexual, but he is sexually confident. His sexiness comes not from looks but from sexual know-how. He knows he's charming the pants off her, because he knows she wants it as much as he does. Maybe more.

There are scenes in *The Goodbye Girl* in which Dreyfuss actually makes Marsha Mason blush, yet they have all their clothes on. That's chemistry. That's great romantic comedy. His performance harkened back to the golden age of screwball comedies, but he brought to it a modern sensibility. At thirty years old, he was about to become the youngest person to receive an Academy Award for Best Actor. There have only been a few times in Oscar history that an actor won in the Best Actor category for a comedy. In 1934, Clark Gable won it for *It Happened One Night*; in 1940, Jimmy Stewart for *Philadelphia Story*; in 1965, Lee Marvin for *Cat Ballou*. Now, you could argue those actors won for a variety of reasons, but anyone who has seen *The Goodbye Girl* knows Richard Dreyfuss won an Oscar for his comic staccato delivery of "I sleep in the nude, au buffo" and, of course, the much repeated ". . . and-I-don't-like-the-panties-drying-on-the-rod." Here was an actor who won an Oscar for being singularly funny. It hasn't happened since.

The Goodbye Girl formed a lot of ideas I had about how to do physical comedy. I find that I can't do a scene with physical comedy in it without thinking of Richard Dreyfuss. He packs funny. He sits and does yoga funny. He cracks his neck funny. His *Goodbye*

Girl character's effeminate portrayal of Richard III in his Off Broadway debut was inspiringly funny. But he also has pathos. There's a scene in the film in which Elliot comes home drunk after he's bombed on his opening night of what is billed as the first gay portrayal of Richard III. He's crying, "I was an Elizabethan fruit fly . . . I was putrid. Capital P. Capital U. Capital TRID!" We are laughing at his humiliation. Then he makes an unexpected turn and we see the tears are real. I love this scene, because you never see it coming. You never see a hint of vulnerability in Elliot, underneath his confidence and bravura, until the moment he lets his guard down and shows us that his humiliation has been real. In that moment you realize that maybe Elliot's smart-ass routine has been an act all along. Maybe that cockiness hides a lot of doubt and insecurity and pain. Maybe, in that moment, we are given a glimpse inside the real Richard Dreyfuss who once said to me, "I like to play characters that are self-aware." I knew that without his even telling me, because it reminded me of the night I saw *American Graffiti*, when I was in the backseat of someone's car and I thought, I want to be like him. Both the character and the man who is playing him. I want to be all those things that Richard Dreyfuss is: funny, confident, outspoken, sure of myself.

Not long after I first saw *The Goodbye Girl*, I made my grandmother take me to the actual location of the apartment in the movie—at 78th Street and Amsterdam Avenue, in New York City. Someday I will get here myself, I thought.

Trying to emulate Richard Dreyfuss didn't just help my acting career; it also helped me in my real-life teenage world. One night, four of my friends and I were driving around our small town, doing nothing. I was in the backseat, as usual. It was too late to do anything, too early to go home. Eventually we settled on just parking our car in the town green. Pretty soon other kids in their cars started to gather, until there were about ten or fifteen cars parked on the green. Kids were sitting on the hoods of their cars, not smoking, not drinking—it was just a spontaneous gathering of kids talking, having fun, and being kids. I was just about to get up the courage to talk to a boy I had a crush on when suddenly we were surrounded by two police cars. Nobody knew what was happening. Lights were flashing. Sirens going. The police jumped out of the car, hands on guns, and the kids were just stunned. I guess they thought we were doing something illegal. What they found was just a bunch of kids doing absolutely nothing! They spent some time interrogating us, searching our cars, and then told everyone to go home or we would be arrested for what they called "illegally gathering." Kids were getting into their cars, but I was just furious. I spoke up loudly, trying to stop kids from going home.

I said with a great sense of moral outrage, "You know we don't have to go anywhere. This is the town square, of our town where *our* parents pay the taxes. We're not doing anything illegal. We're just talking."

And I began to rally everyone. "Do you understand the outcome of the police arresting a bunch of kids for talking to each other? We should let them arrest us. This will be front-page news. Nice kids being arrested for talking to each other in the town green. The town meeting place, going back to Colonial times!"

I had found my voice, and it sounded an awful lot like Richard Dreyfuss's. Just like Hooper, I was speaking up for my beliefs, confronting local authority.

I think I even impressed the police when I came up with, "And there isn't even a prison in our town. How would we all fit in the car? There are twenty kids here."

I really wanted the police to arrest me, because I knew I was right, but I was so Richard Dreyfuss-y that I managed to convince the police officers that arresting us was a really bad idea, and eventually they just got into their cars and drove off. I was a hero for about an hour. It was the first time that I remember being noticed for something other than just being funny. The cute boy I had wanted to talk to came over to me. I still remember the way he kind of nodded his head at me, as if he couldn't believe I had spoken that way to a cop. What he didn't know was that I had nothing to be afraid of. I couldn't wait to shake the dust off this town and get to New York, where I would claim my destiny as an actress. Eventually one of my girlfriends told me she needed to drive me home. I still had to get in the backseat, but that night and for a long time after, I could tell the girls in the front seat thought, *She's going somewhere we are not.* From the quiet dark of the backseat I looked up at the moon and smiled. I had become, for a little while, Curt from *American Graffiti.*

When I moved to New York, I actually tried to get an apartment in *The Goodbye Girl* building. It's a movie about hopes and dreams and emotional triumphs. I had come to New York City to follow my dream to become an actress. I had known all the time I was sitting in that backseat that I would get there.

Years after I had moved away from New York to Los Angeles, I had the privilege of working with Richard Dreyfuss. The film was *Lansky,* and I was playing his wife. We were filming a scene in the bedroom. Richard was giving me some direction about how I should cry while he opened some drawers to pack for a trip. He said, "Now, when I open the first drawer, I want you to give me a little cry, and I'll be taking the clothes from the drawer and putting them in the suitcase. Then when I open the second drawer, you'll give me a big cry and I'll slam the first drawer, then you'll give me a big cry and say, 'Meyer, please!' and I'll slam the second drawer and turn around . . ." I was lost. All I could think of was Richard Dreyfuss packing and being funny in *The Goodbye Girl*. My tears dried up and turned to laughter. I just covered my face with my hands and pretended I was crying. The director came in and pulled me aside, and said, "Is there a problem? It looks like you're laughing."

"Yes, there's a problem," I said. "The man packs funny! He won an Oscar for packing funny!"

Richard Dreyfuss said, "I wanted to be Spencer Tracy because I knew I would never be Errol Flynn."

I wanted to be Richard Dreyfuss because I knew I would never be Farrah Fawcett or Christie Brinkley. So my question is, Now do you see why it's so important to know who Spencer Tracy is?

CHAPTER SEVEN

Screaming for Marty

"Look at how good I look in a turban. I need to be in *The Last Temptation of Christ*." Funny, I never got the call.

When I was at my first acting school, the faculty would ask first-year students to play minor parts in some of the senior stage productions so the teachers could chart our progress. I was tapped for a small role in a William Inge play called *Natural Affection*. *Natural Affection* told the story of a juvenile delinquent violently acting out against his mother. I played the neighbor who lives across the hall. I was thrilled. Then I actually read the play. I had two scenes. In the first, I'm coming home from a date. I had a couple lines. My second scene was the last one of the play. I enter their apartment looking for the mother's boyfriend, calling out "Bernie! Bernie!" The boy—angry because he has to go back to reform school—picks up a kitchen knife and stabs me to death. Then, as I lie dead on the living room floor, he drinks a glass of milk. Curtain. The End.

Now, William Inge wrote some great plays and films: *Picnic, Come Back Little Sheba, Dark at the Top of the Stairs, Splendor in the Grass* . . . *Natural Affection* was just not one of them. The last scene was just about the worst, most mixed-up ending of a play I had ever read. I also had proof. There were only thirty-six performances of it on Broadway. Something needed to be done to fix this turkey.

Have I mentioned I was a know-it-all? I'm a know-it-all. But only about one subject: the movies. I know the movies. I love the movies. So I knew what needed to be stolen *from* the movies. I said to the director, "What if the neighbor is like a darker version of Holly Golightly from *Breakfast at Tiffany's*? She's Holly a few years after the movie. Things haven't worked out for her; she's kind of beat-up, a boozer, living next door in a sea of bottles."

The director was pretty busy, you know, actually directing the play, and this was a walk-on role, so he didn't much care what I did. "What, Illeana? I guess so . . . we'll be getting to you soon." I immediately took this as a yes and went backstage to get into character. Mainly by fastening a gigantic rhinestone clip in my hair à la Audrey in *Breakfast at Tiffany's*. I waited, and I waited.

There was one problem. We could never get past the intolerably long first act to get to my entrance. It portrayed the mother's adjustment to her delinquent son, his Oedipal complex, her abusive boyfriend Bernie, and, somehow, her obsession with polishing inlay furniture. As I said, thirty-six performances on Broadway. Since I had to sit there, waiting for my entrance, I had a lot of free time to come up with *other* ideas I thought would save this play. I sidled up next to the director and whispered, "Have you thought about how we are going to do the ending?"

He stared at me, as if trying to remember who I was. "What, Illeana?"

I said, "The ending? The ending where I'm killed by the son?"

He scratched his head as if he hadn't even thought about it, so I said, "What if it's like a Hitchcock movie?" assuming he would just know what I meant.

I discovered Hitchcock through a wonderful book and series I saw growing up called *The Men Who Made the Movies*, by Richard Schickel, and I am proud to say I still have my first-edition copy. It was through this documentary—a series of interviews with directors from Hawks to Hitchcock—that I began to understand the process of moviemaking that I had first experienced on the set of *Being There*.

In *The Men Who Made the Movies*, Hitchcock shows examples from his films to illustrate how to create drama and suspense. He describes the film *Frenzy*, which features a murder scene and is a great example of how to create almost unbearable tension. He doesn't show the girl's death, but rather shows the killer enter the building where she works. The audience knows he's the killer. She doesn't. He cuts to the outside street, and the camera pulls out. Imagining the girl's demise is much worse than actually seeing it. This lesson stayed with me and was invaluable when it came to pitching a new ending to *Natural Affection*.

I said to the director, "What if I come over looking for Bernie, Mom's boyfriend, but he's not there. I start flirting with the boy. I start taking my dress off. But the dress gets caught over my head. While I'm laughing and stumbling around, the kid picks up a knife and starts to come at me. I don't see the knife coming at me, but the audience does."

I saw the wheels turning and the director starting to get excited. "Yes," he said. "We do have the issue of him stabbing you, and this would solve that because we wouldn't have to see it. I like it. We'll get to you soon."

Every day I would engage the director about the ending. He seemed to enjoy my enthusiasm for planning my own murder. Then, during one rehearsal, I was talking about the ending, which, by this point I had all worked out, and he snapped at me, "Illeana, you can stay and watch, but you have to stop talking to me; it's very distracting. We will get to you." I was so hurt; I decided I wouldn't come to rehearsal for three days. When I was called to return to finally do my scenes I would simply act my part as written. I'd just sit there, read my Ruth Gordon autobiography, and just get on with it. No fanfare, nothing. Fine. I was leaving rehearsal, and the director stopped me. He wanted to talk to me because *he* was hurt that I had stopped coming to rehearsal!

"Where have you been?" he said.

I was flabbergasted. "I thought I was getting on your nerves?"

"You were," he said, laughing. "It's funny; you are so irritating when you're here, but when you aren't here I really miss you. Please come back!"

I have since identified this as one of my most lovable traits: You can't stand me when I'm around, but when I am not around, you really miss me! Anyway, I came back, and the ending, lucky for me, was still el stinko. With just days before our opening performance, we rewrote and restaged it—with some help from the master, Alfred Hitchcock. I am not being facetious when I say this was probably one of my first great collaborations with a director.

We couldn't have real blood onstage, since it would of course stain everything, so we came up with this idea that the boy would stab me with the dress over my head, and I would immediately fall behind the couch. Behind the couch, where no one could see, were a bucket of stage blood and some thick pillows. We timed it so that I would scream and stab the pillow while he dipped his knife into the bucket of blood. Every time he raised the knife, there would be more and more blood on it. The effect was chilling, and you never saw anything except the bloody knife and my legs thrashing around from behind the couch. What you *imagined* was happening was so much worse than seeing it. Thank you, Alfred Hitchcock!

The first night we did the show was crazy. The minute the dress was twisted over my head and the boy started walking toward me with the knife, the audience went nuts. They started screaming, "No! He has a knife! Get out!" It was so intense it actually scared me.

I refused to do the curtain call, because I didn't want to ruin it for the audience. How could I get up and take bows after I'd just been killed? The director, who had by this time become my biggest ally, shook his head at me. "Fine, Illeana; you're the director."

When the play was over—and it was a big success, by the way—he said, "You know, you have one of the most bloodcurdling screams I have ever heard. You could make money with that scream."

I joked, "Yeah, Special Skills: bloodcurdling screams!" Little did he know that I would take his advice and that scream would take me far.

A few years later, I had graduated from the Neighborhood Playhouse and had become involved with a company called Goodwater. We were doing an Off Broadway showcase comprising mostly actors and writers who happened to be assistants to many of the great filmmakers in the Brill Building in Manhattan. The Brill Building—at 1619 Broadway—had once been Tin Pan Alley. Then it became a notable film and production house. Directors such as Jonathan Demme, Spike Lee, Paul Schrader—you name it—all had offices there. A friend in our show was working as an assistant for the film director Frank Perry. He had an office next to Peggy Siegal's and was also a client of hers. Peggy was a very famous publicist—still is—handling all the biggest movies of the era. He had overheard that she needed a new assistant because hers was moving on to work for Martin Scorsese, who was also in the building. My friend recommended me. I passed my interview, and pretty soon I had my dream job. Every day I learned something invaluable about show business. Like, be prepared.

On my first day of work, I rode the elevator with Warren Beatty and Elaine May. They were actually discussing *Ishtar*, which they were editing, in the elevator. I thought, Man, an elevator ride with the right director might land you in a movie.

A lot of my duties involved inviting and escorting famous people to premieres. My roommate would tease me, "That's what you do? Invite famous people to parties?"

"Yes!" I would say excitedly. I mean, the fact that I had Neil Simon's home number and Walter Cronkite's and could call them and invite them to a party—as if we were friends—well, who didn't want to make calls like that? Also, the fact that I knew who

Joe Mankiewicz and Garson Kanin were, or that Adolph Green was *married* to Phyllis Newman but that his *partner* was Betty Comden, was finally identified as an important skill. Dream job!

One day I was on the phone with David Denby, who was then a very important movie reviewer for *New York* magazine. (He is now a very important reviewer for *The New Yorker*.) Well, part of representing the film was screening it for reviewers. Peggy always wanted to let a filmmaker know in advance if a review of their film would be positive, so one of my jobs would be to call a reviewer and gauge their reactions after a screening. Mr. Denby—to put it mildly—did not receive these calls well, but I made them nonetheless. On a daily, sometimes hourly, basis.

"Hello, Mr. Denby—I'm calling from Peggy Siegal."

"No, I do not have a reaction to *Beverly Hills Cop II*." Click.

Peggy Siegal came walking in as I was looking at the phone. "Did you call David Denby?"

"Yes, Peggy. He just hung up on me."

"Call him back."

"What? No, Peggy, he just hung up on me."

"Call him back."

"But——"

Just then, Frank Perry came running in and looking around. He stopped and did a double take at me, pointing his finger. "You're an actress, right?"

I smiled wryly. "Yes, Frank. I'm an actress who answers the phone for a living."

"No!" he said. "Put the phone down."

I looked at Peggy. "What about Denby?"

She said incredulously, "You're an actress?"

"How would you like to yell at Shelley Long?" Frank said

excitedly. "We have a part that we forgot to cast. It's a few lines. Do you have a monologue you could do for me?"

What's crazy is that (a) I did have a monologue I could do for him. Because I really did believe that any elevator ride could lead to a job, and now it had. And (b) that he needed to hear a monologue to see if I was qualified to yell at Shelley Long.

I followed Frank into his office. He lied. I had to do two monologues to see if I was qualified to yell at Shelley Long—but I got the part!

"Great," he said. "We are shooting this right now. Come with me."

He took me by the arm and started leading me out of the office.

"Peggy," he said, "I'm taking her."

Since Frank was also a client, there wasn't much she could do. Peggy, bless her heart, let me leave work, but only if I agreed to return after I was done shooting to complete any work I had missed that day. Glamorous showbiz. Still, dream job!

The next thing I knew, I'm driving downtown with Frank Perry—who had made such great movies as *The Swimmer* and *Mommie Dearest*—to shoot what would be my first speaking part in a movie. I was in a daze. They sat me in a chair, slapped some makeup on me, handed me a baby, introduced me to Shelley Long, and bingo, I was acting in a movie. I handed back the baby, said goodbye to Shelley Long, apologized for having yelled at her, and was back at work that night eating pizza and wondering what the hell had happened. But I was in a movie. There was visual proof.

This story, which sounded as if a famous publicist like Peggy Siegal had made it up, immediately made its way through the halls of the Brill Building. I was excited because people finally started identifying me as an actress. One of these people was Martin Scorsese's assistant, who asked for my résumé.

"Let me have it," she said, "I'll keep it on file. You never know when Marty is casting something."

I didn't tell her that I had actually *tried* to audition for the movie *The Last Temptation of Christ.* I sent a picture of myself wrapped in a turban to the casting director and signed it, "Look at how good I look in a turban. I need to be in *The Last Temptation of Christ.*" Funny, I never got the call.

Remember *Natural Affection*? The play in which the director said I should put bloodcurdling screams on my résumé as a special skill? To pad out my very few credits—and to be funny—I had actually put it on my résumé. "Special Skills: Great legs, bloodcurdling screams." I knew one of them would get me somewhere. That was the résumé I handed Martin Scorsese's assistant. Months later, Martin Scorsese had finished filming *The Last Temptation of Christ* and was doing what they call ADR (additional dialogue recording) on the film. They were in a real rush to get the movie out. The studio was pushing for an early release because there was a lot of controversy surrounding the film, and people were beginning to protest it.

I was at work and I got a call from Marty's assistant. It sounded very conspiratorial: "Hey, I was reading your résumé. Do you really have a bloodcurdling scream?"

So I told her the whole story about the play. She said, "OK. This is top secret, but Marty needs someone to dub some screams for Barbara Hershey. If you *really* have a great scream . . . "

I assured her I did.

"Can you come down to the third floor at five o'clock and scream for him?"

"Sure," I said, not thinking that this entire conversation was in the least bit odd. I mean, I had just landed my first part in a movie in an equally ridiculous way, why would my second possible acting job be any different?

At five, I made my way down to the third floor to scream for Martin Scorsese. I really didn't know what to expect. He was sort of a mythical figure in our world: He worked right down the hall from us, but no one ever saw him. We would hear about him, or occasionally read something about him that his staff had left behind in the Xerox machine. I wasn't the biggest fan of his most important movies such as *Raging Bull* or *Taxi Driver*. But I loved his offbeat movies: *Alice Doesn't Live Here Anymore*, *The King of Comedy*, *After Hours*, *New York, New York*.

I found the mixing stage and opened the door. It was a very dark room. Once I was inside people started introducing themselves. Marty, of course; his editor, Thelma Schoonmaker; her assistant, Gerri Peroni; the producer, Barbara De Fina; plus the sound-mixing and ADR team. There was some small talk, and then Marty finally laughed and said, "OK. Let's hear it."

I was trying to be professional, but when I said—a little too seriously, I guess—"I just want to prepare you; it's really loud," everyone started laughing.

Marty said, "Yes, bloodcurdling, right?" There was some more laughing.

The whole thing did feel a little silly, but, I mean, wasn't this an audition of some sort? I thought to myself: I'm a trained actress. I'll take it seriously even if they don't. I went up to the mike, took a deep breath, and I swear I thought everyone was going to burst out laughing again. Then I got very quiet to get their attention. I took another deep breath, made myself cry, and started screaming my guts out. There was complete and utter silence. Then all at once everyone started to applaud. Marty was particularly impressed.

"Oh, my God! That is awful. How do you do that?"

I deadpanned, "I work for Peggy Siegal . . ."

Big laugh at my boss's expense, of course. But I was trying to build a rapport based upon Peggy Siegal's colorful reputation.

Marty said, "Listen, we're going to have a loop group come in tonight—background noises, 'Kill the Romans!,' that sort of thing. Would you want to be a part of that?"

I had no idea what he was talking about. I said, "Yes, that sounds great."

"We'll have some fun," he said. "There'll be pizza."

"Any more screaming?" I asked.

More laughing.

"No. No. We'll get to that."

I called my roommate and told him I wouldn't be home for dinner. I had landed my second part in a movie. Sort of. Even he had to admit that working for Peggy Siegal was turning into what I had always insisted it was, a dream job!

That night, I returned to the third floor to find out exactly what a "loop group" was.

Marty was right. There was pizza! There was also a bunch of people from Marty's office. Some of them I knew—assistants, editors, folks who worked for him, including an actor, Paul, who was in my theater group. Marty loved Paul because he bore a striking resemblance to a character actor named Dan Duryea, who was famous for playing villains. You can see for yourself in *Goodfellas* where Marty cast Paul as the "Terrorized Waiter." Others I was meeting for the first time, such as the director

Michael Powell. Michael was a very famous British director, who had made *The Red Shoes* and many other films. He was a mentor to Marty and was married to Marty's editor, Thelma Schoonmaker. Wow. I'm going to be making crowd noises with Michael Powell. Dream job!

We started, and at first we did crowd reactions. Oohhs and Ahhs. Happy crowd sounds. Angry crowd sounds. You name it. Then we took turns doing individual crowd lines to replace dialogue that was unusable for various reasons. Marty would just call for someone to go up to the mike and try something. As the night wore on, things started to get really silly. Marty had us doing deliberately crazy and inappropriate accents, or *Godzilla*-like bad dubbing. It was thrilling to be a part of something so creative. And there was pizza! My only clue that Marty liked what I was doing was that he kept asking me to go up to the mike and do something different. This was confirmed the next day when I got a call from his assistant, who said, "Marty really likes your voice. He wants you to come back and do some other voices in the film."

Over the next few weeks I would go down to the third floor to replace a line here or there. I was Jesus' mother, Lazarus' sister—you name it. Then came the screaming. There were two big screaming scenes. One, as I said, was for Barbara Hershey, who was playing Mary Magdalene. Pretty simple. The other was for Lazarus' sister, Martha. When I first saw the scene, and how long it was and what it involved, I was stunned. It depicted the entire fall of Jerusalem. There was running and screaming. There was fire, and more running, and buildings falling. How the heck was I going to match all this action? Marty just smiled and said, "Should we go for one?"

To say that I was scared was an understatement. A week ago

I didn't even know what looping was, now Martin Scorsese is calmly just waiting for me to save his picture.

"OK. Here's what I'm going to do," I said. "I'm going to do one hundred jumping jacks, make myself cry, and just go into it."

Marty nodded, as if he were thinking, Oh, that sounds reasonable. Two heart surgeons just nodding in agreement as to what needed to be done for the patient.

Sheer and utter fear pushed me forward. I solemnly went to the corner and turned my back while Marty and Thelma waited. Then I prepared emotionally. As much as you can prepare for playing the falling of Jerusalem. Basically I made myself cry. Then I did a hundred jumping jacks, and ran around the room screaming and crying like a lunatic. "Jerusalem is on fire! Run for your lives. They're killing everyone," etc. Rent the film. I will get a residual check and you'll see what I'm talking about. Those are my bloodcurdling screams, all right.

Marty and Thelma seemed very pleased, and then I went back upstairs to Peggy Siegal. I thought that would be it. The next day his assistant called and said Marty wanted me to dub an *entire* character's part. He needed to replace the character's voice because she had a thick New York accent. It did not fit well with Willem Dafoe's lower register, and he thought my voice would match better. It would be about ten lines spread over three scenes. Down I went to the third floor again. I was under strict orders from Marty's assistant not to tell anyone that I was doing this, so I never told Peggy Siegal that I was moonlighting with Marty and Jesus.

That's right. What was amazing about this round of looping was that I got to do all the scenes with Marty himself, while he played Jesus opposite me. By this time I was less intimidated and we started to talk more about movies—although with Marty mostly he talks and you listen. I did manage to make him laugh again. I told him that I loved Liza Minnelli and that my grandmother had taken me to see *New York, New York* on the opening day, but the violent story line had kind of gone over my head. "It was like an MGM musical and then all of a sudden Liza Minnelli is getting beaten up, and then, Oh, now we're back to singing and dancing."

He asked me about directors I liked and I mentioned Joseph Mankiewicz, because I was reading a book about him. The next day he gave me another book about Mankiewicz that he thought I would like even more because he felt the book I was reading was slanted a little negatively. And if he mentioned a film I hadn't heard of, he would immediately get a tape of it made so I could watch it. "Oh, you haven't seen *Letter to Three Wives*? I'll get you a copy." I mentioned an obscure documentary I had seen as a kid called *Sherman's March*, and Marty brought me a copy of it so I could see it again. One day I said to him, "Marty, I once saw this movie about this father that goes nuts, and all I remember was a glass of milk—" He cut me off. "Nicholas Ray! *Bigger Than Life!* I'll get you a copy." Back at my desk at Peggy's, I would look at the clock, counting the hours till it was time to go downstairs for my next film lesson with Marty.

I always thought I had two people to thank for my relationship with Marty (aside from my favorite boss, Peggy Siegal!). The first was director Howard Hawks. During one of our talks, Marty tossed an obscure one-liner at me, "That's it—I close the iron door!"

And I screamed, "*Twentieth Century!*"

Marty was floored. "How do you know *Twentieth Century*?"

"My favorite movie! Howard Hawks."

The other was Mel Brooks. We were taking a break, and as Marty walked out the door he said over his shoulder, "I'll be right back; I'm going to wash up."

It immediately struck a chord with me because it sounded like this Mel Brooks–Carl Reiner routine from the record *The 2000 Year Old Man.*

I paraphrased, "That's right, you go save France; I'm going to wash up."

I had no idea the impact it would have. Marty just stopped, and spun around. "Mel Brooks! *2000 Year Old Man!* How do you know that?"

For the next twenty minutes we proceeded to go through every routine on the album. Then Marty actually started to brag that *he* was on the *2000 and Thirteen* album they made as a follow-up in 1973.

"You can hear me laughing," he said. "I'll bring it in so you can listen to it." And he did. We sat in the third floor studio of the Brill Building and Marty played the *2000 and Thirteen* album for me and said, "That's me. Do you hear it?"

We were laughing like two idiots until the sound mixer interrupted and said, "Um, Marty, we really need to get back to work now."

How do you not love a director who in the middle of this huge controversy over *The Last Temptation of Christ* brings you the *2000 and Thirteen* album so you can hear him laughing? One day, we were finished working, and we walked out to the elevator together. I didn't know what button to push for him, so I said, "Are you going back upstairs?"

And he kind of stammered and said, "Where are you going?"

And I said, "I'm going back upstairs to Peggy's."

And then, just a little too quickly, he said, "I'm going back upstairs, too."

It was one of those awkward moments where I thought: I don't think he was going back upstairs. I think he wants to ride in the elevator with me. We got to the ninth floor, and again there was this odd, "I'm going this way; which way are you going?" "Oh, so am I" kind of awkwardness. Eventually he ended up walking me all the way to Peggy's office. It was after hours, and the office was empty. He kind of peeked in, and said, "So . . . this is where you work." I said, "Yes," pointing out my desk. And Marty said, "Oh, is that your little desk?" And again I thought: Doesn't Martin Scorsese have more important things to do? I watched him walk down the hall. Before he turned the corner, he turned around once more and waved. I waved back. I got back to my little desk and just smiled to myself.

On one of my last looping days, Marty told me he was casting the part of Rosanna Arquette's friend in his upcoming segment of the anthology film *New York Stories*. I loved Rosanna Arquette; she'd been in *After Hours*, which was one of my favorite of Marty's films at that time. My honest-to-God reaction when he mentioned *New York Stories* was that I thought he was just talking to me about his work, the way we had been talking every day about movies and work. I was young and earnest and really just wanted to do a good job. I had too much respect to say, "Hey, Marty? Any parts for me in your next film?" I was trained by Peggy Siegal that working with directors like Norman Jewison, Barry Levinson, and Brian De Palma meant you would never dream of pushing an agenda by telling them you were an actress. I later auditioned for Norman Jewison, and he was shocked to find out that I even *was* an actress.

So the first couple of times that Marty mentioned casting this role, I brushed it aside. It was Thelma Schoonmaker who said when Marty left the room, "Illeana, I think he wants to see if you are available to audition."

Oh, my God. Now I get it. The next time the subject came up, I was ready.

Marty said, "Yeah. You have a kind of Rosanna Arquette quality. I've seen a couple girls for the part, but they haven't been right."

This time I made sure I was clear: "Yes. I would love to audition for *New York Stories*." I made the appointment myself through his assistant. I didn't have an agent. It's kind of astonishing to think how far screaming for Marty has taken me.

The appointed day came, and I literally walked from Peggy's office down the hall to audition for Marty and his casting director Ellen Lewis. Ellen went on to cast some of the greatest movies of all time, including *Goodfellas*, *Forrest Gump*, and *The Birdcage*, as well as *Cape Fear*. When I finished reading my sides, I asked, "Do I have the part?"

They said, "We can't tell you that! It's not how it works."

I said, "But if I have the part then I can go tell Peggy that I have to quit because I'm going to be in *New York Stories*. She will be really impressed."

They laughed, conferring for a minute before they said, "OK. OK. You have the part."

It was all a little surreal, since part of me was disappointed that I wasn't going to be able to work with Peggy anymore. I had learned so much from her. In one year I had worked on *The Un-touchables; Moonstruck; Good Morning, Vietnam; The Princess Bride; Fatal Attraction;* and many more. Peggy took it in stride. She immediately got an item placed about it in the *New York Post*'s buzzy "Page Six." Actress working for famed publicist lands part in Scorsese movie. Again, a story that sounds like a publicist made it up, only it was true. On my last day of work at Peggy Siegal's I sat at my desk finishing last-minute assignments. I worked on the press kit for *Bright Lights, Big City*. I talked to Charles Grodin about some upcoming press for *Midnight Run*. I said goodbye to the girls in the office—all of whom went on to great things. I smiled as I thought of that first day when I crossed the lobby of the Brill Building and imagined that an elevator ride might lead to working with a director, and now it had. Little did I know it would also lead to a ten-year relationship. Like I said, dream job!

CHAPTER EIGHT

What's It Like to Work with Robert De Niro?

The scene that launched "You're the girl from *Cape Fear*."

Everywhere I go, every movie I do, every relationship I have ever been in, every red light I've ever been stopped at, I am invariably asked: "What's it like to work with Robert De Niro?"

I'll be at an airport with guards going through my bags, making sure I'm not a threat, and suddenly one of the TSA folks will look at me very earnestly and say, Can I ask you something? And I think it's going to be about my illegally stashed weapon, or the pot brownie someone planted on me, and instead he or she will say, "Hey! What's it like to get your face bitten off by Robert De Niro?" I'm sorry, is that a security question? I'm pretty sure it's not.

A week before *Cape Fear* came out, I went on David Letterman's show. In *Cape Fear*, I played Lori, the jilted colleague of Nick Nolte who is attacked by Max Cady (Robert De Niro) after he picks her up in a bar. In the pre-interview for Letterman, I went over all my questions with the producer, but when I sat down, Letterman surprised me out of the gate by going off script and asking, "So what's it like? Having Robert De Niro beat the crap out of you?"

And people always get an interesting look on their face when they ask me. Like I'm going to offer up some amazing insight. Something profound: "He covers himself with soot ashes, then incants the words of Stanislavski, *An Actor Prepares*." Something mystical: "He only works at sunrise, with his body facing east." Something ridiculous: "Well in between takes of getting beaten up we did Three Stooges routines." I've always thought that if I *did* say any of those things except for the last one, which is actually true, people would smile knowingly at me and say, "Yes. That's what I thought."

People's curiosity about this matter is a testament to one of our greatest living actors, and since it's my legacy forever to be the girl who got her face bitten off by him in *Cape Fear*, I'm going to try to answer the question. So what *is* it like to work with Robert De Niro?

To give this some context, I'm going to go back to acting school—that first acting school I went to, where the headmistress thought I had no future. I heard that she was later run over by a bus. I had nothing to do with it, of course. But maybe just as she couldn't see my huge talent right in front of her, she couldn't see that enormous bus coming at her, either. My friend and fellow acting student was Elias Koteas. Elias is a wonderful actor who has created some edgy performances in films such as *Crash*, *The Thin Red Line*, and *Zodiac*. He is very serious, and he had a lot of ambitions, but his *main* ambition back then was to be in a movie with Robert De Niro, hopefully one directed by Martin Scorsese. He was obsessed with all things Robert De Niro. I mean, he would make me eat at the Belmore Cafeteria, because "That's where Travis Bickle ate in *Taxi Driver.*" When I told Elias that I had never actually seen *Taxi Driver*, he was outraged and dragged me to a double feature of *Mean Streets* and *Taxi Driver* so that I could experience the genius of his favorite actor, Robert De Niro. I remember coming out into the light after seeing both films back to back and thinking, Jesus, I want my mommy! Take me to see *Lassie Come Home* or a Danny Kaye musical. Life can't be that dark. Elias just laughed. He was wearing an army jacket and contemplating getting a Mohawk at the time. (I'm kidding.)

Part of the reason Elias thought it was his destiny to work with Robert De Niro was that Elias bore a striking resemblance to him. He had all his mannerisms down, too, which made the comparison more obvious. He was not above stalking him, either. Elias started lurking around the set of *The King of Comedy*, which was filming near our school, trying to get spotted by De Niro so he could hopefully get a part in the movie purely based on their resemblance. Now, unbeknown then to Elias, *The King of Comedy* is a movie *about* a stalker and Elias *was* spotted by De Niro, and he actually thought he might *be* a stalker, and someone from production told him to get the hell away from the set. This, of course, thrilled Elias. It was a sign that it was only a matter of time before he fulfilled his destiny and worked with De Niro for real.

I just wanted to be in show business. I thought *my* destiny was to do comedy. Be on a sitcom. At the time, I couldn't dream a dream big enough that included working with Robert De Niro or Martin Scorsese. I was a comedian. How would I ever in a million years end up working with Robert De Niro or Martin Scorsese? After I was in *The Last Temptation of Christ, New York Stories, Goodfellas, Guilty by Suspicion, Cape Fear*—five movies in a row, all with Martin Scorsese or Robert De Niro—I ran into Elias, and he good-naturedly accosted me. "You!" he said. "How did *you* end up with my life?"

Elias did eventually work with Marty on *Shutter Island*, and I was thrilled for him.

It was early in 1989 that I first met Robert De Niro. It was right after the premiere of *New York Stories*. I was in a dark hall on my way to Martin Scorsese's apartment to discuss being in a movie called *Wiseguys*, later changed to be called *Goodfellas*. At the time, Marty was living in a very tall, very modern building on West 57th Street named Metropolitan Tower, nicknamed the Razor Blade Building. The elevator that took you to his penthouse apartment on the seventy-fifth floor was so fast it was like a rocket launch. After you lurched to a stop and got off, the effect was always the same: complete disorientation, nausea, and confusion about which dimension you were in. Everything was pitch-black, as if you were in an air raid, so your eyes had to adjust like a raccoon's as you made your way down the hall. There was also this loud screeching sound—day and night—that Marty assured me was the wind whistling through the glass and steel, but it made you feel as if the building were going to crash to the ground.

So, there I am, making my way down the dark hall, and the wind is blowing like a haunted mansion at Knott's Scary Farm—Marty's Spooky Hallway Ride—and who did I see coming the other way but Robert De Niro. There was no official word that Robert De Niro *was in* the movie, or even considering being in the movie, so I got a secret little thrill that maybe that's why he was leaving Marty's. I smiled politely at him as I passed by and respectfully and quietly said, "Hello." He politely nodded back, said, "Hello," and we both kept walking. I did notice that he was wearing large horn-rimmed glasses that I thought made him look very sophisticated. Like Clark Kent. It was a good look.

Marty opened the door for me, and I said, "I just said hello to Robert De Niro. Does that mean he's going to be in the movie?"

And Marty looked a little concerned and said, "You recognized him?"

I laughed, and said, "Of course. He's Robert De Niro!"

And he said, "But he was wearing a disguise."

And I said, "Marty, he was wearing glasses."

And Marty said, "I know, he thinks *that's* a disguise."

And I said, "Well, you might want to tell him it's not working, because he looks like Robert De Niro with glasses on."

I'm not sure if Marty did tell him, but I never saw him wear those Clark Kent glasses again.

The casting of *Goodfellas* was top-secret stuff. I was privy to hearing about and sometimes even seeing every actor or actress that was even in consideration, but I was sworn to secrecy. Listen, I knew that *I* was in consideration, and Marty wouldn't confirm or deny if I was going to be in the movie, and we were in a relationship. That's how top-secret it was! There was a building excitement that Marty would be reunited with both Joe Pesci and

Robert De Niro, but names like Tom Cruise, Bruce Willis, and John Malkovich were also being mentioned. I let the De Niro casting issue drop, but it did not seem accidental that The Godfather had paid Marty a visit.

The next time I saw Robert De Niro was on the set of *Goodfellas*. I became a fixture on set, sitting quietly behind or near Marty absorbing everything that happened on what is often called the best film of the '90s. I was afraid not to go, because I would miss something. One day they were shooting at the Copacabana, which was near my apartment, and Marty said, "We're doing something pretty interesting today. You should come down and see it."

It was of course the famous Steadicam shot entering from the back of the restaurant. Another day we were jammed into the Hawaii Kai on Broadway. It was ancient, and inside everything was made of straw and grass. Marty said, "Careful, this place has fleas"—and let me tell you, it did. I was at a booth watching Joe Pesci and Ray Liotta act the "But I'm funny how? Funny like a clown?" scene. And then there was Mr. De Niro. Word was spreading about *Goodfellas,* and actors, mobsters, you name it were requesting if they, too, could come down just to get a glimpse of Robert De Niro. In some neighborhoods a carnival-like atmosphere developed and folks were having cookouts and sitting in lawn chairs outside places where they were shooting. It was like they were a part of the atmosphere and Marty harnessed that energy and put it into the film.

It's hard to explain the impact of Robert De Niro at the time he and Marty were making *Goodfellas.* He was a god in New York. I mean, there were actors—Vincent Gallo, for one—who had agreed to be extras just to brag that they were in *Goodfellas* with him. I had just been watching and had been happy with that, but now I was going to be in a few scenes with him. In one scene, I was going to have a line right before his. Elias was right. How did I end up with his life?

Marty created an atmosphere on the set that was fun and homey, like a large Italian family, but the scenes with De Niro always changed that dynamic. His presence brought a tension and energy that I had never experienced before or have since. When he walked on set everyone stopped talking, and it was like, boom, something important is about to happen. We were shooting the famous Christmas scene in the bar where Robert De Niro chews out Johnny Roastbeef for having bought a new Cadillac. All of Brooklyn was outside cheering—as I've said, people were having barbecues and drinking wine and applauding every time an actor walked into or out of the bar. It was past midnight, but nobody wanted to leave. When they were shooting that scene and De Niro opened the door and revealed the Cadillac there were hundreds of people to the side that the camera had to avoid. Inside I had a front-row seat watching Robert De Niro. Enough time to get pretty nervous because my first line in *Goodfellas* was coming up. We had been shooting in the bar a few days, and there was going to be this very long, complicated tracking shot, with most of the cast involved, and I had a line during it to Julie Garfield, which was "If I even look at anyone else, he'll kill me." The camera then holds for our reaction, and then moves on to De Niro and Joe Pesci, and the scene continues. It was like an eight-minute shot. We rehearsed it almost all day. Finally Marty said they were ready to shoot. And even though I had told myself, Don't screw this shot up. Don't do anything phony. Don't do anything that makes Robert De Niro go over to Marty and say, "How did that bad actor get in my movie?" I didn't quite pull it off. The first stupid thing I did was to try to get a laugh. I thought, Let me goose my one line in the scene like a bad actor. So the camera is tracking along, there are twenty people in the frame, all these actions. Out of the corner of my eye I see the camera getting to me, and all of a sudden I become Eve Arden. "If he catches me with *anyone*, he'll *kill* me!" then I downed a glass of wine to button it. It was dreadful, of course, awful and hammy. I knew it immediately, and so did Marty. He yelled out, "Cut. Cut. Technical difficulties." Everyone started groaning. Everyone else had been brilliant. Marty came over to me and whispered into my ear so no one could hear it but me: "Don't do that again." Then he laughed, "Sorry, everyone, sorry," running back to the camera, "Our fault. Our fault. Technical problems." Twenty-thousand-dollar mistake, Marty later told me. He never let anyone know but me, but he cared enough that he wanted every actor in the frame to be perfect.

People always ask me, what did you learn from Marty? A thousand things. That was one. Sensitivity. A love for actors and their processes. I did it right the next time. Wait, the next hundred times, because we continued to shoot the same scene for the next fourteen hours!

There was a lot of downtime between shots, and this is where I learned the first surprising thing about what it's like to work with Robert De Niro: He's really funny! He loves to laugh. I was in a sketch-comedy group at the time called Manhattan Punch Line, and I dabbled in stand-up. I had a couple routines that Marty was aware of, so in between takes he brought De Niro over to hear them. I used to do a pretty good Shelley Winters impression. She was then a blowsy older actress with a kind of warbly voice who had an association with the Actors Studio. She would make the talk-show rounds babbling about her association with De Niro or Marilyn Monroe. She had this habit of sort of rubbing her rather large breasts and saying, "When Bobby and I were at the Studio with Marilyn, I taught Marilyn how to be sexy." So I would do that impression for De Niro, adding, "When Bobby and I did *Bloody Mama*, he asked me for advice, and I said, 'Bobby, don't eat fish off the truck; go with the chicken. Here, have some of my breasts.'"

I had another routine called "Raging Bullwinkle." Basically, cartoon characters Rocky and Bullwinkle acting out a scene from *Raging Bull* as Jake and Joe LaMotta. So with Robert De Niro and Joe Pesci both staring me down, I did my Rocky the Flying Squirrel. "You're nuts! You let this girl ruin your life!"

Then Bullwinkle, "Rocky. Did you fuck my wife?"

Then Squirrel, "How could you ask me that? I'm your brother."

People ask me if making *Cape Fear* was scary. No. Doing "Raging Bullwinkle" for Robert De Niro and Joe Pesci was much scarier! But I got my laugh. I made Robert De Niro laugh. And if my only interaction with De Niro had been being in *Goodfellas*, watching him work, getting to say a line before him, making him laugh, I would have been content. Little did I know. Irwin Winkler produced *Goodfellas*, and he wanted me to audition for a part in *Guilty by Suspicion*, which he was directing. I didn't get the part for which I had auditioned, but Irwin still wanted me in the movie, because it dealt with the Communist blacklist, and my grandparents, Melvyn and Helen Gahagan Douglas—who was the first Democratic woman elected to Congress from California—had been in the thick of all of that. He offered me the part of Nan, Daryl Zanuck's assistant. It was a small part, but I would have a couple scenes with Robert De Niro, so I said sure. This is where I learned the next interesting thing about what it's like to work with Robert De Niro: It's not so easy. It's like waking up and realizing you're on a tightrope one hundred stories up with the world's greatest tightrope artist and wondering how the hell you got there.

There was an actor in *Guilty by Suspicion* who found himself on the tightrope. He couldn't believe he was acting with Robert De Niro. He just thought, I am not good enough, and it threw him. He was so intimidated that he just froze in De Niro's presence. The scene would begin and he'd start flop-sweating, and it was brutal. He confided in me that he was pretty sure that De Niro thought he was miscast. He kept saying, "I don't know why I'm here." No amount of my encouraging him could boost his confidence.

I saw this happen on *Goodfellas* a couple of times, too. Actors would "go up" on their lines—they'd forget what they were saying, or suddenly be like I once had been: really, really bad. It happened to me with my only line in the movie! It suddenly occurs to you, Oh, he's like the world's greatest actor. How long is it going to take him to discover that I am a hack? You have to work against this fear that he is judging you in the scene. So, on *Guilty by Suspicion*, every time I was scared or thought I was awful or didn't deserve to be acting with Robert De Niro, I remembered making him laugh on the set of *Goodfellas*. I discovered making him laugh made me less intimidated of him. Pretty soon every time he saw me he expected me to do something funny—and now I couldn't wait to see him. It almost got me into trouble.

One day we were shooting a scene, and I only had one line in it, something like "He's not in," and *that* was the day that Steven

Spielberg and Mike Ovitz, the head of Creative Artists Agency, decided to visit the set. Imagine you're doing a scene with the world's greatest director and world's greatest talent agent watching you and you have one line in it. Pitiful. Now, I knew Bob's next movie was going to be the remake of *Cape Fear*, and Steven at the time was possibly going to be directing it. So we're doing the scene, and De Niro walks up to my desk, looking for Daryl Zanuck in the movie, and says, "Is he in?" And I have to say very solemnly, "He's not in." Well, De Niro turned to walk away, and I gave it a couple beats and then yelled out to Ovitz, "What do you think, Mike? Have you seen enough? Ready to sign me? When do we start *Cape Fear*, Steven?"

It was pretty ballsy—we were still shooting the scene—but being a comedian at heart, I went for the joke. Luckily for me, Bob busted up, so everyone else followed.

There was a poster shop on Hollywood Boulevard—sadly, it's no longer there—that I went to because I wanted to give Bob a thank-you gift after filming ended. I had this small part in *Guilty by Suspicion*, yet he went out of his way to be gracious to me, and I really appreciated it. So I was in there, looking around this dusty shop, and I actually found lobby cards from the original *Cape Fear*, so I gave them to Bob as a wrap gift. We were standing outside on the old Goldwyn lot where my grandfather had once been under contract. I remember De Niro's tearing the paper off and smiling that wonderful, iconic smile as he looked at the cards. Back-to-back movies with Robert De Niro. Not bad.

I went home to New York, and things had changed—now Marty is directing *Cape Fear*. He tells me that there is a part that I'm right for, but that it's not up to him. I will have to audition for Robert De Niro. If Bob doesn't think I'm right, I won't get it.

I watched the original movie, with Barrie Chase playing the part of the drifter Diane Taylor, which in the version Marty was directing would be Lori, an attorney who gets involved with Nick Nolte. Again the casting was top secret, but I knew I could do this part if I got the chance. I auditioned first for the same casting director from *New York Stories*, Ellen Lewis, and then it was time for De Niro to approve me. There wasn't really a script at that point so we improvised some scenes, specifically the bar scene, and I was cast in the movie. I remember everything about that audition, including what I wore. It was a white shirt with a Peter Pan collar and a short black skirt. The only thing that changed when we filmed the scene was the color of the skirt. Marty liked the Peter Pan collar because he thought it made me look like a nice Catholic girl, which I was. Still am!

Because of Robert De Niro and *Cape Fear*, people know my name. And if they don't know my name they always recognize my face—probably because of the harrowing and controversial rape scene that we shot, where part of my face is bitten off. A lot of folks thought the scene was gratuitously violent. I can only say, sadly, that it was based on actual events Bob had researched. To make it truthful, I also spent time with a criminal attorney in Florida's Broward County Courthouse doing my own research to prepare for the scene and its aftermath. After a seventeen-hour day and fourteen hours of shooting that scene, Bob went over to Marty and said, "I think she's done." I went back to my hotel room and cried. I had gone to places I didn't know I was capable of. On the second day, the mood on set was so somber that Bob and I lightened things up by doing Three Stooges routines between takes just to let everyone know I was OK, that we were . . . acting.

Later, when the musicians were recording the score with Elmer Bernstein, they got to the rape scene, and several of them walked out, saying they should have been warned. It was considered so disturbing it was censored in Sweden.

A week ago, I sat next to a girl in a movie theater. She gasped when she saw me. She said, "My God, that scene in *Cape Fear*. It gave me nightmares for years!" I'm often asked if I was scared. The answer is no. The first scene I shot in *Cape Fear* was the bar scene, and believe me, *that* was a lot scarier.

It was my first big scene in a movie, and I had a lot to prove. I knew instinctively that I was going to be judged as to whether or not I deserved to be there, but I was ready for it. I had decided I was going to do this laughing thing. I knew I would have to play drunk, but I also thought: It's Robert De Niro in the scene, and Marty is the director. I'm in good hands. I just have to listen to whatever these two geniuses tell me to do, and do it.

My journal from the first day reads, "I was watching my Sanford Meisner Documentary at 5:30 A.M. and getting last minute inspiration. I am dressed like Audrey Hepburn. I am pretending to be Ruth Gordon. Faith. Achievement. Victory. And Oh yes, fasten your seatbelts!"

It's my first day on *Cape Fear*, and I am just excited to be there. I'm walking to the set from my trailer—it's the first time I've had a trailer—and I'm in my costume. I've got my makeup on. My hair looks cute. I'm smiling at folks as I walk, trying to make eye contact with someone as if to say, "I'm in a movie!" but no one knows who the hell I am. I'm still happy. I get to the set, and I'm the first one there. It's a real bar; we have the whole place to ourselves. I sit at the bar waiting, looking around, and the crew is talking. Nobody is talking to me. I thought one person might, you know, mention my cute outfit, or my hair, or something, but nothing. So I think, I know what I'll do. I'll just make myself busy. I ask props if they will make the drink I'm drinking in the scene, a Sea Breeze. It was an inside joke I had with a friend, and I figured this little joke will give me some confidence. I explain to the gruff props guy how to make it—we're in a real bar, after all—and he just looks at me and says, "You're drinking wine. I got the grape juice already poured" and walks away.

Marty gets to the set, and finally Bob. The first assistant director immediately asks Bob if he needs water. He gets Bob water. Bob doesn't drink it, but it's there if he needs it. No one asks me if I want anything, but I'm fine. I don't need water. At this point I'm like a racehorse. I'm raring to go. I'm ready to act. My whole life has led to this moment. "Listen and answer under the given circumstances," Sanford Meisner advises. We start to rehearse the scene, and I'm going for it. I say my first line—a little drunk, a little loud, and I'm laughing and banging the bar—and De Niro says very quietly, "blah, blah, blah, blah, blah, blah, blah, blah."

Yes. He actually said the words "blah, blah, blah, blah . . ."

I continue with my lines, which sound totally bizarre coming after his "blah, blah, blah." We do the entire scene that way. I talk. He says, "Blah, blah, blah, maybe I'll move here . . . blah, blah, blah, I move over there."

I have no idea what is happening. I mean, this never happened on the set of *Goodfellas*.

I look at Marty, and he's nodding at Bob as if this is totally normal. He doesn't even make eye contact with me. Rehearsal ends. The director of photography, Freddie Francis, thanks Bob and he gets up and leaves, followed by Bob's hair-and-makeup team. Marty follows him. The first assistant director, Joe Reidy, smiles at me and says, "We will need you in forty-five."

I slowly walk back to my trailer, thinking, I had all these things planned that I wanted to rehearse, and I don't even know what the hell just happened in there. So much for watching the Meisner documentary that morning. The basis of Meisner technique is listening and answering truthfully. I thought Robert De Niro would be great, like he always was, and I would just work off him. I didn't think I would have to do anything. The clock is ticking as I wait in my trailer, and now I start to get really insecure. I'm like all of the others I have seen fold before Robert De Niro. I'm like the guy from *Guilty by Suspicion*. I'm on the tightrope! I start to think, I'm awful; I have no idea how I got here; I don't deserve to be here; I'm only here because of Marty, and he's not even helping me, he's in the trailer with Bob, probably telling him to do the whole scene like that, "'Blah, blah, blah' . . . Bob, it's brilliant!" and we have to do this scene in forty-five minutes. My first big scene in a movie. It's happening. This disaster will be filmed.

When I was at the Neighborhood Playhouse studying Meisner technique, the hardest thing for me was called Emotional Preparation. You imagined you won the lottery or your dog died for some emotional fuel, and then you began the scene. Sanford Meisner would look at you and say, "Start the scene again, and this time come in crying and make the bed." You'd be standing outside the door, trying to make yourself cry, thinking, My mother is *dead*. My *mother* is dead! No, she's not. No, she's not. Finally you'd enter, put your hands over your eyes and fake-cry, and hope that your partner had something better than you had.

As I was sitting in my trailer, I began, probably for the first time in my life, really to emotionally prepare. I thought about my character, Lori. She was in love with Nick Nolte's character, Sam. They were involved and he had stood her up. He had humiliated her, made her feel unloved, and she was going to show him that she was attractive. That she could be loved. And she was self–destructive. She was going to hurt Sam by hurting herself. That emotional nuance was buried deep in my homework. For me, that was what the whole scene was about. I took Robert De Niro the famous actor—an actor I admired—out of the equation. I'd never met him before. Only I knew the outcome of my emotional preparation. I was going to sleep with the first guy who sat down next to me at the bar. I was gonna take that guy home. Something I had never done before in my entire life because I was a nice girl. But I was going to do it tonight. For fun. It just happened that that person was Max Cady. So all the flirting, all the laughing, all the drinking was to get him to take me home.

I had been profoundly affected by the murder of a classmate my first year at the Neighborhood Playhouse. She was walking home alone from seeing the play *Hurlyburly*. As she entered her building a man took her by knifepoint to the roof, raped, and murdered her. A classmate had offered to walk her home, but she had declined. That momentary decision cost her her life. There had also been the tragic "preppie murder" case, which also occurred while I was in acting school. A girl named Jennifer Levin went into Central Park with a boy after they had just left a bar. It was a bar near my school that a lot of us frequented. That clean-cut, good-looking boy, named Robert Chambers, was convicted of manslaughter after the half-naked and badly bruised corpse of Jennifer Levin was found. He claimed that she had died during "rough sex." I was haunted by that case and how her decision, that innocent lapse of judgment to leave the bar with him, had cost her her life.

I always use music to prepare. There is usually one song, or a set of songs, that gets me into character, and for the bar scene it was Etta James. There is an undercurrent in her music that makes me uneasy. It makes me feel kind of boozy and out of control. I put my Etta James tape on, listening to it again and again till I began to feel drunk. People don't think training is important. Sure, when everything is working you don't need it, but when I find myself in trouble, I think, Thank God I can fall back on my training. Luckily, it worked that day. I listened to the music and did my emotional preparation. There was a knock on my door and this time I was really ready.

I walked to the set, like a fighter going into the ring. I could hear nothing except the Etta James playing in my head. I was confident this time because I had a secret. There was something I knew for certain. Robert De Niro was going to pick me up. He was going to pick me up, and take me home, and this was going to be the greatest one-night stand of my life. That's all I knew. I just had to do whatever it took to make that happen.

I sat at the bar and started to fake-laugh. Ha. Ha Ha. Ho Ho Ho. Let me tell you, you start laughing with a hundred people looking at you like you're an idiot, and it's a little embarrassing, but I didn't care, because I had a secret. It was like the more people were rolling their eyes at me, the funnier I thought it was. And De Niro was looking at me like he wasn't quite sure what I was doing, but he was intrigued, I could tell. A fire was in his eyes, and I was pretty sure I was causing it. He started topping me now, coming alive, and the scene started cooking. I knew I wanted to use this desperate kind of laughing. I kept on laughing, banging the bar, telling jokes, and somewhere along the way I was laughing for real. Pretty soon the whole set was laughing. It was wild. So many folks have asked me if I was really drunk. No. I felt drunk, though. I remember ordering a Sea Breeze in the scene because I knew if I said it, the props guy would have to make me one. It's something a drunk would do. I got my Sea Breeze. I think I drank fifty of them. The scene was going so well that Bob conferred with Marty, and they decided that the best way to shoot was with two cameras simultaneously so we could both stay in it but also ad-lib. We kept the plot points the same but improvised most of the scene. The cameras kept rolling, and when we got to the end, we just started again. Later, when I watched myself in the rushes, with everyone around me laughing, I couldn't remember half of the things I said. My favorite compliment came from Nick Nolte, who said to me, "Are you sure you've never done drugs?"

Bob and I sat on those bar stools for hours. When it came time for lunch, I didn't eat. I just stayed in my trailer, in my "drunken Etta James stupor" until we were ready to shoot again. I was ready to get back in there. Keep punching. I was in the zone. Fourteen, fifteen hours later, we are done. All day. One scene.

The next day, I got to the set, and I was walking along and now everyone was smiling at me, nodding at me, patting me on the back. "Good morning, Illeana. Would you like some coffee, Illeana? Can I get you something, Illeana? That was a great scene yesterday, Illeana." They had a chair for me. It was a director's chair, and it had my name on it. I had seen my grandfather's name on the back of a director's chair on the set of *Being There*. Now I was seeing mine: ILLEANA DOUGLAS. People ask me, when did you know you'd "made it"? That was the day. The day after the bar scene in *Cape Fear*. When I felt like I had earned the right to be on a film set. When everybody knew my name.

You get into the ring with the greatest fighter of all time and hope that you become a fighter, too. You can run away, or you become what you most want to be. *That's* what it's like to work with Robert De Niro.

CHAPTER NINE

Happy Just to Be Alive

Welcome to set. A complete re-creation of the 1972 Andes plane crash, 12,000 feet up in the Canadian Rockies.

I was flying to Canada to start filming the movie *Alive*. It was based on the plane crash in the Andes of a Uruguayan rugby team. They had to resort to eating the bodies of their dead companions to survive and were finally rescued, seventy-two days after the crash, when Nando Parrado and Roberto Canessa trekked for ten days through the Andes to find help. There were forty passengers and five crew members onboard, and only sixteen came out alive. It is an amazing story of the triumph of the human spirit, and one of the greatest survival stories of our time.

Looking out the window of the plane, I saw the snowy peaks of the Canadian Rockies, where we would soon be shooting. It was bittersweet. I was a working actress now, and that meant traveling from job to job, and yet everything I wanted was back in New York. Still, I hoped *Alive* would be like climbing a mountain and reaching the summit, finally finding that unattainable something that was missing in my life.

The previous year had been a roller coaster for me. I wrote in my journal, "My life is divided in two parts. Pre and post *Cape Fear*." But there was spillover from starving actress to working actress. *Cape Fear* had not come out yet, and the day I was scheduled to be on my first talk show ever—David Letterman's show—I was still selling furniture out of my apartment to pay the rent. Dave had seen *Cape Fear* and loved it, but aside from him, no one really knew who I was when I went on his show. When I sold my last table just days before the movie came out, I signed the bottom CAPE FEAR. That's how sure I was that my life was about to change.

I had been invited onto *Letterman* because a friend of David's, Hank Gallo, had seen me perform as a comedian at Stand Up NY and recommended me. (Stand Up NY was originally owned by Cary Hoffman, who let me perform there and actually thought I had a future as a standup.) It was quite a break to be on *Letterman*—it meant national exposure, and Hank had risked a lot to get me on the show, assuring the producer, Robert Morton, that I was funny and could tell a good story. I remember being called for the longest pre-interview "audition" of my life, during which

I proceeded to tell the producer every even remotely funny thing that had ever happened to me.

We settled on a *Zelig*-like experience I had had when the Secret Service occupied my dressing room in Ford's Theatre, in Washington, D.C., on the night that President George H. W. Bush came to see a performance of a play I was in, called *Black Eagles*. The morning after seeing our play, which was about World War II, the president started the ground war against Iraq. Like Leonard Zelig, we became a footnote in history.

The night I was on *Letterman*, which was my first national television appearance, I followed Jacques Cousteau, and he bombed. He sank. He was like a dead fish stinking up the joint. How many more bad aquatic metaphors can I give you?

I was in the makeup room, and Robert Morton came backstage, ashen. "Jacques was *not* funny," he said. "Dave is *not* happy. Are you *sure* you're going to be funny?" I assured him I would be, but he wanted to go over everything I was going to say. He began coaching me on every line and joke. Suddenly he was like Warner Baxter in *42nd Street*, shouting at me, "OK, Dave is going to ask, 'How did you prepare for your part in *Cape Fear*?' and you'll say what?"

I would answer robotically with my prepared material, "I have older brothers; I'm used to getting beat up." I hadn't been that nervous, but now, as we made our way down the hall toward the stage, I felt like an unskilled comedy surgeon, getting instructions from another doctor before I entered the Letterman operating room, famously kept at 58°.

I don't remember anything that happened, but afterward Robert Morton came up to me, put his hand on my shoulder as if he were a priest, and said, "That went well. *Dave is happy.* You will be back." I felt anointed.

Overnight I became "that girl from *Cape Fear.*" I was walking down the street, and someone yelled out, "Hey! I saw you on *Letterman*! You're that girl from *Cape Fear!*" I knew I'd never have to sell another table. When the movie opened a few days after my appearance on *Letterman*, the phrase became my constant companion. I was at a party in Los Angeles when Barbra Streisand—sounding very much like Barbra Streisand—suddenly looked at me and said, "You're that girl from *Cape Fear.* You were very good." People (such as Roddy McDowall) called and took me to lunch. I was pulled out of a line of people waiting for tickets to watch the filming of *Seinfeld* and was asked, "Why are you standing in line? You're that girl from *Cape Fear!*"

I was auditioning a lot but with mixed results. It took three auditions to get a role in Spike Lee's *Jungle Fever.* The night we shot, the cinematographer, Ernest Dickerson, laughed at everything I said. Spike, if he really liked something, gave you a kind of half smile. He was a great, albeit tough audience. The part got cut. I worked with Woody Allen in *Husbands and Wives.* It snowed the day we shot, and I could not believe I was staring at another great cinematographer, Carlo Di Palma, as he lighted a set. I thought, My God, I have made it. I will probably be in every Woody Allen movie. Annie Hall Douglas.

My part got cut. I went to an early screening and nobody had told me I was no longer in the movie. I think Marty was more upset than I was. The nerve to cut another director's girlfriend out of your movie. I wrote in my journal, "I am an actor. I go from job to job. Although the job let me down, I will continue to prosper." I was right. After all that work trying to be in a movie, the producers of *Cape Fear*—Amblin Entertainment and Steven Spielberg's producers, Frank Marshall and Kathleen Kennedy, who I had met at the premiere—put me in *Alive* and I could not have been more grateful. I wrote, "It was a good thing, because I had no more furniture to sell."

I was looking out at the Canadian Rockies and thinking, Here I was, a working actress. Going from job to job. About to shoot *Alive*. But I was worried. It was March 13, 1992. Friday the 13th. I was flying on a plane over mountains about to shoot a movie about a plane crash, based on the real life crash in the Andes of a plane that had also flown on Friday the 13th—on October 13, 1972. I was reading the book that our movie was adapting, *Alive*, by Piers Paul Read, trying to keep it in my lap, understanding that it might not be what your fellow passenger wants to see you reading. The guy next to me noticed it and reminded me, good-naturedly, that it was Friday the 13th and asked, "Are you at all superstitious?"

As we were passing over the mountains there was some turbulence, and I laughed it off, but it got me thinking that I *was* superstitious. But I figured that flying on Friday the 13th to make a plane-crash movie was either a good omen, or a really, really bad one. There were other things I was scared about. I was leaving Marty for what would be our first separation in four years. Would things be the same when I got back? He was also about to shoot *The Age of Innocence*. I was supposed to have played the small part of Daniel Day-Lewis's sister, but I had to give that up, since the shooting of *Alive* forced us to be on set every day whether we were on camera or not. The juxtaposing of our films did not go unnoticed by Marty and me. He would be depicting the life of upper crust New York society, shooting in mansions that featured sumptuous banquets. I would be living in the Canadian Rockies, possibly sleeping in a tent, starving, with a bunch of guys on top of a mountain. He packed me off with three books, *Silence*, *The Bridge of San Luis Rey*, and *The Brothers Karamazov*. They were all about suffering!

Alive would be a long, arduous, physically and mentally demanding movie. I knew that because back in sunny California, the director Frank Marshall and his wife, the producer Kathleen Kennedy, had personally interviewed actors to make sure they knew what they were in for. There would be risks. We would be living in the wilderness of the Canadian Rockies in a place called Panorama. There would be bears there! I would be the only woman in a cast of men to fly by helicopter to the Delphine Glacier—12,000 feet up—where we would shoot most of the film. The temperature would reach 30 below in minutes. Blizzards and whiteouts could develop instantly. We would very possibly be snowed in. We would shoot six-day weeks. There was also no end date; you were simply agreeing to be there for the run of the picture. However long it took. To re-create the accuracy of the story of *Alive*, we would be contracted to lose up to fifteen pounds on a special "survivors" diet.

You'd think I'd be running for the door, right? That's what was so awesome about Frank and Kathy. All the while they were detailing the dangers that could surround me, they had huge smiles on their faces. After all, they explained, they'd worked in the Venezuelan jungle for *Arachnophobia*. Shot in the Serengeti for *The Color Purple*. They made *Alive* and its disturbing story line seem like a picnic. No pun intended. Frank said, "We wanted to shoot it in the Andes, but we couldn't figure out a way to get the equipment there, so we found the last sister plane of *The Fairchild*, the exact plane that crashed in the Andes, and replicated the crash site." They wanted total authenticity. He took out storyboards and showed me side-by-side photos of a recently destroyed airplane in the snow on the Delphine Glacier next to pictures of the actual plane-crash site in the Andes. I was staring at the pictures, and for the first time, I got it. We would be shooting on a mountain. In the snow. On a mountain!

"Do you get altitude sickness?" Frank said at the audition. "You might be throwing up a lot at first, but you'll get used to it!"

Here I was, this dyed-in-the-wool New Yorker, used to my creature comforts and my twenty-four-hour food delivery, but the more Frank and Kathy described how hard it was going to be, the more they made it seem like an amazing adventure—something I might be able to talk about for the rest of my life—if I lived through it, of course.

I came out of filming *Alive* not only alive, but reborn. Like all births, it didn't come without some pain and suffering. Yes, I threw up. Yes, it was freezing. Yes, there were times, I thought, I cannot do this. Yes, I had a nervous breakdown over a baked potato. But that's not what I remember. It's the first line of the movie: "We were part of a grand experience." I couldn't have said it any better.

Let's start with what everyone remembers about the movie. The plane crash. There was never a time I saw *Alive* with an audience when the sequence didn't get applause. We shot that crash scene for four weeks. Imagine four weeks of getting dressed, made up, and reenacting the same horrific plane crash. Just the crash. We hadn't even got to the scenes yet. That's the attention to detail I had seen the day Frank and Kathy had shown me pictures and storyboards. By starting with the crash, they set the tone of the film, because it gave us discipline, and we all got to know each other very well during those long days buckled in our seats.

To create the images, they used different planes, each to create a different effect. For close-ups, your section of the plane was separated while a wind machine blew potato flakes in your face, or it was rotated at a 45-degree angle to better record your anguish. The moment I have been asked about the most is when two passengers are sucked out of the back of the plane. This was created by having a plane twenty feet in the air on a hydraulic lift, which was then dropped fifteen feet while two stuntmen attached to rigging were yanked out the back. The day that we shot it, we knew this was a big stunt, but none of us actually knew what was going to happen, because Frank wanted to record our genuine fear. Well, we were all in our seats on the set plane, and suddenly it dropped fifteen feet in the air. The guys went flying out the back. Instead of screaming and acting scared, everyone just gave this simultaneous "Whoaaaa!!!" as if we were on the best ride of our lives.

From over the loudspeaker we heard Frank say, "Cut. Cut . . ."

The plane slowly went back up the hydraulic lift to what was called "first position" to try it again. We knew we had ruined the take. Frank, bless his heart, came inside the plane shaking his head at us. We were bad kids. We felt terrible, but he was grinning at us. He said, "Don't do that again."

We were miles away from any city, so Frank and Kathy went to a small town nearby called Invermere and rented out an entire theater for us. We used it to watch movies that might inspire us. Nothing current. Just classics that we had never seen, all with adventure themes, such as the original *Flight of the Phoenix* and *The Great Escape*. None of us had seen *The Warriors*, a movie Frank had worked on, so we put in a request for that. I can't remember enjoying a film more. I have a lasting memory of the cast of *Alive* hooting and hollering at the screen. Afterward, Frank told us stories about the filming of this Walter Hill classic. We bonded over nights like that, because the days on the mountain were long and challenging.

From the beginning, there was something familial about *Alive*. John Patrick Shanley—the Academy Award–winning screenwriter of *Moonstruck*—had written the script. In a hotel suite in Vancouver, the entire cast gathered to read the script aloud for the first time. We were all getting to know one another, and everyone was nervous and excited, wanting to do a good job, because John would be sitting there listening to us speak his words, which were so beautiful, they were like poetry. John wouldn't have any part of the seriousness. He volunteered to read the stage directions, which he did, acting out everything in a loud and boisterous manner, making everyone laugh. I was so happy to see John, who had always had faith in me. He gave me a hug after the reading and said, "What did I tell you? Did I tell you you'd be here?"

I had an association with John when I was working for Peggy Siegal. Peggy had done the publicity for *Moonstruck*. Some of my favorite conversations were talking to John while I was supposed to be working on *Moonstruck*. He was such a funny, humble, and talented artist. The fact that I had known him in my previous life made working on *Alive* seem like destiny, and he was thrilled that I would be playing Lilliana Methol, until the day I called him for some clarification about a line I was having an issue with. Frank had said to me, "John's the writer; you'll have to talk to him."

In real life, Lilliana Methol had been eating the bodies of the dead before she died in the avalanche. For the film, John thought it worked better dramatically if Lilliana was revolted by the idea and died without ever eating the bodies. We were discussing the script and John said, "I don't want a comma out of place." Needless to say, I did my scenes exactly as they were written. There was a time in movies that when an actress had an issue with the script, she spoke to the writer and respected his wishes.

But to this day I'm not sure he ever correctly explained why my character is singing Burt Bacharach's "The Look of Love" the night before she decides she will finally eat human flesh!

We all felt the responsibility of playing real people and were fortunate to have the actual survivors of the Andes crash there to guide us. I wrote in my journal, "I feel like Nando Parrado is God, because he was closer to God than anyone I have ever known."

I was raised a Catholic, but I hadn't been to church for years. I was an actress. I was raised as a hippie. I didn't know what I believed in. I believed in movies. I believed Audrey Hepburn was a saint. I believed Billy Wilder was God. When we recited prayers in the film, like the real survivors had, with Nando there watching, it had a profound effect on all of us, and I think you can feel that in those scenes.

He told me, "There were so many times I could have died. My will to die was as strong as my will to live, but I know that God saved me. I must repay that debt every day by telling people how lucky they are to be alive." One of the ways Nando expressed this enormous love he had inside him was by hugging you. Nando was a great hugger, and this became a real hugging movie. We were going through a lot of difficult emotions; sometimes you didn't know if it was about the film or a real incident. One time an actor was crying, "My dog died; my dog died," and I said, "I'm so sorry; when did it happen?" And he looked at me very strangely and said, "When I was a kid." It was an eerie moment. Nando just took a hold of the actor and started to hug him, while he experienced this long-repressed memory. Knowing that it was more important just to hold him, not judge him, Nando let the actor cry in his arms. He had this ability to hold you long and hard until you felt safe. You could truly feel the love he was radiating. One time we were shooting, and I scratched my cornea. This cloud appeared on my left eye, and I couldn't see out of it. Nando took me in his arms, and calmed me down. He personally wanted to take me to the hospital. It was a long drive, and I was pretty scared, but he just made me believe I was going to be OK. On the way back from the hospital we drove to this abandoned Western town where they had shot *The Grey Fox*. We walked the empty streets, looked out at the fields, and watched the sun go down together. He said to me that the most important thing for us to project in the film was that life was beautiful and worth living.

Our other tech advisor, also a survivor, was Roberto Canessa. If Nando was the kind and loving supportive father figure, Roberto Canessa was the tough love father I also needed. Nando was serenity. Roberto was strength. I was complaining to him about something that was happening in my life, and he said, "You'd better grow up, because you're not a little girl anymore." It was like being slapped in the face. Yeah. Try not to whine to someone who managed to walk out of the Andes alive. Roberto told me I had to be stronger than any of the men on the film. "Lilliana never cried," he said. "Remember that." We were filming the avalanche scene. I was buried under the snow, in a specially designed set we called the mausoleum. I had a breathing tube that was about to be pulled from my mouth. From above, I could hear the muf-fled noises of the crew and the actors. From under the snow I heard the cameraman Dave say, "Illeana is packed in snow! Let's move!" My head had a gigantic ice cream headache going through it, but I had to pretend I was dead. I couldn't scream in pain. I couldn't move. They pulled the breathing tube. All I had now was the trust that the actors would pull me out to safety. We shot it again and again, until my face was scratched with snow and ice. My hands and feet were numb. Each time something would go wrong, Frank would say to me, "Can you do it one more time?" I'd think, I cannot do this. I can't feel my face. But somehow I found the strength to continue. I didn't want to let Frank down. The hardest thing about climbing under again was that you knew how scary it was going to be. In the years since *Alive*, I've been on a lot of sets, and folks have said to me, "You don't complain much, do you?" I've just laughed.

We were shooting a very difficult scene, the one in which we decide that we will eat the bodies of the dead. We had gone on a three-day fast before it to get into character. For two days Frank pumped the soundtrack of *The Mission* over loudspeakers to get us in the mood before we shot. It felt so real, and I had never been more proud of the work we all did over those two days. Saturday night came, and to reward us, Frank said we were all going out to dinner in Invermere. The cast, the survivors, everybody. We could have anything we wanted except for bread, pasta, or dessert. We got to the restaurant—The Windy—before Frank and Kathy and associate producer Bruce Cohen arrived, and we saw pasta with four cheeses on the menu. It sounded incredible. We were so proud of ourselves that we were going to get away with this, and we all ordered it. The waitress looked at us and said, "I'm really sorry, but Frank and Kathy already called ahead. You can't have the pasta." They knew our every move!

Later that night, Frank pulled me aside and told me there had been something wrong with the focus, and none of my close-ups was usable. They would all have to be shot again. At first I thought it was a joke, but he was not kidding. I slowly walked backed to the table and told my castmates what had happened. I was reeling. How on earth would I be able to re-create that scene alone, without the rest of the cast? Some of the actors gathered around me. Ethan Hawke was kneeling next to me; Josh Hamilton was holding my hand. Jack Noseworthy, Christian Meoli, Kevin Breznahan. They said, "Illeana, we'll be there for you, OK? Don't worry." If I had climbed the mountain looking for something, I was beginning to find it.

On the day we reshot the scene, every actor in the movie was there for me off camera. It's hard to describe the feeling you have when your fellow actors do something like that. When they let you know, as Jack Noseworthy had said in his thick Boston accent, "Honey, we got your back." Ethan was doing his same lines again off camera, and he was just tearing it up, drawing everything I had in me out of me again, and shouting at me, "If we want to live, we're going to have to eat!" He'd lost fifteen pounds by then.

Someone recently asked me who the most surprising person I've ever worked with was. Ethan Hawke. Ethan so dramatically affected my life that when we finished shooting *Alive* I wrote him a thank-you note. I told him that knowing him had changed me. And it did. He was an artist. He may have looked like a shaggy puppy, but he was one of the most inspiring people I have ever met. Ethan made me excited and hopeful about music, movies, art, books, you name it. His authenticity and daring to be an artist affected me.

I was doing a film after *Alive*, and I just didn't feel like I fit in in the same way I had on that set. Ethan, who was on his way to Texas, drove sideways to Wilmington, North Carolina, just to cheer me up. "Fuck 'em," he said. "Stop trying to please everybody. Just do your work." And he was right. The night he got there I watched Ethan walk into a roomful of strangers, introduce himself, and just start playing the guitar. I'll never forget it. I thought, I want to be like that. Just fearless.

On *Alive*, Ethan's condo was the hub of late-night discussions with the cast about movies, music, sex, lack of sex, food, lack of food. All I wanted when I got home was cherry pie. We painted pictures. We played music. Wrote songs. Read scenes from plays by Sam Shepard. We were pretty "artsy." We all talked about wanting to make movies like the ones John Cassavetes had. It was Ethan who said to me, "You need to direct. I'll help you." And he did. When I got home from *Alive*, I used to joke, the rest of the cast bought cars; I made a movie. I wrote and directed and starred in my first short film, *The Perfect Woman*. Ethan helped me cast it, and he was also my clapper.

We borrowed a camera from Marty—one he had got from none other than John Cassavetes—to shoot it. *The Perfect Woman* was later bought by Miramax. I remember standing backstage at the New York Film Festival. It was playing the closing night before *The Piano*, and I was standing next to Harvey Weinstein, and he said, "I'm going to buy this movie," and he did. Here's how I thanked Ethan. He had never seen the film *East of Eden*, so I asked Marty if he could screen it for him and some of the cast of *Alive*. Maybe we could even invite Elia Kazan himself to talk about it. Marty had never met Mr. Kazan, but he invited him, and sure enough he came. It led to a lasting friendship between the two masters. Picture the scene: this group of hot young actors, jammed into Martin Scorsese's screening room, watching *East of Eden* with Elia Kazan. There was the emotion of the film. The emotion of watching it with Kazan. Marty watching it with Kazan. The lights came on, and there wasn't a dry eye in the house. It was pretty special. That was all because of *Alive*. *Alive* awakened the artist in us. I've fallen off the mountain a few times since then, but it was on the set of *Alive* that I accepted that I *was* "artsy." I was an artist. I would die for my art. Well, almost.

For three days I had been starving myself in an attempt to be "in character" to shoot a part of a scene that had never been completed. The problem was the weather would change so rapidly on the mountain that many times you would be in the middle of shooting a scene when the weather suddenly wouldn't match what you'd been shooting. So you'd have to start to shoot another scene. The call sheet, which lists the day's scenes, was six pages long! It read, "Under cloudy conditions to be completed: list of scenes. Under sunny to be completed: list of scenes." I needed sunny conditions to complete this scene in which I was supposed to be very hungry. The sun kept going down before we got to my scene. It had been five days of Frank's telling me, "I promise. We'll get to it tomorrow." It was my own idea simply to stop eating. We had done one fast already, but I wanted to take it further. Starve for my art! And I was starving.

The sun went down, and I was sitting in the snow on what they call an "apple box"—there were no chairs—and Frank came up to me that fifth day shaking his head, grinning with the usual "Sorry, Illeana; we'll definitely get to it tomorrow." We had been there so long, I forgot what civilization looked like, and I guess the conditions finally got to me. I stood up and said, "That is it. That's it! I'm leaving." And I walked off the set. Problem was, we were on a mountain. I still remember the look on Bruce Cohen's face as I just started to walk past the plane set and out into the snow. I mean, we were forbidden from walking away from the boundaries of the set. It was quite dangerous, but I was walking somewhere, stomping off in the snow. Pretty soon Frank Marshall was told what was happening, and he and Bruce came after me in a snowmobile. I'm stomping along, and I could hear Bruce talking in hushed tones, explaining, because clearly I had lost my mind, "Frank, she hasn't eaten in three days." And Frank's saying, "Can we get her some food? Is there anything here?" And Bruce's saying, "I think we have some baked potatoes left over from lunch." The next thing I knew, they were radioing base camp. I heard the second assistant director tell Bruce, over the walkie-talkie, that the potato was on the way. Then the second assistant director came snowmobiling out to Bruce and Frank with the potato. Handed it to him. The second A.D. said to Bruce, "This is all that was left." I saw this shriveled, burned little baked-potato half. Frank shook his head as Bruce handed him this measly little thing. But he's the director; he's in charge. He is going to get me to eat. He starts pushing this potato at me, saying, "Illeana, eat the potato. C'mon. You have to eat something." He had the little shriveled half a potato in his hand, and he was saying, "Please. Illeana, please eat the potato." And I was starving, and I wanted that potato so bad, but there was another part of me that was so stubborn; I just did not want to accept that fucking potato because it was like accepting that I was wrong, that I needed help. I was so tired. I was so hungry. I was looking into Frank's eyes. He was holding out the potato, and I was like a wounded animal as I took it from his hands. I put that cold, hard, shriveled potato in my mouth and started to chew. Much-needed blood sugar started to flow to my brain. Frank walked out to the snow, and I just collapsed in his arms crying. "We won't tell Marty about this," he said, and I started to laugh. My director was holding me in his arms. Holding me till I felt safe. And eventually, true to his word, we did get that scene.

When *Alive* was over for me, my knees buckled under me as I tried to walk away from the plane. I knew things would never be the same in the real world as they had been on the mountain. Love. Trust. Safety. We had distilled everything that was good in one another. I had learned so many life lessons. I was wearing a plastic T-shirt designed to give me some protection from the snow. On the back one of the cast had written, I TASTE LIKE CHICKEN. I weighed 112 pounds. I had worn the same filthy dress for four months. I hadn't bathed or showered in weeks. I had cried over a baked potato. Frank Marshall hugged me. We had all become these great huggers. Kevin Breznahan said, "Illeana was our wife, our girlfriend, our sister, and our mother." Nicest thing anyone ever said to me. The last night I was there, Ethan and Josh Hamilton and I rolled downhill together outside Ethan's condo. There was no more snow on the ground. It was spring. We decided that if there was a heaven, it looked like the stars above us.

In the morning, I boarded a single-engine plane to Calgary. I eventually flew for sixteen hours, no sleep, one plane to another, finally landing in Wilmington, North Carolina. I had become what I had always wanted to be, but there were sacrifices. *Alive* went over schedule, and now I was flying straight to another movie, *Household Saints*. I hadn't seen Marty in four months. He said to me, "What do you want to eat when you get home?"

I said wistfully, "Cherry pie."

I was on the set of *Household Saints*. And it was hot. Close to a hundred degrees. I missed the snow and cold of the mountain. The movie took place in the '50s, so they had cut my hair, dyed it black. I was in a black '50s dress. We were shooting a wedding scene. It was supposed to be in Greenwich Village. Someone handed me a baby to hold. I was trying to ground myself, but nothing seemed familiar to me. I had no idea who I was or what had happened to me. I was a cannibal. *No*, I was a housewife. I was standing next to Tracey Ullman, who was the lead in the film. She was the star of *The Tracey Ullman Show*. I idolized her, but I was so disoriented that I was still searching for something to say to her when she said, "Someone just told me you were shooting a movie on a fucking iceberg?"

"Something like that," I said quietly. The days went by. I was so lonely, but there was no one around who could hug me until I felt safe.

Now, I don't remember this—it was told to me after the fact—but when I finally did make it home, apparently I ate an entire cherry pie, by myself. Marty planned this special dinner for me, and invited Daniel Day-Lewis and Winona Ryder, who were in *The Age of Innocence*. We were at the dining room table and everyone was laughing, and I said, "What?" and Marty said, "You just ate that entire pie!" I looked, and the pie plate was empty.

I said, "Oh, my God. Why didn't you say anything?" And Daniel said, "You seemed to be enjoying it." Now I started laughing. We were all sitting at the table, laughing. I looked at the empty pie plate. I looked at Marty. I was home. We were going upstairs. Marty was screening *Sullivan's Travels* for Daniel and Winona. They had never seen it. I think I laughed more at *Sullivan's Trav-*

els than any movie I had seen. "There's a lot to be said for making people laugh" learns the director, played by Joel McCrea. I had climbed that mountain, and attained that missing something I would be able to talk about for the rest of my life. I was, as Nando had hoped, "happy just to be alive."

CHAPTER TEN

Uncle Roddy

Hugo's restaurant on Santa Monica
Boulevard. Photograph by Roddy McDowall.
"You're not going to like these photographs,"
he said, "but someday you will!" As with
everything else, he was right.

It's not good to break down in tears when you are trying to
make a good impression on a Hollywood legend, but luckily
for me Roddy McDowall understood actresses and their frailties.
I met Roddy right after I had auditioned for the part of Janice,
the suspicious sister of Matt Dillon in the Gus Van Sant film *To*

Die For. I was pretty despondent by the time I arrived at Hugo's, the restaurant where Roddy had chosen to meet me. I was convinced I was not going to get the part I so desperately wanted.

Sometime after *Cape Fear* came out, Roddy McDowall contacted my Los Angeles agent. I received the following message with utter astonishment, "The actor Roddy McDowall called and he would like to take you to lunch, and snap some pictures of you for his latest book." Roddy was well known for his photography books of actors, a series called *Double Exposure,* so this was quite an honor.

Then it dawned on me. Wait a minute, Roddy McDowall, *the* Roddy McDowall? He wants to take pictures of me? Why? No, this is great. It will be great. Don't be nervous. I already knew a lot about him. There wasn't a celebrity bio I had read that hadn't had Roddy McDowall in it. Roddy McDowall was the confidant of Elizabeth Taylor, Natalie Wood, Montgomery Clift—basically everyone. Can I ask him about Elizabeth Taylor and what happened on the set of *Cleopatra?* The cult classics *Inside Daisy Clover* and *The Loved One?* His friendship with Montgomery Clift? Can I bring my copy of *The Legend of Hell House* and have him sign it? Can I bring *my* crappy camera and take pictures of *him*?

We set a date to coincide with my audition for *To Die For.* I was flying to Los Angeles for my *second* audition for the film. For the first audition, I had flown out to Los Angeles on January 16, 1994, and spent the night at the home of my former roommate, Steven, in Santa Monica. We had gone over all my scenes, had some wine, and said good night. I was feeling very confident and couldn't wait till the morning. I was sleeping on the floor in the living room and the next thing I remember, the earth was moving. Up and down and sideways. Pictures were falling from the walls, books came tumbling down, and dishes were crashing around me as I scrambled in the unfamiliar house to find Steven's bedroom. We held onto each other for dear life and prepared for the end. Two actors' lives tragically cut short. The shaking stopped, we went outside to see the destruction—even filmed some of it with my new toy, the video camera Marty had given me—and then, typical actress, I wondered if I was still going to have my audition in the morning. I even tried to call the studio. Yeah. No one answered. I had been upstaged by a really, really bad earthquake!

So I was back in New York when I received the call about Roddy McDowall's wanting to meet me. I know you know that, but I wanted to write it one more time. Roddy McDowall called and wanted to meet me! I was not going to let L.A.'s largest earthquake stop me from auditioning for *To Die For*. Auditioning for a part I thought I had been born to play.

My plan was to go to the audition and then meet Roddy McDowall and hope that I had some good news to share with him. "Roddy, I've signed on for the picture." Something like that. Roddy chose the place. It was a restaurant called Hugo's on Santa Monica Boulevard. Another good sign.

I knew all about Hugo's. The first time I went to Los Angeles was to work on *Guilty by Suspicion*. Marty insisted I had to have breakfast at Hugo's. "Every morning!" he said. "Make sure you're seen!" Hugo's was sort of an in-spot in those days. "You never know who you'll meet there."

So every morning I went to Hugo's and had breakfast. He was right. I saw a lot of famous folks. Didn't meet too many of them, but I saw them for sure. Then, at one of my last solitary breakfasts at Hugo's I see James Woods. There is nothing like the thrill of seeing a movie star, especially one you admire, swagger through a power-breakfast room, table-hop here, smile at someone there. Oh, wait—he's smiling at me. James Woods is smiling at me. He paused to say hello. My first welcome-to-Hollywood hello. (Something I reminded him the night when I spilled goat cheese on him.)

I remember calling Marty and telling him, "Marty, you're right. Hugo's is the best! I just met James Woods." Long silence from the other end. "Stay away from him." There were no hard feelings. They worked together years later on *Casino*!

When I went to meet Roddy McDowall, it was an unusually rainy day and I was still wearing my audition outfit, because I didn't have time to change. Here I was back at Hugo's. My place, I thought as I entered. Not only was I actually going to experience dining with someone there, but I was also going to meet Roddy McDowall. My first impression was of course to notice the instantly recognizable expressions and mannerisms and impish voice that I had seen and heard so many times in so many of his films. He would tilt his head, and I would think, Oh, my God, it's Cornelius from *Planet of the Apes*. Stay focused, Illeana. The next thing I noticed was the impeccable, Old World way in which he dressed and carried himself. His crisp white shirt cuffs were turned up over a baby blue V–neck sweater, which was covered by a tan Members Only cargo jacket. Wonderful cologne. He turned his gold ID bracelet on his left hand as he spoke. It's a cliché to say you want movie stars to live up to who you hope they'll be, but Roddy was everything I had hoped for and more. Charming, funny, gossipy. He dropped the name of a beautiful French starlet from the '30s and said, "She brought the clap to Hollywood—Gershwin, everyone had it." He had stories about everyone, always with a wonderful aside—usually about their private lives or loves. I was in heaven.

Then he ruined it by asking me how the audition had gone. I sighed and started to describe the scene to him with as much humor as I could muster. Auditions are always competitive, but the line of twenty-plus girls who auditioned for *To Die For* was a who's who of successful actresses, including two future Academy Award winners. We could have all left and filmed another movie. There was that much talent. I was sandwiched between two really successful gals, and I was convinced that someone more famous than I would get the part. It had nothing to do with the work. The work had gone well. And I knew I had allies. At one point, I was struggling with the reader—the person who is hired to read opposite you during the screen test. She was stumbling over the lines, and Nicole Kidman, who had been watching, piped up and said, "Do you want me to read with you?"

Actress looks directly into camera: That's what's called a good sign.

A bad sign? Buck Henry had his feet up on the desk the whole time I was there, rocking back and forth in this high-end office chair. Rock, rock, rock. When you are auditioning, and maybe this is just me, you survey the room when you walk in and think, Hmmm, who do I need on my side? Along with Gus Van Sant, producer Laura Ziskin, Nicole Kidman, and some Sony execs, there was the towering giant of a screenwriter, Buck Henry. Hadn't counted on that. Twice nominated for an Academy Award— Best Writing, Screenplay Based on Material from Another Medium, for *The Graduate,* and Best Director, for *Heaven Can Wait.* Let's throw screenwriter of *Catch-22, What's Up, Doc?,* and co-creator of *Get Smart* into the mix, too.

There he was, feet up on the desk, chewing gum, having seen a million auditions, not impressed, not laughing at any of my jokes, and why should he? He's Buck Henry. He cowrote *The Graduate*! Not on my side.

Now, that's what the scared actress is assuming he's probably thinking. When is lunch? Or, I wonder how big my on-screen writing credit is going to be? What's the hotel like in Toronto? I remember all through the audition thinking, this is going very well, and if I can just get Buck Henry to stop rocking in his frigging office chair it will go even better. Nicole Kidman gave me a secret smile as she said goodbye, or maybe I was assuming that, too. Gus took a Polaroid of me. That might be a good sign? I was recounting the entire experience to Roddy McDowall when he stopped me.

"Do you mind if I take some pictures? You're very . . . expressive."

"Sure," I said reluctantly. I hadn't expected him to take pictures right there at the table. I mean, I didn't even have any makeup on, but I think he sensed something was going on with me emotionally. He took out his camera and began snapping away. I was trying to smooth my hair, trying to look pretty for the camera, and I started to feel really self-conscious. Roddy McDowall had photographed some of the great leading ladies of our time. In fact, stop reading this right now and go pick up his four-book *Double Exposure* series, and you'll see what I mean. As he snapped away he asked me, "Do you think you have the part?" I wanted to laugh and say, yes, of course, I have the part—but all of a sudden I was pretty sure, in fact I was convinced, that I did not have the part.

I looked down at what I had chosen to wear for the audition. A white Capezio bodysuit with tights, Doc Martens boots, and some crazy short jumper I had bought at a Village flea market. Pseudo–Audrey Hepburn chic was the look I was going for. I had worn it so often it was already starting to rip under the arms. I mean, who wears something like that to meet Roddy McDowall? Would he notice? And now photographs would prove that I actually wore things like that to try to get parts in movies. I began to feel ridiculous and out of place in Hollywood. Meanwhile, the rain was coming down. I hadn't valet-parked, because I wanted to save money. Always thinking of money. I would have to make sure that Roddy got into his car before I did so he wouldn't find out. What kind of actress doesn't valet-park?

Roddy was snapping away, and I started to unravel. "No," I said. "I don't think I got the part. I don't have a chance." Then came the tears. I was convinced that another actress had cinched it. I said to him, "I saw the way she hugged everyone goodbye."

I'm not sure why, but I started to tell Roddy about the pressure I felt coming out here and competing against actresses who had already "made it" in my mind. About the pressure of having a famous boyfriend like Martin Scorsese who was so successful, and what would he think if I didn't get the part. I was revealing insecurities I didn't even know were there. Listen, I'm sure if I had had the clap I would have confessed that to him, too. He was a very good listener.

Roddy put down his camera, and handed me a handkerchief to dry my tears. "Oh, you poor dear," he said sympathetically. He started talking to me as if we were old friends, and I felt as if we *were* old friends. I'm sure a lot of other actresses had cried on his shoulder: Natalie Wood, Tuesday Weld, Elizabeth Taylor, and that actress with the clap. He was everyone's confidant. Now he was becoming mine.

"Now dry your eyes and listen to your Uncle Roddy," he said. "It's so important to find joy in this business, because as the years go by, people will try to steal that joy, so that is something as an actress you must hold onto. Marilyn could not hold onto joy. All we have is the joy of the work, and if they could kill that joy, they would. Marty, or Spielberg, they are beyond feeling any happiness in the work. They know better. But that is both a blessing and a curse."

It was like a secret actor-to-actor pep talk. Those words, and the fact that they came from him, set me straight. It gave me a confidence that I could wear like armor to all future auditions. Here was a man who was in his sixties then, in some of the greatest movies of all time, and he told me he was still auditioning. He had no bitterness. He was a child star who went through the studio system and had many ups and downs in his career. I took his advice to heart. I was on my own path, and I didn't need to compare my career with anyone else's. Soon we were back to laughing and gossiping. He dropped this brilliant aside involving two actresses known for playing prim and proper ladies on-screen, one a British redhead, the other a cool blonde.

He said knowingly, "The ones who play the virgins. They're the ones who sleep with everyone." Snap. Snap. Snap.

He paused, putting his camera down again and making a Cornelius expression. "You are not going to like these pictures," he said. "But when you are older you will." He was right, of course. He made the sun come out for me that rainy afternoon at Hugo's. From that day on, he became my Uncle Roddy. Always there to lend a sympathetic ear or to have a nice gossip with. When I told him I was cast in *To Die For*, he laughed and said, "You see now. All that worry for naught." We started to write back and forth. We would send each other silly postcards that he would sign, "With love to I.D." The nickname stuck. Given to me by a Hollywood legend who never stopped working.

Roddy came to New York to be in *A Christmas Carol*, and it was a joy to see him onstage. He and Marty had crossed paths over the years, but they had never really met, so this was perfect. We arranged for a dinner at Marty's townhouse. Roddy arrived with his signature Members Only jacket and a long red scarf. There was my Uncle Roddy to approve my choice of a boyfriend. He loved Marty, of course. They were both film nerds and heavily involved in film preservation. Roddy was on the board of governors for the Academy and Marty had his own organization called The Film Foundation. Roddy had been caught up in an FBI sting about copyright infringement over his vast private film collection. Marty was helping him untie the rights for a movie Roddy had directed nicknamed *Tam-Lin*. We would look forward to his visits. He'd show up at the townhouse with at least three cameras in hand. He took some wonderful formal pictures of us, and then what he called "snappy snaps," just for fun. When we were out in Hollywood we would often have dinner at Roddy's house. In the garden there was a gigantic statue of him as Cornelius from *Planet of the Apes*. Hysterical. These were no ordinary dinners. You would be sitting next to Maureen O'Hara, who was next to Steve Martin, who was next to Gore Vidal. Hard to know whether to eat your peas or just stare at Gregory Peck and try not to scream, but Roddy always made sure to include everyone in the conversation. He was so gracious that way. After dinner he brought out an autograph book that everyone had to sign. Marty drew a little self-portrait, signing it, "From your fan and admirer." I wrote, "To My Dear Uncle Roddy—I could listen to your stories for all eternity."

Roddy had been keeping autograph books going back to when he was twelve years old. John Ford, the director of *How Green Was My Valley*, had given him his first one as a way for the child actor to keep out of trouble when they were shooting. It became a lifelong habit for Roddy. He took out his first autograph book to show us. It was thickly bound green leather. He read entries from John Ford himself, the entire cast of *How Green Was My Valley*, and his next film, *Lassie Come Home*, which was where he met his lifelong friend Elizabeth Taylor. We were just in awe, holding something that contained so much movie history. It was Roddy who convinced me that I had to start keeping a journal. "You're going to meet a lot of interesting people, I.D. And I'm one of them, so start writing!" I did, and I will forever be grateful. It was Uncle Roddy, along with Gregory Peck, who sent me a letter inviting me into the Academy of Motion Picture Arts and Sciences after I had come a few votes shy of an Oscar nomination for the very movie I didn't think I was ever going to be in, *To Die For.*

He was not a fair-weather friend, either. When Marty and I broke up, it was a decision Marty made, and many of his friends who had known us as a couple sadly became distant. Not Roddy. He took me by the shoulders and said, "Now listen, I.D. You know this will mean absolutely nothing as far as you and I are concerned." It meant a lot that he reassured me in that way. But that was Uncle Roddy. Class all the way. Also, Elizabeth Taylor had been divorced seven times, so I'm sure his shoulder was used to being cried upon. I needn't have worried. I moved to Los Angeles in 1998, and the parties at his house, the memories, the formal portraits, as well as the "snappy snaps," continued. I was at a brunch at the home of George and Joan Axelrod, my future in-laws, and Roddy started taking pictures of me once again. I had no makeup on, there was a sleepy smile on my face, and I said, "Roddy, you're always taking pictures of me when I'm not ready." But he insisted, saying, "Those are the best kind."

Roddy was part of a circle of intimate friends, along with the Axelrods, who went on Sundays to visit the greatest movie star diva of all time: his best friend, Elizabeth Taylor. In my next book I *will* tell the story of how Elizabeth Taylor came to my beach house, fell in love with Gabriel Byrne, and broke her nose, but for now let me stick with Uncle Roddy. He deserves it.

We were driving back from Elizabeth's house in Bel Air down Benedict Canyon to Roddy's house in the Valley. We were going pretty fast. It's a winding and scary road, and I finally felt I knew him well enough to ask about "the accident." He pointed to a bend in the road and said, shaking his head, "That's where it happened."

I was referring to Montgomery Clift's car accident during the shooting of *Raintree County*. I had certainly read enough celebrity biographies to know that Roddy had been there the night it happened. After Clift left a party at Elizabeth Taylor's house in Benedict Canyon, his car had gone off the road in the fog and hit a telephone pole. The accident left him permanently disfigured and addicted to pain pills and eventually booze. Out of respect, I had never asked Roddy about it, but I thought it was important to know the history. He told me he had tried to help Clift many times, as others had. Roddy was a private man who kept his private life separate, but I could tell by the way he spoke about him that Roddy felt a deep love for the man he could not save.

"He couldn't look in a mirror. You couldn't have a mirror any-where around him. Once his looks were gone, he couldn't cope. A tragic figure, because he was surely our finest actor."

I have always loved film history, and I thought it was impor-tant to try to get stories from all of the greats of Hollywood so that those stories remain alive, and I think Roddy knew that about me. I told him that with his permission, I would include that story in my journals. The journals he had urged me to keep.

Beyond his memories, Roddy gave me something even more personal. It was a deeper appreciation of older actors and our re-sponsibility to care for them. For years, before anyone was aware of it, Roddy visited elderly and mostly forgotten actors at the Mo-tion Picture Home in Woodland Hills. It was a retirement home and hospital for actors, some of whom could not afford health ser-vices. Roddy started an organization called Roddy's Girls, which was a group of seventy-five of his lady friends who built a rose garden at the Motion Picture House—I was lucky enough to be-come one of Roddy's Girls. It's not hard to imagine that Roddy had seventy-five lady friends. He probably had a hundred and seventy-five. He was a friend to all of us, making each one of us feel special and loved. He probably knew all our secrets, too. Thank God he took them to the grave.

When I got married there was Uncle Roddy to give me away. My mom just fell in love with him. But that's how he was. He took your arm and made you feel as if you had known him all of your life. It was around that time I learned he was sick. It was cancer, but he refused to admit it or discuss it. This was a man who never complained, never spoke of anything negative, and al-ways had an optimistic outlook on life.

"I.D., I want you to have this," he said, putting a Tiffany vase in my hands. "I'm not leaving anyone anything; I am simply giving things to friends that I feel they will enjoy." I did not want to admit to myself that he looked very thin in his Members Only jacket.

The last time I spoke to him, I was in Chicago filming *Stir of Echoes*. The movie was going great, and we talked about that. My marriage not so much, and we talked about that, too. He got me laughing and gossiping and reminiscing about all our happy times together. He could always cheer me up telling wonderfully indiscreet stories. He could drop names like Ava, Audrey, Grace, Elizabeth, Natalie, Irene—he had an irrational love of all things Irene Dunne—and it wasn't name-dropping. He'd been on a first-name basis with all of those amazing actresses. "And now good night, I.D.," he said. He died in October 1998 at the age of seventy.

Everyone needs an Uncle Roddy. He was more than my uncle. He was my angel. I like to think my angel is in heaven right now, having a nice gossip with Mata Hari or Marie Antoinette, or the French starlet who brought the clap to Hollywood.

CHAPTER ELEVEN

A Director To Die For

Am in the zone, if not in a trance. Gus Van Sant instructing me to skate over Nicole Kidman's grave on Lake Simcoe, Ontario.

Not all that long ago, I was shooting a movie called *Picture Perfect*, directed by Glenn Gordon Caron, when one of my favorite experiences happened with a director—up until we met Mike Nichols together, that is. Glenn was under quite a bit of pressure. After a very long day, we had a huge setup that was going to take place in Times Square at dusk. It was summer, hot and humid, and we were shooting at rush hour with thousands of people behind barricades screaming while we tried to rehearse a scene with Jennifer Aniston, who just *happened* to be starring in *Friends* at the time.

Glenn was trying to set up the shot, and it was so loud you couldn't hear anything. I could tell he was getting frustrated. He just wanted this experience to be over.

"This is a nightmare!" he said over the roar of the crowd.

Meanwhile, I was giddy. Of all the movies I've done, I have to say in that moment I may have reached my personal nirvana of being exactly where I wanted to be, doing exactly what I wanted to be doing.

I was wearing a hat, and I said, "Glenn, please let me wear my hat. I want to be like one of those actresses in a movie from the '50s who looks up, wide-eyed, as she arrives in Times Square and is wearing a hat!"

Glenn looked at me like I was absolutely nuts. Over the noise, this beleaguered director said, "You seem pretty excited." I couldn't believe that he wasn't. I thought about the time when I was a kid staying with my grandmother in Queens. Al Pacino was shooting a scene from *Dog Day Afternoon* in Brooklyn. This event had been covered in the *New York Post*. I begged my grandmother to take me so we could watch the filming. We took the subway to Brooklyn and stood for hours behind the barricades to get a glimpse of the people making the movie. I think I might have seen the top of Al Pacino's head—and it was still exciting.

Now, on the set of *Picture Perfect*, I made Glenn Gordon Caron stop everything to take the moment in. I said, "Glenn. Look at us. We are shooting a movie. In Times Square. There are thousands of people screaming. They're *outside* those barricades. They would do anything to be *inside* the barricades. We're *inside* because *we're* making a movie."

Inspiring words from my grandpa: "Always order a club sandwich." Best advice he ever gave me!

Enjoying the perks of being an "inner city youth" in the musical *Two Gentlemen of Verona*. Yes, those are jazz hands.

My roommate and acting school buddy Steven Rogers and me posing like movie stars circa 1925. I got this raccoon coat as an homage to Rudy Vallée. Steven went on to become a successful screenwriter of many romantic comedies.

Are you talking to me? My other acting school chum Elias Koteas (on the right) doing his best De Niro. Years later he would ask me, "How did you end up with my life?"

Answering the phones for publicist Peggy Siegal: Marty calling me post-Oscars after losing Best Director for *The Last Temptation of Christ*.

First trip to Hollywood. Priorities. Clean Joe Mankiewicz's star on Walk of Fame. Then try to call Billy Wilder. Years later his grand-nephew, TCM's Ben Mankiewicz, would thank me for being the family maid.

Me photographing the billboard of *Goodfellas* outside Warner Bros. for Marty.

Robert De Niro, Marty, and me on the set of *Cape Fear*. Marty is staging what took two days to shoot.

Typical day on the set of a mountain. Frank Marshall said *Alive* would be a great adventure, if I lived through it! Tough conditions brought the cast and crew together.

This picture makes me hungry. Ethan Hawke and me on the set of *Alive*. Wonderful actor, and his singing and guitar playing are pretty good too.

A last-minute costume change from director Gus Van Sant made this scene even more chilling. *To Die For* is one of my favorite films. Photo by screenwriter Buck Henry.

What can I say? I played Matt's sister in *To Die For* and his wife in *Grace of My Heart*, and playing his wife here in *Grace* was more fun. Just a brilliant and intense actor.

Didn't get to talk about *Happy, Texas*, but I love this picture, and I love the movie. Miss Schaefer, y'all!

Favorite picture from a set ever. Director Glenn Gordon Caron and me shooting *Picture Perfect* (starring Jennifer Aniston . . . hmmm, whatever happened to her?) laughing about how lucky we are.

I should have married Uncle Roddy. My best-best man, Roddy McDowall.

I interviewed Jerry Lewis for the 2014 TCM Classic Film Festival. I'm getting some last-minute direction from The King of Comedy backstage at the El Capitan and enjoying every moment.

Meeting Joseph L. Mankiewicz got me in trouble with another director, Martin Scorsese. The caption reads, "Twenty years ago this pose would have been blurred."

Clockwise from top: Well, I blame him for everything. Dennis Hopper, Griffin Dunne, and me on the set of *Search and Destroy*. Finally I would learn, "That's what it's all about, man"; Always sing in the key of Liza. Meeting my idol Liza Minnelli at the 2013 TCM Classic Film Festival opening-night screening of *Cabaret*; Shooting a "Friday Night Spotlight" for TCM in Atlanta. I got some dress advice from Jerry Lewis; Shooting a sex video with Tom Arnold on the floor of IKEA for my branded web series *Easy to Assemble*. The only mandate from IKEA was to "keep the aisles clear." *ETA* lasted four seasons; A last-minute casting change brought Peter Fonda / Captain America / the other half of *Easy Rider* into *Grace of My Heart* as my guru "Dave."

This look of amazement suddenly came over his face, and he said, "I want a picture of us. Right now, together. Right at this moment!" He called over the photographer, and we snapped the picture. It's my favorite picture with any director I have ever worked for, because it truly captured the moment. That moment was joy. And I am wearing a hat.

My first love was acting. My second love was, and still is, the director. It could have started when I read Richard Schickel's book *The Men Who Make the Movies*. I found myself fascinated with the men who make the movies as much as the movies themselves. Some actresses fall for their directors of photography, because they make them beautiful. Some actresses fall for their leading men, because they start to believe the words the men are saying—"I love you; I want you; I need you"—are true.

My first memory of a director goes back to the set of *Being There*, watching quietly in the shadows while Hal Ashby directed my grandfather and Peter Sellers. I was mesmerized but conflicted. Part of me wanted to dance in the light with the actors. Part of me preferred the comfort and safety of watching, in the dark, next to the director. I could hear things that no one else heard. Secrets, laughing, mumbling. Things the actors didn't know about. The director was part god, part mad magician. But the actors were the magic trick itself. This question, of what side of the line am I on, has always been a factor in my own actress-director relationships.

I've always had a theory that the need to direct is an obsession with trying to re-create and somehow make sense of your childhood. You can look at any director's films and see that even if the stories are completely different, the themes are the same. You could tie those themes to their childhood. The most obvious example is Hitchcock. As a child, his father sent him with a note to the local police chief. The chief looked at the note and led Hitchcock to a cell and locked him in it for five minutes. Hitchcock was confused and terrified because he had done nothing wrong. When the policeman let him out he said, "That's what we do with naughty boys." Hitchcock claimed he was haunted by this incident, and that's why many of his films deal with an innocent man wrongfully accused of a crime. Another common thought is that directors are voyeurs—happier to watch and control the action rather than take part in it. It was Hitchcock who said he loved Grace Kelly because of her *willingness* to be submissive.

Sometimes directors are superheroes trying to save the girl. Sometimes they are the sadistic fellows trying to punish the girl. Again and again and again. I have certainly been at the hands of a director, asked repeatedly to do a scene, over and over again, only to be told that, I *still* didn't have it right. It's times like that I think to myself, Hmm, I wonder who he hates more, his mother or his father?

Sometimes this need for control is not simply to manipulate actors and circumstances but rather to attempt to change the outcome of some event from the past. Director John Frankenheimer was one of the most intimidating people I have ever met, and I learned a lot from him about being fearless. He knew I had ambitions to direct, so he chose me to be part of a select group that saw various cuts of his films. I asked him if we could continue our conversations over lunch, and we did, always at Orsini Osteria Romana, on Pico Boulevard. The first time we had lunch, he said very loudly and very directly, "Illeana, you're going to get much more out of this than I am, so you're going to pick up the check." After a screening of his TNT film *George Wallace,* one of the HBO executives wanted to remove fifty seconds from a cut, and he wouldn't let them.

"I will walk," he said. And he meant it.

At lunch, I asked him where he had found the bravery to say something like that, and he said, "Illeana," and he paused for dramatic emphasis, "my life has been about seconds and inches." Frankenheimer was both seconds *and* inches away from Bobby Kennedy the night he was shot at the Ambassador Hotel.

My first professional experience working with directors was not on sets. It was working for Peggy Siegal helping to publicize some of the best films of the '80s. For each project, Peggy would assign who would be responsible for handling each member of the cast during the press tour and release of the film. All the other girls wanted to be around the movie stars. There were bidding wars over who would get to work with Kevin Costner or Andy Garcia in *The Untouchables*. Nobody *ever* wanted to work with the director—unless you enjoyed constant runs to CVS to pick up their Maalox or Xanax prescriptions.

The glamour was being with the movie stars. Picking up their jewelry or clothes for events and premieres. Ordering champagne for their suite at the Four Seasons. Sometimes eating their untouched fruit plates after the press junkets. My absolute favorite task was spending an afternoon trying to get the supermodel Paulina Porizkova to attend the premiere of *Moonstruck* with Nicolas Cage because Cher's date was going to be the band Bon Jovi. Yes, the entire band! I told you this was a dream job! Porizkova declined—or rather, "her people" declined on her behalf. She had a boyfriend at the time, Ric Ocasek. Years later I teased her about this when we worked together on *Wedding Bell Blues*. With the director, there were no *Vanity Fair* photo shoots or *Premiere* magazine profiles, but I learned pretty quickly that being around the director was where *all* the real action was.

Working for Peggy Siegal, I probably learned more about the psychology of directors than I ever did on any film set. I understood their moods and sympathized with their pressures, and learned to duck when things went wrong and objects went flying.

People say that directors are egotistical, and they are, but that's also their game face. I had a director privately tell me, once a journalist left the room after reading him aloud a bad review of his film, "If you let them think you care, they will eat you alive." The funny thing is, I never ever mentioned that I was even an actress or even had aspirations *to* act. I thought of myself as the director's little helper, and it was a role I enjoyed. I also sensed that it was a relief for them be around one person who wanted absolutely nothing from them but to listen and learn.

The directors I worked with assumed I wanted to be behind the scenes, and in some ways, I did. If I had ever said I wanted to be an actress, the relationship would have instantly changed. When I became identified as "an actress," I lost the power I once had to communicate with directors as if we were equals. For example, after *To Die For* came out, my wonderful agent at the time, Jay Moloney from CAA, said to me, "Illeana, who do you want to meet? Anyone at all. I'll make it happen!"

"Billy Wilder?" I asked.

He rolled his eyes, saying, "Someone that could hire you. Someone that would put you in a movie!"

I said, "Not everything is about getting a job. It's the privilege of meeting someone whose work you admire. Plus I have an in." Billy had worked with my grandfather on *Ninotchka*. A few days later Jay called me with Billy Wilder's home phone number.

The fact that I can write that I actually called Billy Wilder still gives me a thrill, but I am a little mortified about how the conversation went. Mr. Wilder himself answered the phone. He was friendly but curt: "Young lady, I appreciate very much that you would like to meet me, but I'm in no position at this time to offer you a job."

"No, I understand that, Mr. Wilder. I was just hoping to talk to you about some of your movies. You wrote *Ninotchka*—my grandfather, Melvyn Douglas, was in it—I would be very curious to know about working with him and also Ernst Lubitsch."

"Young lady, I am no longer *directing* pictures. You should be spending your time meeting directors that will put you *in* pictures, not *talk* about the pictures."

There's nothing like being lectured by Billy Wilder. Still, in that one brief phone call, I felt like I got a taste of what it would probably have been like to be directed by Billy Wilder. He would have had very little patience. Sentiment would make him uncomfortable. He was easily frustrated by actresses looking for jobs. I always wondered, If I had identified myself as a director, would the conversation have gone better or made more sense to him?

The next example of how my relationship to directors changed once I became an actress involves an equally impressive director, Joseph L. Mankiewicz. He was charming, witty, engaging—all the things I expected. A good director needs to feel like he is directing. A good actress needs and wants to be directed. It's a symbiotic, often seductive relationship.

So it's probably a good thing I never worked with Joseph L. Mankiewicz, who was rumored to have had love affairs with most of his leading ladies. Joseph Mankiewicz was right up there with Wilder for me. Some of my favorites films of his are the pitch-perfect *All About Eve*, *A Letter to Three Wives*, and the romantic *The Ghost and Mrs. Muir.* I had seen Mr. Mankiewicz at a number of Peggy Siegal's premieres, most notably Barry Levinson's *Good Morning, Vietnam*. The after-party was held at the legendary restaurant '21', which was prominently featured in *All About Eve*. When I saw Mr. Mankiewicz walking through the very rooms that he had so brilliantly captured in some of that film's most unforgettable scenes, I thought: Once again, movies and real life have collided. We were looping *The Last Temptation of Christ*, and Marty was impressed that I was reading the Mankiewicz biography *Pictures Will Talk*, by Kenneth L. Geist, but he winced and said, "It's not a very flattering book" and brought me one he much preferred, *More About All About Eve*, by Gary Carey with Joseph L. Mankiewicz, along with his own biography, *Scorsese on Scorsese*. Interesting way to court someone. Stop reading the book about the other director. Here's a book about me. Thought Joe was a bastard? What do you think of this guy?

Obviously Marty admired his work, so around the time of *Cape Fear*, I asked Marty if he might reach out to Mr. Mankiewicz and invite him to the premiere, and then we could have dinner with him. One of the things that was endearing about Marty is that whenever I would suggest meeting some of these Hollywood greats, he would suddenly become insecure.

"Why on earth would Joe Mankiewicz want to see *Cape Fear*?"

That's when I'd remind him that first of all, he was doing it for me, and second of all, "Um . . . you're Martin Scorsese! You're a great director. I'm sure he'd be thrilled to meet you, and see *Cape Fear*!"

Marty was always surprised whenever he found out that another director admired *his* work, too. He looked at Mankiewicz as if he were in another pantheon of Hollywood history.

Well, Mr. Mankiewicz did indeed attend the opening of *Cape Fear*, and a few weeks later, we arranged to meet him and his wife, Rosemary, for dinner at a restaurant he loved near his home in Bedford, New York.

Marty was meeting him as the *director* of *Cape Fear*. Mankiewicz gave him an overall critique of the film, which was very insightful; Marty was humbled by his praise. They talked about cameramen and lighting. Technical things. Then Mankiewicz turned to me, the *actress*. He proceeded to completely dissect my character, Lori Davis. He broke down every choice I had made; he read deeply into my character's psyche. Now, I hadn't even told Marty some of the homework that had gone into my emotional choices, but Mr. Mankiewicz had picked up on little nuances I had played as if he were a psychic. His blue eyes bored into mine. As he spoke it seemed there was no one at the table but the two of us. He wanted to let me know that he, and he alone, understood me. I felt like I was being redirected in *Cape Fear* by Joe L. Mankiewicz himself, which did not go unnoticed by the other director of *Cape Fear*, Martin Scorsese, who was glaring at us across the table.

When he finished, I said, "Mr. Mankiewicz, did all of your leading ladies fall in love with you? Because I think I'm in love with you right now."

He smiled and said, "All actresses want to be psychoanalyzed. They don't know who they are, so they want to be *told* who they are. If a man can do that, then any woman will fall in love with him."

He said it in jest, but I thought there was tremendous truth to it. I was certainly putty in his hands, and he knew it. Tell me who I am, Joe? Tell me who you want me to be, Joe?

We took some pictures, and he said he would sign them and send them along to us. A week later they arrived. I am sitting next to Mr. Mankiewicz, and I have a huge smile on my face. So does he!

The caption read, "For Illeana—twenty years ago this pose would be <u>blurred</u>!" At first I didn't understand what it meant, but Marty grabbed the picture away from me.

"*Blurred*! How dare he!"

My other director explained it to me.

"*Blurred*! You would be *moving* around! Get it!?"

Marty refused to let me hang up the picture. I loved that he was jealous of an eighty-one-year-old, even if it was Joseph L. Mankiewicz. And what a memorable, sly line written by this witty screenwriter/director to his actress.

Still, looking at the picture, and Marty's reaction, I realized that's all I was to Joe. I was the "actress." I had lost the ability to communicate one-on-one with directors as I had when I was working for Peggy Siegal. I was conflicted that I would be on only one side of the camera now. Luckily for me, one director changed that. He was the director of *To Die For*: Gus Van Sant.

In the 1990s, Gus Van Sant was the one director with whom I dreamed of working. I loved watching his films, but I could not put into words why they touched me so much. There was an emotional sensibility to which I related but could not place. The movies played like dreams, with haunting images and gritty performances. I remember seeing *Drugstore Cowboy* and thinking,

What the hell was that? It was an assault to the senses. It was like listening to Pink Floyd in a darkened bedroom. He had the audacity to take a matinee idol, Matt Dillon, and make him a drug addict, and the artistic vision to film an ending with him where death seemed almost welcoming and romantic, like Juliet's swallowing poison.

Then came *My Own Private Idaho*. It was not so much a film as an experience. I could feel the cold and desperation of these two hustlers. This was a movie that took you somewhere. I could actually smell this film. The embers in a fire, the dirty leather coats that smelled of smoke, the old houses and the open fields. Again, I'm going to say images. Images set to music. Houses falling from the sky. The safety of the home smashing to bits on the ground.

Van Sant's *Even Cowgirls Get the Blues* may not have been well received critically, but the images and color of that film, and the boldness and daring of the filmmaker, stayed with me. This was a director who was part Nick Ray, part Warhol, part Bergman. Gus Van Sant? Was he even American? I wondered. When I met Gus at my audition for *To Die For*, he was quiet and completely different from what I had expected. Soft-spoken and unassuming. He was from Connecticut, for God's sake. Grew up in a town very near me. He would go on to be nominated twice for an Academy Award, for having directed the quietly brilliant *Good Will Hunting* and the historically powerful *Milk*. His directing style *appears* to be simple, and that may be part of his genius, because the emotional depth of his characters is boundless.

But this was 1994. He was directing *To Die For*, based on the novel of the same name by Joyce Maynard. I had dreamed of working with him, and now it was happening. I was playing the part of Janice, a professional ice skater and the sister of Larry, played by Matt Dillon.

We were in Toronto shooting the ending of the movie, in which I skate over Suzanne's body. I had grown up ice-skating, but for the movie I had trained for six weeks to be able to perform like a professional ice-skater. Back in New York City, Gus had sat in the living room of my apartment while he and the costumer Beatrix Aruna Pasztor and producer Laura Ziskin chose outfits for me to wear in the movie. For the final scene I would be head to toe in a tight, form-fitting black-and-gold ice-skating outfit. It was stunning and very close to what I had seen the real ice-skaters wear when I was training. The day before the shoot, Gus decided to change my beautiful outfit to this absolutely nutty pink fuzzy sweater, with a scarf and poodle skirt. I looked like a little girl in the 1950s—not the beautiful and evil black widow. I was trying it on for him in my trailer, and I was looking at him as if to say, Gus, this is nuts, I look like cotton candy. At least can we lose the pom-pom on my woolen hat? Gus was his usual sort of quiet and understated smiling self. He said, "Oh, really; I kind of like it." That's all he said. And Gus was very collaborative. I could have probably got away with wearing my black outfit, but I trusted Gus, and I wanted to be a vision of what he wanted me to look like, even if I didn't understand it. After all, he was the director.

It was snowing when we shot the scene. I passed by David Cronenberg, who had just finished shooting his scene as the hit man the Marettos hire to kill Suzanne. Buck Henry, the screenwriter, stood to the side and took pictures. I was in this crazy outfit. The wind was whipping across Lake Simcoe and it was hard to just stay upright on my skates. The camera was attached to a

LUNA crane, and as it rose above me, it was shaking so much that I thought it was going to come crashing down. Again and again we shot it, with Gus standing behind me on the ice in his parka. I was a skater in the zone, if not in a trance, as I glided out to my position trying not to blow away. Then the sun came out, and we finally got the shot. Of course when I saw it in the movie, it all made sense. I was in one of Gus's visions, surrounded by crystals of ice; I was frosty white and pink. The goddess of death. Smiling innocently. Just stunning. It is one of my favorite images of any film I've ever been in. Quietly powerful, like much of Gus's work.

That night I was at the bar with Gus and Buck Henry. Buck was telling stories about *Catch-22* and *The Graduate*. I made fun of Gus because he drank whiskey sours—straight up. It reminded me of Connecticut. How could someone as hip as Gus drink whiskey sours? I thought, Why would I be anywhere else but here? Making a movie during the day, hanging out hearing stories at night. I was always seeking out Buck Henry for stories. One day I saw him at lunch, and I had my tray about to sit down, and he said, "Illeana, you can sit here, but you can't ask me any more questions about my movies."

I had never really socialized with a director on set besides Marty, and Gus blurred those lines by hanging out with the actors, letting them see dailies—which was verboten with many directors. All that artistic stimulation I had missed from being just "the actress" came flooding in. Gus created an environment of collaboration, and he was never threatened by opinions. I remember shooting one of my first scenes with Nicole Kidman. Let's stop for a minute and remember how friggin' great she is in *To Die For*, shall we? She had a black hat and veil on. She asked me rather directly, "What about you, Illeana. What do you think?" I saw the costumer, Beatrix, nervously looking over her shoulder, but I did not want to lie, so I said, "I think it looks like you just killed your husband. It's too much."

She said, "That's what I thought" and took it off, adding, "Thank you" as she smiled at me.

That camaraderie of looking out for each other was a reflection of the environment Gus created. At times, *To Die For* felt like a home movie. One day I was kidding around with Matt, and he accidentally broke my thumb. Gus, rather than hiding it, wanted to incorporate it into the movie. "We have to take advantage of it," he said excitedly. "It's real. She's a skater, and she fell and broke her thumb." It worked for the documentary feel of the film. When you look at a movie like *To Die For*, you can tell how Gus was breaking the rules as a director, because it's really an independent film mixed with a studio film. Juxtaposing the documentary style improv within a Buck Henry script. Brilliantly casting people such as Joaquin Phoenix, Casey Affleck, myself, opposite the china doll beauty of Nicole Kidman. I always thought *To Die For* was wrongly identified as a black comedy. To me, it was more of a film with a social commentary. Part Mankiewicz in its storytelling (for example, the flashback technique used in *A Letter to Three Wives*), part Wilder in its cynicism (like his very dark film about fame, *Ace in the Hole*). A fascinating look at American values told through the eyes of its victims and its victorious murderess, Suzanne Stone. True, the film's "You aren't anybody unless you're on television" no longer plays as satire. In that way, *To Die For* predicted the future and the culture of celebrity.

I always kept mixtapes that I would listen to in my trailer to get me in the mood for various scenes. Gus would come in sometimes just to hear what I was playing, which for that film was usually a '60s mix of the Beatles, Neil Young, and Donovan. That sort of thing. Gus was in my trailer when he heard Donovan's "Season of the Witch." I was thrilled when it turned up in the movie's last scene as the background music while I'm skating.

Another time we were shooting Matt Dillon's funeral scene and Gus came to my trailer and said, "Do you have any sad music?" In the scene, Nicole plays a song for everyone at the graveyard. Well, the song I picked out was "Imagine" by John Lennon. We did the scene, and it evoked strong emotions. Gus said it worked so well that they would have to get the rights to use it. It turns out that "Imagine" cost too much, and that's a shame, because boy, did that song work for that scene. In the end, they used Eric Carmen's "All by Myself," which, if you notice, is slightly incongruous with everyone's performance, but I was thrilled to be able to contribute some musical ambience, like an emotional DJ.

I learned so many things from Gus Van Sant as a director, but one of the most important was trust. And lenses. We were shooting one of the scenes in the ice rink. Gus was playing the off-camera interviewer of the fictional documentary about the murder. It was the first time I'd done a movie in which I was essentially acting along with the actual director. In the scene Gus is the insensitive nosy reporter asking questions about the death of my brother, but he was also directing me.

Normally you tell a director what you are going to do, but because he was the antagonist in the scene, interviewing me, I stayed in character never letting him know how I would answer the questions. He also threw a lot of questions at me that were not in the script, and I was answering them in character as Janice, *not* Illeana. What I thought might be an emotional moment was coming up in which I say, "And that's the last time I saw my brother." I had noticed that whenever reporters were interviewing victims of crimes the cameraman seemed to sense when the person was about to become emotional—and zoom in for a close-up. The victims would be asked about their childhood, and they would be laughing, in the middle of this happy memory, and all of a sudden they would form a mental picture of the person, and be overcome with grief, realizing that the person was dead and never coming back. And then they would apologize for crying. Why do people apologize for crying? I wanted to do something like that, but I didn't want to tell Gus I was doing it. I wanted him to be caught off guard and see how he'd handle it.

We are doing the scene; Gus said, "Tell me about your brother." I started to share these wonderful stories using an emotional preparation of my own to form my own mental picture, and I started crying and said, "I'm sorry; can we stop?" Just as I had suspected, the astute director of photography, Eric Alan Edwards, and Gus did not stop—they even zoomed in on my crying face and just let the camera go, waiting patiently for me to continue. And I was truly emotional. It happened very organically. Finally I said, "That's the last time I saw my brother."

Gus had not expected me to start crying, but he had reacted like a documentary director photographing his subject, catching me in this seemingly private moment of grief. A sense of relief washed over me, because I knew I had nailed it. There was some discussion with the director of photography and then Gus pulled me over to the side. He was, again, his quiet and understated polite self. He said, "Man that was . . . that was really good." He was smiling, and I was happy.

"But we had the wrong lens on. Do you think you could do that again?"

Wrong lens? What did that mean? It was the first time I had ever heard that from a director. I remember my takes on *Alive* were ruined because they were out of focus. Now it's the wrong lens? To this day, whenever I'm doing an emotional scene I ask two questions: "What lens is that?" and "Are we in focus?" Then it's "OK, good to go."

My heart sank. We were standing on the ice rink and I kicked my skate into the ice. I said, "No, I can't do that one again. That was perfect, but let me see what I *can* do."

I told Gus, "I need to emotionally prepare again. It will have to be something different. I'm going to listen to some music. Can I have a minute?" It was one of those moments on set in which you're trying to pull a rabbit out of a hat and the producers start pointing to watches and talking about overtime, and the director has to make a decision if it's worth it.

Gus said, "Take all the time you need."

Emotional preparation is not my strong suit, but I grabbed my Walkman and found one of my mix tapes with the theme song to the movie *Alive*. I hoped this soundtrack, which evoked so many nostalgic memories for me, would conjure the emotions I needed to re-create what had happened so organically.

I skated, and I listened. I was circling the rink and could see that Gus was as calm as could be. The producers had their heads in their hands. I must have skated that rink for ten minutes until I had it. I nodded to Gus, and we filmed it, and that's what's in the movie. It wasn't inspired, only the first take had that, but the second take was as close as possible to the original version.

What's important is that this was my first technical collaboration with a film director. Before that, I just showed up and was emotional; I didn't worry about technical things. Gus taught me about how having the right lens was important. How you could calibrate your performance to the size of the lenses, meaning how big your face was going to be on-screen and how much emotion you would see. It's pointless to cry in a wide shot, for instance. You'll never see it. Another thing he did that was very helpful was to explain what the shot was going to be "by the numbers"—the numbers that sync up to where the camera moves—and how the positioning of the camera could help me with my performance.

I was acting for the camera, and the camera became my friend. Gus picked up on my interest and began to explain the shots to me, and the decisions that were behind them. One day when we were shooting a scene and he wasn't sure where to put the camera, he said, "Illeana, if you were shooting this what would you do?" I loved his use of overhead shots, which he used a lot in *Drugstore Cowboy*. That final overhead of Matt Dillon, as I said, is a killer. I said, "Gus, I think we should go with an overhead," and he laughed, but that's what we did. It was the first time a director took my suggestion, and it made me more invested in the scene.

I had another scene that was very technically complicated with lots of camera tracking, extras passing me, etc. It ends with a close-up of my taking a phone call in which I learn that my brother is dead. I have to go from laughing to crying in an instant, with the camera landing inches from my face. I knew there was only one way I could get to the scene emotionally. I asked Gus if *he* could be off camera and tell me something very specific about my own brother, and then hand me the phone. My reaction, which is in the movie, came from Gus's telling me that. It was this combination of acting with and for the director that I think made my character, Janice, so memorable. You think of a documentary like *Grey Gardens* and part of what makes it work is the off-camera relationship Edie Bouvier is having with the Maysles brothers, Albert and David, who are filming her. Some days I felt that I was in a documentary about the death of my brother with Gus as my interviewer/director; other days I was in a movie playing scenes with my brother, Matt Dillon, or with Nicole Kidman as his killer. But to the audience I was the character they related to—because I was always outside commenting to them on how I really felt about everyone they were watching. *To Die For* crystallized an on-screen performance with which I would forever become identified. I was someone who, like Mike Nichols had said to me when I had asked for his autograph, was both *inside* and *outside* the movie at the same time.

When the film was over, I gave Gus an antique toy gun. Through Marty, I'd got to know Sam Fuller. He directed such classics as *Steel Helmet* and *Pickup on South Street*, plus my beloved *The Big Red One*. On set, Sam had always fired a gun for action and for cut. The toy gun I gave Gus was a symbol of what one great director did—my gift to another great director. Gus's gift to me was a picture he painted of three houses falling from the sky. On the back he wrote, "Be your own flying saucer. Rescue yourself." It became my motto, especially as I began my own writing and directing career working with the most difficult actress I have ever come across: me.

CHAPTER TWELVE

A Woman's Picture

Grace of My Heart premieres at the Venice Film Festival. Allison Anders and I are laughing because our luggage, along with the gorgeous gowns we were planning to wear, did not make it in on time for our opening.

The collaborative experience of working with Gus Van Sant was exhilarating. It inspired me to want to make more movies with the winning combination of *To Die For*: great scripts with ensemble casts that blended an indie spirit with the sheen of studio filmmaking. With Marty's encouragement I began bringing him story ideas, plays, writers, and directors, developing scripts with him to executive-produce through his company, Cappa.

Get out your handkerchiefs. This is going to be weepy. This is a story about a woman named Edna Buxton who wants to be a singer-songwriter but finds that being a wife, mother, lover to the men in her life keeps getting in the way of that dream. Her manager, Joel Millner, creates Denise Waverly out of Edna, and she becomes successful. But it's not enough to be the heart behind the hits.

Edna wants to hear her own voice singing her own music and her own words. She holds fast to that dream and finally finds her voice and makes a hit record. Denise Waverly didn't know that she had to understand loss, pain, and suffering and have this wealth of experience before she could embark on her own journey as an artist. At the end of the story, she learns that a woman's journey is eternal. There are no road maps. Denise's story—it was called *Grace of My Heart*—was pretty close to mine. Mine began with its writer and director, who will always be the grace of *my* heart, Allison Anders. And so *Grace of My Heart* began, and in some ways, it has never ended. Long after the filming of the movie, I have remained close with Allison, as in a really, really long female road movie.

The road movie of *Grace* began, of course, with traveling. I'd been invited to The Sundance Film Festival as a writer/director to screen my short film *The Perfect Woman*, which I had made right after *Alive*. The plot of *The Perfect Woman* centers on thirty different women—from Martha Plimpton to Brooke Smith to Jane Adams to me, all saying what they imagine the "perfect" thing is a man would want to hear. It played in many festivals, but for me the most significant was Sundance, because that's where I first saw Allison Anders's *Gas Food Lodging*.

The greatest power of any film is to make you walk out of it and think, "I don't know who the director is, but somehow she knows me." Well, I walked out of *Gas Food Lodging* thinking I don't know who Allison Anders is, but somehow I have to convince this lady to make a movie with me. *Gas Food Lodging* seemed like an updated take on the melodrama. Her damaged but strong heroines were a force to be reckoned with. Funny, fearless, and sexy.

Marty had given me some interesting advice after *Cape Fear*. Or he cursed me, I don't know which, because his advice turned out to be accurate. He said, "I think the problem you are going to have in your career is that you are always going to be more interesting than your material. So you're going to have to seek out directors who understand how to use you, and to write the part around you, rather than your playing the part. If you find that director," he said, "I will help you get that movie made." Now, at the time, Marty was not really known as a "woman's director" producing "sensitive women's pictures." That was about to change.

After Sundance, I said, "I think I found the director. *Her* name is Allison Anders."

I first met Allison at the kind of place you'd actually see someone stop in a road-trip movie: a groovy diner in Santa Monica called Cafe 50's. I'm sure I was wearing a '60s A-line type dress, because it was a phase I was in that hasn't ended, and I'm sure Allison was wearing a Mexican embroidered dress, since that's all she ever wears. If I called Allison right now, she would be wearing a Mexican embroidered dress. The minute I saw Allison (well after she finished hugging me, because she's a hugger; thank God I had so much hugging experience from *Alive*) I realized that everything about her, from her flaming red hair to her tattoos to her patchouli oil, was cool. She is one cool chick, but she also radiates a warmth that I instantly connected to. Usually when you're an actress sitting down with a director, you're putting on an act of some kind, showing off about how many movies you've done or how confident and poised you are. But Allison was so honest and vulnerable about her life that you couldn't help meeting her halfway. We swapped stories about our relationships, love, marriage, breakups, living in California vs. living in New York. Just as I had hoped, she turned out to be a movie and music buff. It seemed like there wasn't a book, a movie, or a record—down to an obscure 45 of Mary Hopkin's "Goodbye"—that we didn't both love.

It was like going back in time and meeting the best friend I never had in high school: You like Sylvia Plath? I *love* Sylvia Plath. Oh, my God, I was just *talking* about Patty Duke in *Me, Natalie*! Yes! Paul is my favorite Beatle, too!

Every good road trip movie involves fate. You meet the right person at the right time and say the right thing. Allison was asking about how I had met Marty, and I told her we had met at the Brill Building. The Brill Building had played a significant role in our relationship. I knew all about the Brill Building. I knew the gleaming marble and brass lobby where I went to work every day for my former boss Peggy Siegal. I knew its musical history as the original Tin Pan Alley and later as the vortex of rock and roll from 1958 to 1964, turning out the greatest songs of our time. I knew that Sidney Poitier had supposedly slept on the roof when he was a young and homeless actor.

It turned out that the Brill Building was another point of interest that Allison and I shared. She was an expert on everyone who had ever walked its halls and cut records there. Carole King and Gerry Goffin, Barry Mann and Ellie Greenwich, Leiber and

Stoller. Speaking of the halls, fun fact: Every floor of the Brill Building makes a continuous square loop, and the floors are linoleum so you could easily roll pianos around. Fun fact: I learned how to roller-skate there. Marty and Thelma Schoonmaker were editing *Goodfellas* on the third floor and I would roll past them, cruising the wonderful linoleum halls.

Allison and I hugged goodbye, and after this incredibly fun first meeting . . . we decided to make a movie about Anne Sexton, an alcoholic poet who killed herself! Ultimately, there were a lot of rights issues with the Anne Sexton estate, and we were getting very frustrated that it wasn't moving forward, so we started talking more and more about doing another movie. Maybe something that would be a little more up. Everything was leading us mysteriously back to the Brill Building. Allison sent me a bunch of TV programs, music documentaries, and videos about the California music scene, including *Shindig!, Hullabaloo, T.A.M.I. Show,* and a documentary about the Brill Building called *Girl Groups: The Story of a Sound,* which explored some of the darker aspects of that history. I started reading an interesting book by Ronnie Spector and Vince Waldron called *Be My Baby,* about her life with Phil Spector. We were immersed in girl-group history and the sacrifices so many girl singers and songwriters had made on their way to "making it."

Allison and I both felt like female artists who didn't quite fit in a mold. Maybe this movie would be about everything that was happening in our lives as women—both professionally and emotionally—but with the Brill Building as a backdrop. We had three important things in common: We loved music, we loved melodramas, and we loved movies from the '70s. I said to Allison, "I want to make a movie that looks like it was made in the

'70s. Like Paul Mazursky made it." I was so influenced by women's performances from the '70s; I grew up watching them on-screen, thinking, That's what acting is. Jill Clayburgh throwing up in *An Unmarried Woman*, when she finds out her husband is leaving her. Gena Rowlands having a nervous breakdown in *A Woman Under the Influence*, Ellen Burstyn crying and singing in *Alice Doesn't Live Here Anymore*, Jane Fonda having her first orgasm in *Coming Home*. And I don't want to leave out the great Madeline Kahn and Teri Garr, who both managed brilliantly to combine comedy with pathos. These performances were imprinted on my brain. They took chances, and that's something I wanted to do. When I first saw Allison's work, I knew that those were the kind of movies she was making from a strong female perspective. She followed up *Gas Food Lodging* with the equally spirited *Mi Vida Loca*, about girl gangs in the Echo Park section of Los Angeles.

Still, it would have to have some style, some romance, maybe a man or two to cry over. In the mid-'90s melodramas were thought to be old-fashioned and out of date. Douglas Sirk films such as *Imitation of Life* and *All That Heaven Allows* weren't as highly regarded as they are now. They were thought to be high camp, steeped in sex, shot in lurid color—larger-than-life situations. Allison and I loved melodramas because the stories, even though they were big, were told without cynicism. The plots were motivated purely by emotions—love, sex, greed, jealousy, revenge, etc. In our research for *Grace*, Allison turned me on to Bette Davis in *A Stolen Life* and now my favorite Douglas Sirk film, *There's Always Tomorrow*. I turned her on to *Leave Her to Heaven* and Nick Ray's *Bigger Than Life*. I don't think I ever got her onboard for *Autumn Leaves*. Joan Crawford was too camp even for Allison. In the much-loved gay-themed film I did called *Grief*, there's a line written especially about me by director Richard Glatzer: "Maybe you are a gay man trapped in a woman's body?" Marty used to joke, "If you're a gay man, what does that make me?"

The road trip continued. Allison went home to California to start writing the script, and I went back to New York to co-produce, along with my partner Ruth Charney, and shoot *Search and Destroy*. Then I went to Canada to shoot *To Die For*. We had a delay on set, so I sat down in my trailer and read the entire script while listening to Neil Young. I put the script down, and I wrote in my journal: "I just read Allison's script and it made me cry. I think it could be really great." Then I wrote, "Maybe Matt will walk through the door, and ask me about it so I can say, Oh, this? Why it's a movie I'm working on with Allison Anders. Maybe you could play a part in it."

When I first mentioned Matt Dillon to Allison, I'm not sure if he was who she had in mind to play the Brian Wilson–type character, Jay Phillips. Matt's the epitome of East Coast Cool, but I thought of him immediately when I read it. Aside from being an amazing actor who is totally dedicated to his craft, Matt is quite the music expert. He and I had developed a great rapport and chemistry on *To Die For* that I thought would translate on-screen to his playing my husband and musical mentor. Jay Phillips also had to deal with the phenomenon of his success and the burden that it placed on his music, putting him in a box. I wondered if Matt could explore those same feelings on-screen. Personally, I couldn't remember a time in my viewing life when I *wasn't* seeing Matt Dillon in a movie. Overnight, he became a part of the lexicon of American girl-crush movies with *My Bodyguard* and *Little Darlings*. And he followed those up with *The Outsiders*, *Rumble Fish*, and *The Flamingo Kid*, which cemented his persona. Let's be clear, Matt is a movie star. That charisma is there off-screen, too. Of all the folks I've worked with, I would say that only Matt Dillon is a movie star both on-screen and off. When you walk next to him, everything moves in slow motion as people turn to stare. The public reactions he got from men and women never ceased to amaze me, yet he always handled himself with absolute composure and aplomb.

I have to mention my favorite interaction Matt had with a fan because it illustrates not only the kind of person he is but also the impact of movie stars, and how we believe they are our saviors. We were out in a bar during the shooting of *To Die For*, and a guy came up to Matt and asked him for his autograph. Matt was totally obliging and just about to sign his name when the guy said, "Can you just write, 'To Debbie—I'm really sorry for everything—don't give up on him—Much Love, Matt Dillon.'"

And I watched as Matt wrote it out exactly as the guy dictated, didn't even look up, and handed it back to the guy, who smiled at him gratefully, "Hey, thanks a lot, Matt."

And Matt said, "Hey, good luck, man." And he meant it: Go in peace, my son. Make that relationship work. That's what the movies do for you. They give you hope. God bless Matt Dillon. That's what I say. Now go watch *Crash*, *Wild Things*, or any movie he's been in.

I got Matt interested in *Grace of My Heart* pretty much the way I fantasized I would except that we had clothes on. That was a joke! I always say: I played Matt's sister, and I played his wife, and let me tell you, playing his wife was a lot more fun. When we eventually shot the scene in *Grace* in which Matt asks me—while we are recording "God Give Me Strength"—if I want to go home with him, I'm supposed to think about it and finally say,

"Yes." But it was hard not to laugh, because I could feel Allison next to the camera almost yelling, "Yes! Yes! Go home with him! What are you, nuts?" We were girls, after all, and only human. Sigh.

I wanted Matt to read the script, because I knew he would be so great as this character, but I didn't want to put a burden on our friendship, so I came up with a plan. The cover of the script had a very enticing image of a sexy girl group called the Shangri-Las—remembered best for the song "Leader of the Pack." I knew the image would catch Matt's eye, so I deliberately put the script on the bedside table in my hotel room, hoping he would notice it. Actors are nosy, and they can smell scripts, and sure enough, he spotted it, picked it up, and started to flip through it.

"What's this?" he said.

And I brushed it off, "Oh, it's a musical about the Brill Building. Nothing you'd be interested in."

Matt's eyes lit up. He loved music almost more than we did. He mentioned the music film he did—Cameron Crowe's *Singles*—about the Seattle music scene, in which he played a grunge-rock musician.

"Yeah," I said with a sniff, "you're not right for the part at all. He's like a Brian Wilson, Beach Boys type. Great part, but you're *really* not right for it."

Matt rolled it up under his arm. "Do you mind if I read it?"

"OK," I said, "but I *really* don't think it's for you."

He called me the next day from his hotel room, asking me a lot of questions about the script, which is always a good sign. The entire casting of the film seemed to fall into place like that. We had Eric Stoltz playing my first husband and songwriting partner, Howard. Our relationship had some shades of Carole King and Gerry Goffin, who was also helping with music. We had John Turturro playing my manager. He bore some characteristics of Phil Spector. Allison said, "I'm not sure what would have happened if we didn't get John because I wrote the part entirely around him." Now we had Matt playing my second husband, Jay Phillips. We were soon joined by two fantastic actresses: Bridget Fonda, playing a Lesley Gore–type singer named Kelly Porter, and Patsy Kensit as another songwriter, Cheryl Steed, who was based loosely on Ellie Greenwich.

Grace of My Heart was the second movie I helped produce—*Search and Destroy* was the first—and it spoiled me forever. This was the height of the glory of independent filmmaking, when you could go to a studio (in our case, Universal) with a few key names attached—like John Turturro, who was coming off an amazing performance in *Quiz Show*—pitch the story to a studio executive (in our case, Casey Silver), and come out with a deal. We also had the strength of Marty as our executive producer behind us, vouching for us. It worked. We were thrilled to get the green light until we found out that Kevin Smith's movie *Mallrats*, which was green lighted at around the same time, got a bigger budget than we did. Thrilled for Kevin—he was a friend and a talented filmmaker—but not so much for Allison. Someone explained it to us this way: "*Grace of My Heart* is a woman's picture." Allison was a woman. I was a woman. The crew had a lot of women on it. The editor was a woman. The music supervisor was a woman. But what makes it "a woman's picture"? It's true that Allison always had candles burning on the set. You know you're working with a woman when you can smell the scent of Ylang Ylang candles while shooting a love scene. It's true we did girlie things. Like, if you so desired, you could list on the call sheet your love status: Married, Single, or Looking. Yes, we'd have tarot card readings and the Norse ritual of the casting of the rune stones to seek wisdom and understanding. And yes, Allison did give me a goddess amulet in the shape of a uterus on the first day of shooting. But does that make it "a woman's picture"?

It was *great* to able to embrace our feminine side. I was brought up around a lot of men and was always taught to keep anything "womanly" private, especially your period. One day Allison had menstrual cramps, and our male producer, Daniel Hassid, got her an ice pack to help her with her pain. I remember seeing Allison up on the dolly, behind the camera, holding this ice pack across herself, looking through the viewfinder. That image of Allison, who so embraced being a woman, gave me the courage to do the same. She set a tone that at times felt so casual you felt that you never had anything to be embarrassed about. I did my first nude scene—and my second and third—maybe my fourth all in one movie, thanks to Allison. Allison made me feel like I was a beautiful woman when I did those love scenes. When a man makes you feel beautiful, that's one thing. But when a woman makes you feel beautiful, she's talking about your insides, too.

As the character Denise Waverly grew as a woman, so did I. Allison made me feel it was OK to have an opinion about things. I was playing a woman going through every upheaval that happens in a woman's life. Love vs. career, sexism, marriage, divorce, contraception, abortion, adultery, babies, death, drugs, your mother! It was daunting.

Allison had the first on-screen depiction of a woman's water breaking; we had big discussions about that. I had never had a baby. I mean, did people want to see that? Did people want to see me get an abortion in the middle of a fun musical about the

Brill Building? What I admired so much about Allison was that we could fight passionately about something because we were always fighting to make it better, to make it more truthful. Every disagreement we had, and we didn't have a lot, was about the interpretation of the scene. What would this woman do? What had Allison done? What had I done? The parallels of my life and Allison's life all made it into the movie in one way or another, until I was playing one woman. I was my mother; I was Allison's mother; I was Allison; I was Illeana. And while all that was happening, the cameras just happened to be rolling. Sometimes it felt like I was filming my own life as it flashed before my eyes. When Mick Fleetwood had to drop out of the film, Bridget Fonda's father came in to replace him, and Peter Fonda—Captain America from *Easy Rider*—was cast as my hippie mentor, Guru Dave. I had blamed Dennis Hopper for making *Easy Rider* because it made my dad become a hippie and start a commune, and now I was a hippie shooting on a commune with Peter Fonda. When I looked at the rushes of my smoking a joint with Peter Fonda I thought, Yup. My movie life and my real life have come full circle.

Grace of My Heart became a musical melodrama with the personal tone of a '70s film. A love vs. career story in the vein of *A Star Is Born*. "Not the Barbra Streisand version!" I hear Allison saying. All right, I would be lying if I didn't say that *Grace of My Heart* was, yes, an excuse for me to re-create my favorite actresses' performances, outfits, and hairstyles all in one movie. If I did the director's commentary, you'd hear me say, "Oh, here's me doing Liza in *New York New York*; that's Judy; that's Ellen Burstyn in *Alice Doesn't Live Here Anymore*; Goldie Hawn from *Cactus Flower*; there's Audrey Hepburn's ponytail, trench coat, flats." I was shameless. And Allison knew it, so she would keep a strict eye on me if I veered toward camp. As in the time I tried to get away with Barbra's Afro-permed look from *A Star Is Born*. I walked onto the set to do this very serious scene, and Allison took one look at me and said, "No. Illeana. This is not a Barbra Streisand movie." I slunk back to the trailer.

In the middle of our nice melodrama, Allison went all female Cassavetes on me! Allison wanted to see me angry, and that was a pretty scary thing. I was taught to be a nice girl. Nice girls don't get angry. I remember getting reamed by Sanford Meisner at the Neighborhood Playhouse when I couldn't slap an actor across the face. He said, "You're either a lady or you're an actress. Which is it?" I sat down, humiliated. Of course I had anger in me, but it was not an emotion with which I was comfortable. On *Grace* we were going to be shooting a scene with John Turturro in which he is disgusted with me for giving up on my career and myself. I wanted to rehearse it, but Allison and John didn't want to talk about it; they just wanted to shoot it. John and I worked so well in the film together because Denise Waverly worshipped Joel Millner, and I worshipped John.

Our relationship in the film was also based on Denise's needing his approval, and I wanted John to approve of how I would act the scene, because Denise/I was going to have to get angry and Denise/I was terrified of getting angry with an actor whose approval Denise/I so desperately wanted.

I don't know if John knew I was just scared, but his refusal to rehearse, which felt like he was abandoning me, was the very trigger I needed to tap into the rage that Denise felt from Jay's death. I thought, You son of a bitch, here I am, I adore you, and you won't even help me work out this scene. Well John had absolutely no idea what I was going to do when he walked out there, but he certainly did once we began. I hit him as hard as I possibly could within the context of the scene. I let go of all the anger I had ever experienced, and let me tell you, he gave it back with everything he had. It was electric. It was what I had signed up for. I went from being a "lady" to an actress.

There was another fight on *Grace* that was just as inspiring, only Allison was at its center. We had a very tight, thirty-day shooting schedule, and things had been going very well, and we had been told by one of the producers that we were going to get an extra week of shooting time once we got to Malibu. We were so relieved, because this meant that we would have extra time to work on some of the more emotionally demanding scenes that were coming up with Matt Dillon, who had just arrived. We were in Malibu, and the feeling on the set was jubilant. We were really proud of the work we had been doing, and now we'd have two weeks to finish instead of one. Matt had arrived and was in the makeup trailer getting ready for his first day.

I needed to get approval for an outfit so I went to Allison's trailer and knocked. I heard someone say come in, so I stepped up, and there, sitting on the ground, was Allison, surrounded by all of the producers, and she was casting those Norse runes! The ancient stones that foretold the future. Yeah, when you go to the director's trailer and she's casting the runes with the producers to see how the day will turn out—maybe not a good sign. Apparently, Allison had just been told that we were not getting our extra week after all. The tension seemed pretty thick, so I said, "Why don't I come back later?"

I stepped out of the trailer and was about twenty feet toward the makeup trailer when the door opened and Allison's uterus-shaped goddess amulet went sailing through the air. The producers started filing out of her trailer and down the steps, and Allison hurled her runes at them as they walked out. Then she came down the steps with her purse and started to head for her car. The female producer tried to stop her, and Allison started hitting her with her purse, and then the female producer started hitting her back with *her* purse. And they're having a full-on girl fight! Meanwhile, I looked up and saw Matt Dillon—in his wig—watching the entire thing. He pulled me aside and said, "You want to tell me what's been going on here?" I laughed and said, "Well, Matt, these things are bound to happen on a sensitive woman's picture."

Everyone was OK, and pretty soon we were all hugging and forgiving again. Allison did sustain some serious damage to her goddess amulet, but that's the passion she had for the film. She was willing to fight for it. We got those extra workdays back, by the way. She got us those days back.

Some battles we lost. There were a couple of beautiful scenes with Eric Stoltz that were cut. One was a scene that showed the complexity of Denise's and Howard's personal and professional relationship as married singer-songwriters. To me, it reflected the challenges of a man loving a woman who was changing. Howard understood that for Denise to grow as an artist they would have to say goodbye. Yet the scene held out hope he would still be there and hinted at a happy ending for them. Allison even wrote a scene in which Howard comes back; he appears like a mirage, walking over a sand dune outside Denise's beach house. Marty thought that a happy ending was a cop-out and would be too sentimental. He felt that Denise must end up alone, having made it on her own. Art winning out over happiness I guess. Maybe I'm an optimist but I would like to think a woman can have both love and a career. Of course, it didn't work for Janet Gaynor or Judy Garland or Barbra Streisand in *A Star Is Born*, or Jill Clayburgh in *An Unmarried Woman*, either, so *Grace of My Heart* ends with Denise alone at her piano, with no man in sight.

It was bittersweet for me, because in many ways I thought Howard was the glue to Denise. He encouraged her metamorphosis and mine. Our scenes evoked the innocence of experiencing things together for the first time. Allison joked that the motto of the first week for me was either naked or crying. Is this Tuesday? I must be naked. Wednesday: crying. Thursday: naked again. I said to Eric, "I feel like I'm being initiated, being naked with Eric Stoltz." All our scenes had a quiet give and take; at times it felt so natural that I wasn't aware we were acting—or that we didn't have clothes on! Howard was my first on-screen love. I looked into his eyes and always felt safe. I did not want to say goodbye to Howard and the wonderful actor who played him, Eric Stoltz.

"Since I lost the power to pretend / That there could ever be a happy ending." So sings Elvis Costello in "God Give Me Strength," one of the wonderful songs from the memorable soundtrack of *Grace of My Heart*. I later asked Allison how she came up with the idea of bringing together Elvis Costello and Burt Bacharach for "God Give Me Strength," or Carol Bayer Sager and Dave Stewart, or bringing Joni Mitchell or Lesley Gore, into the mix. And she said, "I was in a hotel room, and I made a list of all the songwriters from the Brill Building and another list of all the current songwriters." Allison's innovation—much copied since—was to make music that sounded as if it had been written in the past. Her thought was "The era is over, but we're going to give you a little more." Since this was a movie about songwriters from the past, why not pair them up with songwriters of the present? She said, "When I told Karyn Rachtman, the music supervisor, this, she put her head in her hands and said, 'Allison, that's a great idea, and it's going to be very hard to do.'" Not with Allison. After all, she's a woman. She made it look easy.

And now a real road trip story. A few years after we finished the movie, I lost touch with Allison. She was in L.A., and I moved back to New York to do some theater. It was 2002, and I was on a road trip with some friends. We decided to stop in Elko, Nevada. There was a motel that had caught my eye called the Thunderbird. I loved the giant neon winged eagle outside and said, "Oh, we have to stay here."

We cleaned up and decided to grab a bite at a Mexican restaurant near the motel. We walk in, and I hear this scream. It's Allison Anders with her daughters and her mother. We couldn't believe it. We embraced, and I said, "What the hell are you doing in Elko, Nevada?" She said she was on a road trip from Kentucky to L.A., and it was the closest restaurant near the motel where they were staying.

I told her I was on a road trip, too. And I said, "Wait, are you at the Thunderbird?"

"Yes," she said. The enormous neon sign of the winged eagle had caught her eye.

We were staying at the exact same motel, and eating at the exact same restaurant at the exact same time, on completely separate journeys. We never lost touch again, and the journey that began with *Grace of My Heart* continues to this day. I'm not sure about the ending of this female-road-trip movie, but the middle has been fantastic.

They screened *Grace of My Heart* in 2011, many years after its initial release, at Cinefamily, in L.A.; it's a retro movie theater where both Allison and I have a residency programming films. I thought it was a lovely gesture but feared that probably three people would show up. I decided to ride my bike there, very low-key, but as I approached the theater, I saw this long line outside. And I was thinking, What are all these people doing here? It was completely sold-out. Allison and Eric Stoltz and I did a lengthy Q&A afterward. We talked for the first time about some of the deleted scenes and the hope that someday they would be restored. *Grace of My Heart* has endured in a way that even I can't explain. When people talk about it, they almost start to cry, as if it's personally about them. That makes me so proud, because that is what we set out to do. Make a personal film, with some music, some style, some romance, maybe a man or two to cry over, which seems like it was made in the '70s.

In short: a woman's picture.

CHAPTER THIRTEEN

You're a Tuning Fork

Marty surveys the damage in the aftermath of Storm Marlon: Two A.M. at the Beverly Wilshire Hotel.

I have met and worked with so many great actors. I'm always asked who my favorite is. It's not quite a fair question because I met the greatest actor of all time. The actor who towers above all other actors because all actors imitate him in one way or another. Marlon Brando. Really, in my opinion, he invented the modern technique of film and theater acting—sometimes called The Method—which has not changed to this day. But this isn't a story about acting. This is a story of perhaps my biggest show business regret: *not* having sex with Marlon Brando. Oh, and learning that I am a tuning fork.

A few months after *Grace of My Heart* came out, I was in Los Angeles shooting a wonderful little independent film called *Wedding Bell Blues,* directed by Dana Lustig and starring Julie Warner, Paulina Porizkova, and John Corbett. A little *Wedding Bell Blues* trivia: Look for the scene in which I am wearing a *Mean Streets* T-shirt, which was a little homage to Marty, who was my boyfriend at the time. Marty was coming to Los Angeles to receive the John Huston Award for Artists Rights, and I was wearing his T-shirt in a low-budget movie—but hey, that was our relationship. My hotel digs for *Wedding Bell Blues* matched our indie budget, so I was thrilled to move into Marty's more glamorous suite at the Beverly Wilshire for a few days.

Between changing hotels and working on the film, I was scattered. I grabbed my Cynthia Rowley dress out of my overnight bag and I had an egad moment. The dress was not suited for a black-tie event. It was microshort and sparkly. A sense of dread and insecurity washed over me. Why hadn't I brought something more appropriate? What would Marty think? I was getting ready in one of the gigantic marble bathrooms, and Marty poked his head in to check on me, looking impeccable, of course, in his Black Label Armani. I said, "Is this cheap-looking?"

"No," he said. "You look cute . . ."

I said, "I know I *look* cute. What about the dress?" He was standing there, and I could tell something was on his mind, because he didn't laugh, and Marty is the *best* laugher.

I asked again, "Are you sure this dress is all right?"

He said, "OK. I didn't want to tell you before I knew for certain, but Marlon Brando is coming over tomorrow to have lunch with me and talk about a project." Actress looks in camera: Is he kidding?

I knew from experience that Marty was *not* kidding. One time, back at the New York townhouse, Marty had yelled up, "Put some clothes on. Mick Jagger is here." I *thought* he was kidding, but as I tiptoed down the stairs in my nightgown, there, sitting in the living room dressed like a proper English gentleman, drinking tea, was Mick Jagger. "Allo," he said, in his distinctive East End London drawl.

The thought of meeting Marlon Brando was just too much for my brain to handle. "Marty, I can't."

As with everything else, Marty assured me that I *would* be meeting Marlon Brando and that it *would* be just fine. Yeah. That's what he said before my big driving scene in *Cape Fear*. I had never driven a car before, and on the first take I nearly ran over Nick Nolte and half of the crew.

"You'll be fine," he said. "There's a script he wants me to direct. Something with him and Madeline Kahn. I'm not right for it, but I said we could talk about it. Then we'll have lunch."

"Lunch?" I said. "He's Marlon Brando! No, I can't. It's too much."

Marty said, "You'll be fine. Be yourself. Just don't be a phony. He hates phonies . . . and *don't* talk about acting! He hates that."

Great, I thought. I'm having lunch with the world's greatest living actor. And I can't talk about acting?

I said, "Marty. I can't. I can't meet him. I just can't." And I meant it.

There are certain movie stars you just don't *want* to meet. You prefer that they remain cinematic and unreal. That's how I felt about Marlon Brando. He was, and still is, everything to me.

Besides, what on earth would I say to him that would not be fan-girl and insipid? How could I express to him that I had a poster of him on my bedroom wall from *The Wild One*? That I had pictures of him ripped from covers of old *Life* magazines that I had stolen from the basement of my local library? I had watched his films, studied his acting, sought out his television interviews, read numerous books about him. I had just finished a book he'd written about himself called *Brando: Songs My Mother Taught Me*. How do you have a normal conversation with Marlon Brando after you've seen *The Godfather* or *On the Waterfront* or *A Streetcar Named Desire* or *Apocalypse Now*, or even my childhood favorite, *A Countess from Hong Kong*?

. . . Excuse me Mr. Brando, could you please pass the bread, and by the way, everything I am, or want to be, or hope to be as an actor is because of you. No. Impossible. Couldn't be done. Wouldn't be done! I was literally shaking in the bathroom of the Beverly Wilshire Hotel.

Marty just laughed. He couldn't understand why I was so nervous. He repeated, "You'll be fine. Don't talk about acting." I rolled my eyes. Yeah, don't mention that I audited classes with Stella Adler in the '80s and that all she had done was talk about her most famous student—Marlon Brando.

It was time to go, and I grabbed my autograph book.

"Marty," I said as we were walking out the door. "Do you think Marlon Brando will sign my autograph book?"

Marty gave me one of his signature scolding looks. "Be good," he said.

"What?" I asked innocently.

I had started keeping journals and autograph books ever since the first one that Roddy McDowall had given me. He was right.

I had met a lot of interesting people. My journals were packed with entries, photos, and autographs from all sorts of folks I had met and worked with. Marty never made fun of me for carrying it everywhere. And sometimes he even helped me get autographs. In some ways he shared my level of excitement, but there was a limit.

We were riding in the back of a limousine, and now I was the one grinning like a Cheshire cat in anticipation when I got my second "Illeana, be good."

It was a term of endearment, but I knew what he meant. Both of us could easily slip from movie fan to movie fanatic. Marty had confessed that during fittings for *Alice Doesn't Live Here Anymore* he had "acquired" a piece of James Dean's *East of Eden* wardrobe from the Warner Bros. costume department. One time we were having dinner at Elia Kazan's, and I excused myself to use the powder room. They were busy eating so I knew I wouldn't be missed for a bit. Under the pretense of looking for the bathroom, I found myself instead upstairs looking for Mr. Kazan's office. I had to see where he wrote. I found it, and it was everything I dreamed, and I confess, since I always had a camera on me—that was Uncle Roddy's fault, too—I snapped some photos of it. I got back to the table, and Marty knew I had been up to something.

He said under his breath, "Be good."

"What?" I asked innocently.

When I was showing him the photos, I said, "I had to do it, Marty. It's history. It has to be preserved." He shook his head at me and then of course asked for several copies of all the pictures!

We were at the event where Marty was being honored—as a humanitarian—and I'm running around collecting autographs from George Lucas to Sharon Stone in my sparkly micromini.

The stunning and statuesque Sharon Stone says as she's signing my book, "Don't you look like a little starlet . . . " Which of course she meant *so* sweetly but made me feel with complete and utter certainty that I probably looked like a floozy at a dance hall. I suddenly felt ridiculous, walking around collecting autographs from famous people—people I knew—so I went back to the table and deposited my book there.

Marty, far from being embarrassed, asked, "Who did you get?"

"Oh, you know, some people," I said sort of shyly.

Then he collected his award as a humanitarian!

When the evening was over, they were rushing to get us out of there, and I realized in a panic that I had left the book behind at our table. When I went back to retrieve it, it was gone. Inside were all my memories. All my wonderful pictures and poems, entries from Sean Penn and Robert Mitchum, Gregory Peck, Steve Allen and Jayne Meadows, Gore Vidal, and Brian De Palma, from the Toronto film festival. An inscription from one of my heroes, Alain Resnais, whom I met at the Deauville film festival—never to be seen or read again. It was childish, but at the time, my whole identity as an actress was wrapped up in those words and pictures. I had worked with some of these folks, become friends with others. It was proof that I had made it in the movies. Now it was gone, and I was inconsolable.

That was the emotional baggage I was carrying when I met Marlon Brando the next day. I put on a lumpy brown sweater over a thrift-store plaid schoolgirl skirt and thick woolen tights and Doc Martens. It was too late to change. Even though he was always supportive, Marty took one look at me and said, "Is that what you're going to wear to meet Marlon Brando?" There was a knock at the door, and Marty and I exchanged nervous glances.

He repeated his mantra: "You'll be fine. Be yourself."

I nodded. Right now "myself" was busy feeling sorry for myself, so I knew that I couldn't *be* myself; I would have to "act" something. I had once heard Orson Welles say that we no longer place a value on listening. So I thought, That's what I'll act. That's the part I'll play. I will listen with great intensity. I will be Marty's wonderfully listening girlfriend. I will be still and quiet and respectful . . .

Oh, my God! The door is opening! Why am I wearing this ugly brown sweater? There he was, Marlon Brando, and everything I was going to act went completely out the window. First of all, his presence, both physical and spiritual, was enormous. His eyes were a deep sapphire blue—a color I had never seen before—which was arresting enough, but astonishingly, they matched exactly the color of the blue velour sweat suit he was wearing!

I thought, Marlon Brando is wearing a blue velour sweat suit. Who made that for him? Who owns that much velour? Does Marlon Brando know he's going to have to go through the door sideways?

He said very quietly to Marty, "How do I look?"

Marty said, "You look fantastic, Marlon!" He was always a better actor than I.

"Thanks," he said, "I've lost thirty pounds."

Jesus, I thought. From what? Three hundred? I am not going to make it!

"I'm a little embarrassed by my weight," he said. "Do you mind if we order lunch up here? Away from prying eyes? Would that be all right?"

Marty had a suit and tie on—of course, he wore a suit and tie to the beach, but still.

We had clearly been ready to walk out the door, but without missing a beat, Marty immediately agreed that yes, of course, we would order up room service and have lunch in the room; that would be much better, much more intimate.

Marty gave me a slightly panicked look, and I knew to discreetly call down to cancel our reservation. I left the room, and when I returned, Marlon Brando had made himself comfortable on the couch. What I mean by that was that he had taken *all* of the cushions *off* the couch and tossed them onto the floor. Then he had taken one of the square seat cushions and propped it sideways so that it was like a pillow and was lying against it. There was nowhere to sit. He was basically sitting on the *entire* couch. With Brando already seated I had a problem. I could not look at him, and Marty was eyeballing me like, Sit down already.

Opposite the couch were two French provincial chairs. I took the one farther to the left of him, so I wouldn't have to make eye contact, because I was pretty sure that if I did I would burst out laughing or crying, or ask him about acting, or be a phony, or any of the other things that Marty had warned me not to do! I wanted to position myself slightly away from them so I could do my listening thoughtfully act but not intrude upon the conversation. I instantly became a distraction. They were discussing the project, which was a biopic of John Mitchell, the attorney general for Richard Nixon during the Watergate scandal, and his wife, Martha. Marty tried to bring me into the conversation, because my grandmother was the congresswoman Helen Gahagan Douglas, who had run against and lost to Richard Nixon for a seat in the U.S. Senate, and Marty thought that Brando, a longtime liberal, would be interested in that. Marty signaled for me to join in the conversation, and I tried to say something interesting, but it just sailed off into the air, and I thought, yeah. Go back to fake-listening, Illeana. They started talking again, and I felt really stupid and out of my depth. I was thinking, Why did you make me talk, Marty? I can't say words when I'm nervous. You know that! Why am I even here? Marlon Brando doesn't want me here. I should try to excuse myself and go into the other room and leave them alone so they can talk about their project.

That's when I heard Marlon Brando say to Marty, "So this is your lady friend?" and I could feel the gaze of Marlon Brando upon me. Time stopped. People say that's a cliché—until it happens to you. Marlon Brando stopped time, that's how good an actor he was. I could feel the gaze of Marlon Brando boring into my psyche. The gaze of the world's greatest actor—known for his keen observation of human beings—was turned on me.

"Stop everything," he said. "Look at your feet."

Everything stopped while we all looked at my feet—which were inverted toward each other and pigeon-toed.

"That's a sign of insecurity," he said. "Why should you be insecure?"

Was this one of those tests that Marty had talked about? Was Marlon Brando testing me to see if I was a phony? Well, I'm no phony, I thought.

Suddenly a wave of emotion went through me, to him, and back to me, and my eyes filled with tears, and things got very real, very quickly. I was trying to hold back tears and wasn't succeeding.

"My dear girl," he said. "What is it?"

There was a rumbling inside my core. And suddenly this voice inside me just started talking and I couldn't stop it. I said, "I am so sorry, but this is really emotional for me—I mean you're Marlon Brando, and everything I do, or want to do, or be, is because of you, and I am insecure."

And Marty started to laugh really nervously and explain, "She's very emotional, Marlon," and he kind of put his arm around me, as if to suggest, you know, "be good," pull yourself together, kid, but it was too late. All of my insecurity, all of my fears of not being good enough rose to the surface. I decided in an instant not to deny it, but just to live—as my acting teacher Sanford Meisner had taught me—truthfully in the moment under the given circumstances. So I looked at Marlon Brando, and I just started to cry.

Marlon Brando's eyes were now locked with mine in what felt like a mystical connection, and he said, "My God, you're a tuning fork. Now I'm crying!"

We were both crying. Marty ran to get a box of Kleenex, which he handed to Marlon Brando. Then Marlon Brando handed me tissues. Marty started to tell Marlon Brando about how I had lost my autograph book, and how upset Marty was because it was all his fault—that he had hustled me out of there, how they're always rushing him out of places, and that he was planning to surprise me by getting Marlon Brando's autograph for me, and now Marty is crying too!

All this truth rained down on us in a suite at the Beverly Wilshire Hotel. Eventually the tears turned to laughter. I mean the whole thing was absurdly embarrassing and wonderful. What can I say? You simply could not be inauthentic in front of Marlon Brando. He made me "be myself." Any notion that this was going to be a normal meeting was scattered like the Kleenex at our feet. At the feet of Marlon Brando. I was exhausted and starving.

We ordered lunch—Marty and I from the regular menu, Marlon Brando from the Henry VIII–portion size: three orders of shrimp cocktail, two plates of pasta, a couple of steaks, three bottles of wine, some salad. I am not kidding. They wheeled in two enormous tables of food. Is there a wedding? No, we're having lunch with Marlon Brando. Lunch! The thing I had feared was not only happening; it was an *actual* happening! There was plenty of wine, and the conversation never stopped. It floated between funny and profound. We talked about his island in Tahiti, and how he liked to collect rocks and shells there, and about his attempts to harness electricity by keeping electric eels in the swimming pool at his house on Mulholland Drive. We discussed the many abandoned movie projects—Brando and Michael Jackson with Jackson as God, and a project with the Native American activist Russell Means that Marty was to direct. We even talked about acting! Yes, we talked about acting, from studying with Stella Adler, to getting advice for *Julius Caesar* from John Gielgud, to his biggest disappointment, more than any other movie he had done: *The Island of Dr. Moreau*. The behind-the-scenes of that film could make a movie itself, and eventually one version was told in the documentary *Lost Soul: The Doomed Journey of Richard Stanley's Island of Dr. Moreau*.

As we kept talking, the day turned to night, and Marlon suggested we order dinner! We never left the room. We ordered from room service again, with a whole new round of food. This time, hamburgers, French fries, grilled-cheese sandwiches, chocolate cake, ice cream sundaes, more wine, of course.

Marlon wanted us to take our shoes off and move the cushions to the floor and have our dinner that way, so that's what we did. After dinner, the conversation continued, only now it started to become even more intimate. He asked me a lot of probing questions, all very personal, all very intriguing and insightful, of course. He directed a lot of questions to Marty about past girlfriends, our relationship, noting how strong it appeared to be. He was also brutally honest about his own personal life and his frailties. He talked about his weight, his relationships with women, and his deep distrust of men, starting with his own father. I never forgot that he was Marlon Brando, because that was impossible, but we got to a place of trust where I felt I could ask him something he wrote about in his book.

It was late at night, and by that time we had had many bottles of wine. I asked him, because I knew I had to, about his relationship with Marilyn Monroe, and he said, "They most certainly murdered her."

I said, "Do you really believe that?"

"Oh, yes," he said.

The way he said it gave me the chills.

It was past midnight, and we finally said good night to Marlon Brando. We closed the door and were so frightened we didn't even speak. We half-expected him to come back and ask us if he could spend the night and have breakfast with us. We waited a few minutes and opened the door to be sure he was gone. The hall was empty. Marty and I collapsed onto the sofa and just started laughing. We were exhilarated. We were exhausted. We had been in a Marlon Brando movie for twelve hours. And . . . we had pictures!

I want to state for the record that it was Martin Scorsese who said, "Let's take pictures of the room!" The suite post–Marlon Brando was a bacchanalian spectacle filled with plates of food, room service tables, strewn-about couch cushions, and empty bottles of wine. We took turns taking pictures of ourselves in the wake of Marlon Brando. It was like a crime scene. A fun crime scene.

The next day, Marty left for New York, and I was moving back into my modest hotel digs. Then something surprising happened. I got a call from Marty's assistant. She told me that Marlon Brando's secretary had called and wanted my address.

"That must be a mistake," I said. "They must mean Marty's address."

"No," she said. "She specifically said that Marlon Brando wants to send you something; she asked for your address and the correct spelling of your name."

I was in shock. What on earth was Marlon Brando going to send me? And why was Marty not a part of this?

I got back to my hotel, and the largest basket of roses I have ever seen *in my life* arrived. It was like a bushel! A bushel of roses! Even the florist was impressed as he helped me carry it inside. And there was a letter. A handwritten letter on light-blue stationery from Marlon Brando. I read the letter. I read it again. And again. And again. And again.

Now, I'm not going to say what was *in* the letter, because it's personal, but he wrote some very kind words.

Marty's assistant called, and now she was really curious. "His secretary called," she said, "and they want to know if you got the flowers. Jesus! Illeana! He sent you flowers."

"Yes," I said, "it's flowers . . . and a letter."

Dead silence on the phone. "What kind of flowers?"

"It's a huge basket of . . . roses," I said.

"Are they red?" she asked.

"Yes," I said, "and pink and lavender and yellow." Like I said, a bushel.

"Oh, my God!" she said. "Are you going to tell Marty?"

Marty . . . Now, Marty made movies about being the jealous type. Still, nothing had even happened—except that I had received 8 million roses and a very nice letter.

Then another call. Marty's assistant was freaking out as she conveyed another message.

"Mr. Brando would like to invite Illeana to lunch at his house on Mulholland Drive. He will send a car. Any day this week."

I said, "Absolutely, yes, please tell him yes. I accept."

Marty's assistant was aghast: "Illeana, you're not going to do it!"

I said, "It's Marlon Brando!"

She sputtered, "He probably wants to have sex with you!"

I said, "Yes, I will probably have to have sex with him. It's Marlon Brando!"

She then launched into the many reasons why this could not happen under any circumstances. I will spare you some of the reasons—especially those having to do with imagined sexual positions with a man of his girth and how that could either smother or suffocate me. But mainly it was that I had a boyfriend, that his name was Marty, and that if he ever found I was even *thinking* of going, he would cook my goose and personally serve it to Mr. Brando!

We stayed on the phone arguing the pros and cons, but eventually I was convinced that it would be a very bad idea. *She* called Marlon Brando's secretary and declined on my behalf. The little excitement was over.

I was alone in my hotel room with my roses and my letter, and I could actually feel Marlon Brando's disappointment with me when he got the news from his secretary. Hadn't I learned anything? I was a tuning fork! We were on the same frequency! He had just given me the greatest Method master class on being yourself, and now I was being the one thing Marty said he hated—a phony. A phony because I really wanted to go.

And who knows how differently my life would have turned out if I had gone. What great stories had I missed? What wisdom would he have imparted? How many great conversations or Marilyn Monroe conspiracy theories? At the very least I could have seen if he had actually had electric eels in his swimming pool. And who knows if he even *wanted* to have sex with me? What I regret is that I had declined out of fear. Fear of how it would look to Marty. I was Marty's girlfriend, and I had to "act" like it.

I loved Marty, of course, but my identity was becoming trapped under his, and part of me was becoming lost.

I couldn't accept that I had anything to offer anyone except through him, even when it was coming from Marlon Brando. Marlon saw something in me that day, something I couldn't see in myself. I *was* a tuning fork. He wanted more of the feeling that I had given him. Marlon Brando identified in me that I had the ability to affect people. It was real; it was vibrating; it was love. It was the beginning of my believing in myself.

CHAPTER FOURTEEN

The Roulette Wheel
of Insanity

Nastassja Kinski, Gina Philips, Jennifer Tilly, Vanessa
Redgrave, and me all calling our agents on the set of
Bella Mafia.

I do not experience happiness as much as relief when any
movie, or television show or Web series that I am involved
in turns out well, or even moderately well, for that matter. As
Robert Altman said when describing making a film, "A group of
people come together to build a sand castle." I wrote and directed a documentary for the IFC network about the trials and

tribulations of filmmaking called *Everybody Just Stay Calm*. One of my favorite quotes came from director Alexandre Rockwell, who described making movies as "stress . . . a little more stress . . . intense stress!" So if every moviemaking experience is so unpredictable, can you tell the difference between the movies that will be good and the movies that will be bad before they're finished? Can you know when you are shooting that a film will be a flop, a bomb, a cult classic, or a brilliant work of art? Sometimes the answer lies in a coffee shop.

I recently sat down with a first-time director—he had already given me the part—for a nice cup of coffee. We were going back and forth discussing the film we were about to start shooting in three weeks.

The meeting started out great.

He said, "I'm just so excited that you agreed to be in my movie. I wrote the part with you in mind. I'm just such a huge fan."

"Great," I said. "I like fans." And I was a fan of his. I loved the script, but I saw some holes in it, some unanswered questions. So as we sipped our coffee I started asking him questions—which is a habit I have—about what I thought were some missing beats in the script. The more I pressed, the more I discovered that he didn't *have* the answers to my questions. Pretty soon his coffee was starting to get cold, and he was becoming less and less a fan.

"Listen," I said. "You need to know the answers, because if you don't know, then I won't know how to play it, and if I don't know how to play it, you won't know how to shoot it, or light it, or stage it, and we could be heading for a nightmare instead of a comedy, which is what we are shooting in just three weeks." And he sipped his cold coffee and told me, with great confidence, "Illeana, we can fix all of that on the set."

And I knocked over his coffee. Not on purpose—I was making hand gestures, but I did get pretty excited. I said, "No. We need to fix this now. Because when we are on set it will be too late."

He ordered more coffee. I took out my pen and got ready to make notes and waited for him to do the same. Instead he sipped his fresh coffee and said, "I'll tell you what. Can I think about it, and get back to you?"

"Sure," I said, putting my pen away. "Absolutely. It's your movie. I am here to serve."

And I meant that sincerely. If someone doesn't want my help, I am not offended. I may have an opinion—a strong opinion—but I am not offended. You can only warn folks that hey, there's a pretty big iceberg up ahead, and if they don't want to listen, it's up to them, they are the captains of the ship. In my mind, the roulette wheel spun, landing on a problem: overconfidence of an inexperienced director.

To me, a movie is like a roulette wheel with a series of problems where the numbers should be. The wonderful mystery of a movie is that you can never predict those problems, so fixing as many things beforehand as possible, such as answering questions in the script, is a good idea. Because the day you shoot the scene that Illeana asked you about in the coffee shop is the day the movie roulette wheel spins and lands on another problem, such as rain. Rain is a problem? Oh, yeah.

Here is an imaginary scenario in which something as simple as weather can ruin a movie:

It's raining in L.A., which it never does, so you didn't plan for it. You didn't build into the schedule what is called a "cover set." You gambled that it would clear up. It didn't. Problem. You have six hours, and your location has now changed. The scene was scheduled for a park. You paid $2,000 for permits, and you have a park ranger standing by. Make that $3,000 for the day. The scene now moves to the producer's house, because it's free. Problem. You've spent all your money on locations. Now we're all on the producer's porch instead of in a park. Problem. The art department is furious because they never dressed the porch, because they were supposed to be in a park. They need at least two hours to dress the porch properly. Problem. Hair and makeup needs to set up in the producer's house, because the actresses got all wet, and now their hair needs to be redone. Problem. While blow-drying the actresses' hair they blow a fuse. The grips fix it, but now you're down to four hours. Finally you start to shoot. Problem. The producer's neighbor has dogs, and as soon as you start shooting they start barking, and now your producer—who was going to help you rehearse and stage the scene—is trying to get the neighbors to keep their dogs quiet. Problem. You are down to two hours to shoot a ten-page scene. Problem. You're scrambling with the new shot list you drew up with the director of photography when you were driving here from the park but everything is different from what you imagined. Problem. You lose the light in one hour. You have one hour to shoot a ten-page scene, so you start cutting it on the spot. Problem. The scene doesn't make sense, but you'll fix it later. Problem. Everyone is screaming at you and you're screaming back that you're a director not a weatherman and there's another problem. It occurs to you that you never answered Illeana's questions about the script, that day when she appeared to have deliberately knocked over your coffee in the coffee shop. Problem. You're watching and she is playing the scene entirely wrong—in fact, is that an accent? It is all wrong. She is ruining your film with her goofball performance; why on earth did you cast her? Problem. There is no time even to discuss it with her; you are down to forty-five minutes to shoot, and you will fix it in the editing room. Problem. In the editing room your editor tells you that you don't have enough coverage of Illeana and persuades you to cut around the scene and, better yet, reshoot it. Problem. There's no money for a reshoot, and besides, you and Illeana no longer speak.

The point of this imaginary story is that you need to answer every question you can in advance because things *will* come up that you hadn't planned for—that you couldn't have planned for—so you try to solve them before you end up in the middle of a mess of problems: No one is speaking to anyone else, the movie never comes out, and the director is no longer a fan. And that's sad, because I need fans to keep downloading *Pluto Nash* from Netflix so they can keep asking me, "Hey! Did you know *Pluto Nash* was going to turn out like, you know, *Pluto Nash* when you were shooting it?" No. It starred Eddie Murphy. I have since added the "every other" theory to my movie roulette wheel. Every other movie Eddie Murphy does is a hit.

Sometimes every slot on the movie roulette wheel is a problem: crazy actresses, crazy director, actresses don't get along with director, director doesn't get along with anyone—and in spite of the odds, the movie you thought would surely turn out to be a disaster (as one actress wrote in my journal, "like the TV version of *Valley of the Dolls*") turns out to be a big hit.

My favorite disaster movie I was a part of was the miniseries

Bella Mafia, about three buxom broads and their Mafia mama who seek revenge on the men who killed their husbands.

I always thought *Alive* was going to be the most challenging film I worked on. But I was wrong, as I told *Bella Mafia*'s seventy-six-year-old director. That's when I knew I had lost it.

"I worked on a mountain! We flew to the set by helicopter! Fourteen thousand feet in the air! In the snow! For Disney! And it was easier than shooting this scene!"

In my defense, I said that only after the following exchange occurred over a bowl of nuts.

> OUTRAGED ELDERLY DIRECTOR WHO CAN'T HEAR: *"What are you doing?"*
>
> CONFUSED ACTRESS (ME): *"I'm eating the nuts."* Holding out a nut in my hand to show him.
>
> DIRECTOR: *"Are you going to eat that nut? Are you? Because if you eat that nut, I will not shoot the scene!"*
>
> ACTRESS: *"Fine. Take the nuts away."*
>
> (Actress hands the bowl of nuts to the art department.)
>
> (Art department is standing by with the bowl of nuts.)
>
> FIRST ASSISTANT DIRECTOR: *"Losing the nuts!"*
>
> DIRECTOR: *"Hang on. You can't shoot the scene without eating the nuts?"*
>
> FIRST ASSISTANT DIRECTOR (to the art department): *"Holding the nuts!"*
>
> ART DEPARTMENT: *"I'm holding my nuts."*
>
> (By this time the entire crew is snickering.)
>
> INCREDULOUS DIRECTOR: *"Are you saying you can't do the scene* without *the nuts?"*
>
> INCREDULOUS ACTRESS: *"If you have nuts on the table, I'm*

> *going to eat the nuts. If you don't want me to eat the nuts,*
> *take them away."*
> FIRST ASSISTANT DIRECTOR: *"That's a wrap on the nuts!"*
> (More snickering from crew.)
> DIRECTOR: *"I want the nuts in the scene!"*
> (Art department comes back with the nuts.)
> DIRECTOR (to actress): *"Can you do the scene with the nuts?"*

By this time there are tears in everybody's eyes as they struggled to hold back laughter—except for me, because this was not remotely funny anymore. I tried one last fateful time to explain the nuts.

> ACTRESS: *Picks up a nut from the bowl and says, with the very*
> *best of intentions,* "David, she is nervous in the scene. She is
> *meeting her mother-in-law, so as she is nervously waiting,*
> *she thinks about eating a nut!"*
> FRUSTRATED, TIRED DIRECTOR: *"Are you finished with the*
> *nut? When you're finished with the nut we'll start shooting!"*
> FRUSTRATED, TIRED, ACTRESS: (Loses it, references *Alive*—
> she worked on a mountain, blah blah blah.) *"No! David,*
> *no! I'm not done with the nut! What I'm saying is, you are*
> *nuts! You're nuts! So, I don't need any more nuts in the scene,*
> *because you are nuts! I am done with the nuts!"*

And to this day this is my all-time favorite quote from any director I have ever worked for:

> DIRECTOR: *"Fine. You do it wrong and I'll shoot it, and we'll*
> *all go home early!"*

Applause from cast and crew. Probably the funniest scene I was ever a part of not caught on film.

According to my *Bella Mafia* costar Jennifer Tilly, there is *more* to the story. We finally finished shooting the scene, and David, our director, came over to me and said very sweetly, "I was going to have a lovely close-up of you but you took so long with the nuts we ran out of time." And . . . scene!

The affection I have for the cast, the director, and anyone involved in *Bella Mafia* holds no bounds, because I've dined out for years retelling *Bella Mafia* stories.

I have never laughed and cried so much on the same set. We were shooting a farce. We just didn't know it. I made life-long friends and learned that my jokes and stories could be the glue that kept things together. Jennifer called us the Five Bitches of *Bella Mafia*, but to me *Bella Mafia* was more like the Roulette Wheel of Insanity. Anywhere you land there's going to be a funny story, so let's spin the wheel, and see where it lands.

THE SCRIPT

Bella Mafia. What does that even mean? Directly translated it means *beautiful* Mafia. Pretty Mafia? I think we might have some disagreement about whether the Mafia is pretty. Maybe it refers to how a network executive back then sold me on the project, absolutely assuring me that it would be a hit because of the key ingredients: "Tits and guns!"

THE WRITER: LYNDA LA PLANTE

This might be all her fault. She was British, and she was friends with Vanessa Redgrave—also British. Wait a minute. That was it. That was the bait that had got all of us. We all wanted to work with Vanessa Redgrave. They kept saying, "You know we have Vanessa Redgrave. She's committed." That should have been a sign.

VANESSA REDGRAVE

Oh, my god. To work with Academy Award–winning actress Vanessa Redgrave. I had seen every film she was ever in. *Julia*, for which she won an Academy Award, was a film I particularly loved—as well as the television movie *Playing for Time*. She was a genius. Is a genius! Every moment she plays on film, you can't take your eyes off her. When I was in acting school, I saw her in *Orpheus Descending* on Broadway. Life-changing. This was going to be the most thrilling experience of my life. And it was. On the first day, we were shooting a scene, cleaning up after a murder or something, all wearing black slips and displaying lots of inappropriate cleavage. Tits and guns! I was on the floor, scrubbing blood with a brush and crying, when Vanessa whacked me in the face with a bloody towel. I whacked her right back—real Actors Studio stuff. I was so into it. She laughed afterward, saying, "Marvelous! Come back to my room for tequila."

Vanessa took me under her wing, and I thought, This movie is going to be amazing. I'm going to learn so much. The second day we were shooting a scene, and she started to have a discussion with the director over some piece of business involving luggage tags. Simple enough, right? Now, I had no idea that they had had a "history." "No, No, No," she said. "I completely disagree, and so does Illeana. Don't you, Illeana?" I was going to have to decide on the second day whose side I was on. Of course I was going to agree with Vanessa. Who didn't want to have tequila every day? The director never forgave me. I was on his bad, not-hearing-well side for the rest of the production. We were shooting a funeral scene, and Vanessa was wearing a veil. She thought, as true Sicilian widows would, that we should all be wearing veils, but the other actresses didn't want to. Vanessa assessed the situation and said, "But Illeana, *you're* going to wear a veil, right?" Of course, I nodded.

I went to wardrobe and came back with my veil, and the director announced to the entire set, "Now you're holding up the entire production because you wanted a veil!"

Another time we were shooting a dinner scene, and Vanessa insisted the wrong cheese was on the table.

"It would be provolone. Isn't that right, Illeana?"

I nodded, of course. I mean, she was right. We were supposed to be this Mafia family in Palermo eating American cheese? Vanessa said, "I'll be in my trailer, and when you have the right cheese let us know." I followed her like a little pet. Get it right, props! I will never forget the look on the props director's face. His face said, Where the hell am I going to get provolone in Burbank? He found some, God bless him, and we shot it, and it's in the movie. The props fellow wrote in my autograph book, "It was wonderful working with you. I only wish the um . . . working conditions could have been a tad less tense. Anyhow. We made it through!"

Underneath the inscription there is a Polaroid of my receiving oxygen on set. I started having fainting spells during shooting.

The pizza strata:

After work, most of the cast, including Vanessa, would come to my house and eat potluck and watch movies and laugh about the day's proceedings. One night I screened the now camp classic film *Valley of the Dolls*. Sort of gallows humor—although I am a huge fan of this absurd soap opera by an unlikely director, Mark Robson. It was on one of those movie nights that I introduced Vanessa to pizza strata—which is dreadful but easy to make. It's kind of a trashy, low-rent, one-dish pizza made of buttered bread, tomato sauce, cheese, and salami. To my great surprise, Vanessa, who had lived in Italy and was with an Italian, loved pizza strata. Later, on set, Vanessa would come up to me with that melodic voice and say, "Illeana, when are you going to make me some more of that marvelous pizza strata?" One of the many things I admired about Vanessa was that despite the friction on set, she never gave up trying to make a scene better. I really admired that. And I learned to ask questions because of her. A lot of questions.

Vanessa wrote in my autograph book, "I really think I would have cracked if it hadn't been for you! I'm still glad we shared a bucket and brush, and a fixed camera together."

THE DIRECTOR: DAVID GREENE

Where do I begin? Wonderful David gets the credit always for some of my favorite things ever said to me or to anyone on a set. Hands down. Such as "You were late to set so lovely Jennifer is now going to say your lines." Or, when, at the wrap party, after one of the lead actresses gave him a beautiful leatherbound script as a gift, he threw it onto the ground and said, "You were the worst one!" As she ran off in tears, he looked around as if to ask, What did I say?

David was British and looked like a character from a Dr. Seuss story. Wild crazy white hair sticking straight out. Married about six times, bless his heart. He got married for the last time about three days before he passed away. I'm not sure how old he was when he directed *Bella Mafia*—in his late seventies or eighty— but he would not admit that he couldn't hear very well. His favorite expression, which he said so frequently that eventually we all began imitating it, was "What? What? Who said that?" when either no one was talking or when he had his headphones on. After lunch, at about three o'clock, he would stop for "teatime," and I'll let you interpret what "teatime" means. After that he would fall asleep, only to wake up suddenly and shout, "What? What? Who said that?" It was straight out of a Monty Python sketch.

I couldn't wait to meet David because he had an amazing body of work. He had directed one of my favorite TV movies of all time, *The People Next Door*, starring Eli Wallach, about a family dealing with their daughter's drug addiction. Before he disliked me, which began on day two, we spoke at length about the movie, which was so terrifying that it kept me from ever even experimenting with drugs. He directed *Friendly Fire*, for which he won an Emmy for Outstanding Director, and a little miniseries called *Roots*, which you may have heard of—for which he also won an Emmy. But he had also directed the TV remake of *What Ever Happened to Baby Jane?* with real-life sisters Lynn and Vanessa Redgrave. That was the "history" he and Vanessa had carried into poor *Bella Mafia*. Apparently they hadn't gotten along on the earlier film, but that hadn't stopped them from working together again. On *Bella Mafia*, David would groan and say, "What is she doing? God, I *hate* this kind of acting" while the scene was going on. As if Vanessa couldn't hear him. As if we all couldn't hear him. David would say things that any other director might of course be *thinking* but never say out loud! Once, in the middle of a scene, with the cameras rolling, he actually said, "God! I'd love a glass of wine!"

Of course, the cast started sharing these tasty bits of gossip. It made you want to show up early not to miss anything! One day, I was walking to the set, and I was very upset about my swiped dress—which I will get to in a minute—and I passed by one of the producers, and he was shaking. He said, "You missed the worst scene in there."

And I said, "Oh, the scene was bad?"

And he sighed and said, "Well, that, too, but no, the scene between Vanessa and David."

I doubled over with laughter. One particularly long day on the set, they were going at it, and Jennifer Tilly quipped, "This movie isn't going to end, because she's going to kill him, and then there will be the trial of *Bella Mafia*, and we'll all be shooting that."

Like I said, a lot of laughing and crying. And David had an

obsession with *not* crying. There were all these gruesome murders and torturings and funerals, all things you would cry about, but he would become very upset whenever an actress was crying. We were shooting a scene in which one of the lead actresses loses her baby, and she was preparing for the highly emotional moment.

"Where is she?" David said impatiently.

"She's preparing to cry," said the first assistant director, very quietly trying to keep the mood.

"I don't want her to cry!" David said.

The actress walked onto the set, and she was sobbing, ready to shoot this very sad scene. Through her tears she said, "Are we ready yet?"

And David said, "We have four minutes to shoot this before lunch; please stop crying!"

She ran off crying—for real. And . . . what's for lunch?

The problem with all this miscommunication is that by the time we would get to shoot there would be time for only one or two takes. David would look at me and Jennifer and here was his direction: "And you two . . . act up a storm."

Was there competition among the five actresses of *Bella Mafia*? Yes! Was it subtle? No! We were shooting a scene welcoming Vanessa back from prison and all the girls were supposed to run outside and embrace her. Well, someone shoved me, because she wanted to embrace Vanessa, and I went flying out of frame and onto the ground. I started laughing, because of course the take was completely unusable, but to my shock, David yelled out:

"Cut. Print. Moving on!"

I said, "David. I fell in the scene."

"I know," he said. "Very emotional!"

"No, on the ground, David. I fell on the ground. Someone pushed me!"

"Moving on!" he yelled out.

I have a wonderful Polaroid of David in my autograph book that I snapped when he wasn't looking. I knew I would always want to remember exactly what he looked like. I look at that picture and start to laugh. It's the back of beautiful Nastassja Kinski's head, and David is inches from her ear, giving her direction. You can't see Nastassja's face, you have to imagine it, but I have a feeling her eyes may have been crossed.

If David was dismissive with other members of the cast, sometimes it seemed as if he was overdirecting Nastassja. One day David asked her if she was ready to act the scene. We had been called to rehearse, but David told Nastassja to go through the whole performance. Well somehow, Nastassja thought this meant the camera was rolling, so she proceeded to act out this highly emotional monologue. It was brilliant, but no one was filming it! The cameraman was trying to signal David to ask if he should start rolling, but David was just oblivious, waving him off for having interrupted Nastassja! He was completely engaged in "directing" her, and Nastassja obliged in giving one hell of a performance. We all just stood there watching, not knowing what to do. When she finished, David said to her, "That was beautiful, darling—the perfect amount of emotion. Would you like to put one on film now?"

Nastassja said, "I thought you *were* shooting?" She was, of course, wondering why he or anyone else hadn't stopped her. We all felt terrible. Here we were again, up against lunch, and with little time to shoot the actual scene. We all stood helpless, wanting to help Nastassja but not wanting to interfere with David. She said, "Well, now I can't do it with everyone looking at me," which she meant figuratively—but David literally instructed us to turn away and not to look at Nastassja. David said, "No one is looking, Nastassja, you may begin!" I was looking at Jennifer like, What is happening? Why are we doing this? We were all turned around waiting for her to start, but now began the discussion of whether or not there was time. "And . . . that's lunch," said the first assistant director. I grabbed a Polaroid camera and secretly snapped David and Nastassja's picture to put in my journal.

NASTASSJA KINSKI

The first time I heard the name *Nastassja Kinski* was when my grandfather Melvyn Douglas recommended a movie to me he had just seen called *Tess*, directed by Roman Polanski. I followed Nastassja's career ever since and was almost starstruck at the notion of meeting her. In *Bella Mafia*, Nastassja played Sophia, one of Vanessa's daughters by marriage. I thought it might be funny to show Nastassja what a big fan I was, so I brought a movie magazine I owned from the 1980s that had her on the cover to show her on the set. It was from around the time she had been in *Cat People* and *Paris, Texas*, a movie I really love. When I asked her if she would autograph it, she looked at me innocently and said, "Are you making fun of me?" I felt terrible. It was not my intention at all. I loved her. But maybe it is inappropriate to ask your costars to sign your movie memorabilia. There were five ladies in *Bella Mafia*, and there was always an ongoing issue with dresses. Who could, would, or should be wearing what? And how low-cut could it be? Every time I wanted to wear something I would see on the rack I would hear, "Sorry, Nastassja is wearing that. No, sorry, Jennifer is wearing the red."

And cleavage. This one's got the dress with the cleavage. You're wearing a sack. When we shot the poster, there was a brawl over diamond earrings. All the actresses had picked out the same pair of diamond earrings that they each insisted *they* had to wear. And no one wanted to hold the gun. I wasn't a fighter, so I ended up with no earrings and holding a large pistol in the poster. One day I came to work, and I passed Nastassja. She said hello, very quietly, and I noticed something strange. She was wearing my dress.

"Hi," she whispered as she passed. I should mention that Nastassja barely speaks above a whisper. Sexy in real life but tough when you're trying to act with her. I would be with her in a scene, a foot away, and I would look at Jennifer and say, "I can't hear anything. Is she talking?" Jennifer would answer in *her* signature baby voice, "What did you say?" That's why I'm leaning forward in every scene. I could never hear my costars! I headed to wardrobe, and I said, "Guys, I just passed Nastassja and she is wearing my dress."

"I know," they said. "She saw it hanging there and she wanted to wear it."

I said, "But I'm wearing it in the scene."

The wardrobe lady was so blasé by that point. She sighed. "Yeah," she said. "We tried to explain that to her, but she liked it."

I said, "I wore the dress in another scene. So we are both going to be wearing the same dress in different scenes. So our characters share dresses?"

They all shrugged. By that point, fatigue had set in. In the end, the only person who even noticed the double dress was my friend the designer Cynthia Rowley, who had lent me the dress in the first place. She was thrilled, of course, to see Nastassja

Kinski wearing her dress, and Nastassja, as always, looked beautiful. But it was *my* dress!

I was so sad when Nastassja wrote in my autograph book: "Even though we hardly spoke, I want you to know I wanted to. I just get shy." There's a little heart next to it. I was so happy to reconnect with Nastassja recently. She still looks stunning, and I'm pushing for a *Bella Mafia* reunion . . . or intervention.

JAMES MARSDEN

How did he come out unscathed? He was just starting out then, but I knew he had a talent for comedy. How else could he have played Nastassja's psychopathic son, Luka—a Sicilian boy who had been raised by monks and who accidentally killed his entire Mafia family, which drives him mad! He was a brilliant actor, because he got through two days of being tied up and tortured by women wearing slips, and pushing boobs in his face, without laughing. For the record, he did the best "What? What? Who said that?" imitation of David Green.

Jimmy wrote in my autograph book, "Thank you for getting me through the day! *Please* let's work together again!" I'm still waiting for that to happen.

FRANCO NERO

Camelot. The man was in *Camelot*! He had been in so many great films and had so many great stories to tell. He and Vanessa met during *Camelot*, became involved, and were then in other relationships, but they kind of reunited on *Bella Mafia*—in which Franco played Mario Domino, a character on the opposite side of the Luciano family who causes them to lose their family fortune, so he kills himself. There, among the ruins, is a true and lasting miracle. They were married in 2006.

Franco wrote in my autograph book, "You cry very well!"

TONY LO BIANCO

The French Connection. I was in a movie with Tony Lo Bianco, and he was in *The French Connection*! Isn't that cool?

DENNIS FARINA

A prince. He played my father, Don Luciano, and we danced together at one of the many weddings in the show. I will never forget: We were shooting the scene and he had me in his arms when one of the actresses came over to us, talking very quickly and animatedly, and when she walked away, without missing a beat of the dance step, he said in his Chicago-cop accent, "That's drugs!"

In my autograph book I wrote two words under Dennis's Polaroid. "The Best!" It's the kind of thing any actor hopes will be written about them. Other actors will know what I mean by that, but what it means to me is that he is solid, always present, has no ego, and just truly enjoys the work. I never saw Dennis complain, and this was a movie where we could have put out a daily paper filled with complaints.

PETER BOGDANOVICH

One of my all-time-favorite comedies is Peter Bogdanovich's *What's Up, Doc?* It had a hysterical script by Buck Henry (remember him? He kept his feet up on the desk during my *To Die For* audition), David Newman, and Robert Benton. It was always a dream of mine to work with Peter Bogdanovich on a comedy. He had made such an impact on my early moviegoing with his films such as *Paper Moon* and *The Last Picture Show*. Classics. He also directed a really underrated film—another farce, called *Noises Off*, about a crazy British director and an even crazier bunch of actors doing a play in which everything that can go wrong does, and they all end up at each other's throats! It is very funny. But it's not real. *Bella Mafia* was real! We were fighting over dresses! We were pushing one another to the ground and filming it.

I would never have imagined that the first time I would meet one of my absolute idols, he would be acting opposite me as Jennifer Tilly's Mafia-don boyfriend, Vito Giancamo. I was so confused as to who Vito Giancamo was that between takes I asked Jennifer Tilly for some explanation of how his character fit into the plot, and she said in her baby voice, "I should really read the script."

Peter wrote in my autograph book, "I always <u>do</u> enjoy talking with you. Looking forward to the next time." It would take fourteen years, but it was worth it. He directed me in *She's Funny That Way*, which was a real farce in the tradition of *What's Up, Doc?* After he saw the rushes, he called me and said, "You're quite good in the film." Sure, it was no *Bella Mafia*, but I took the compliment to heart. Thank you, Peter.

And now the closer: Jennifer Tilly

I couldn't wait to get to the set every day, pen in hand, ready to write down everything that happened. Then again, who would believe it? I have often joked that I became friends with Jennifer only so I could have someone to confirm the crazy on-set stories.

I learned a lot about humor on the set of *Bella Mafia*. So many people wrote in my autograph book that my sense of humor had got them through what one actor had described as "madness." When something happened, I took my cue from Dennis Farina. I didn't complain; I just made a joke out of it. There were always trailers or rooms for everyone on set but somewhere along the way they started thinking of Jennifer Tilly and me as roommates. I would get to set, and I wouldn't have a trailer, and they would say, "Oh, we put you in Jennifer's room, because we know you two are friends." Well, we weren't really friends. I'm sure they were just doing this to save money, but I never said anything, because of course I wanted to room with Jennifer. Who else could I have a nice gossip with? And I really hoped we would become friends. In the morning I would see Jennifer in the makeup trailer, and we would exchange pleasantries and she would leave, and I would think, I bet she has no idea she is sharing her room with me. I can't tell you how many times I would go to Jennifer's room, lugging my costumes, and she would be lounging on her bed reading a script, or taking a nap, her clothes strewn about, and she'd be completely surprised by—but always gracious about—my arrival. And I would explain that apparently they had assigned me to her room. Again. I would clear a path among her shoes, her jewels, and find myself a spot, always trying to make her laugh with something outrageous that happened on set.

I don't know if I just wore her down, but eventually I would just go to her room whether I had my own room or not. So I could pester her about some of my favorite Jennifer performances, such as the ones in *Bound, Let It Ride,* and of course *Bullets Over Broadway.* We got up to a lot of high jinks together. One time we decided we would overact a scene, playing it with lots of wild hand gestures. So if the line was "There on the table," we would both point wildly at the table as if it were a murder mystery: "*There!* On the *table!*" Or if the line was "They are taking the roof from over our head," we would point madly to the *roof!* Poor David. I think once he almost noticed what we were up to.

The worst outrage of *Bella Mafia* is that we never got to do another movie together, because I love Jennifer to pieces and think she is just wildly talented. She created a type: sassy, sexy, funny— a Jennifer Tilly type—that only she can play even though I have tried to imitate her on many occasions. Except for the cleavage.

Jennifer wrote in my autograph book: "You have a knack of repeating the way something happened and making it hysterical. I laughed until tears squirted out of my eyes. Let's hope we are not in the television version of *Valley of the Dolls!*"

So, what was the fate of the five bitches of *Bella Mafia?* Driving down Beverly Boulevard, I nearly went off the road the first time I saw my face on the huge billboard for *Bella Mafia.* I was holding a big gun, but still, my face was on a billboard! *Bella Mafia* was so well received it won the ratings both nights we played on TV. The longer movie version was sold overseas and did even better. It was a huge hit! Vanessa Redgrave was nominated for a Golden Globe for Best Performance by an Actress in a Mini-

Series or Motion Picture Made for TV. I was signed to a television deal with CBS. There was serious talk of a sequel. Of course I was asked, "Did you know when you were shooting *Bella Mafia* it was going to turn out so well?"

Let's spin the roulette wheel one more time.

The television exposure I received with *Bella Mafia* resulted in a lot of meetings about television shows. I signed on to be in a pilot called *Action*, with Jay Mohr and Buddy Hackett. It was directed by the astonishingly gifted late Ted Demme. We were shooting a scene with Keanu Reeves, who had just filmed a little movie called *The Matrix*. I remember filming a scene on Hollywood Boulevard at four in the morning and thinking, This is going to be the greatest show of all time. I knew it would be the greatest shot I ever did. I was dressed as a hooker, strapped to the side of a limo speeding down Hollywood Boulevard. I could hear Ted Demme laughing as he watched the monitor in the camera car that was towing us along. Chris Thompson, our writer and show-runner, was a genius. Our producer was the über-successful and mythic Joel Silver. I adored the star, Jay Mohr, who I had known from *Picture Perfect*. Jay was brilliant and so fast on his feet. Our costar, the irascible and wonderfully funny Buddy Hackett, was a mentor to Jay and always had kind things to say when we were acting together. Wendy Ward, the child star turned prostitute turned network executive, was the most challenging and rewarding character I have ever played. Her character had been written with me in mind. I had amazing clothes. I looked incredible. Every day we were working with stars such as Keanu Reeves, Sandra Bullock, Salma Hayek, and Ice Cube, making what we felt was the best, most cutting-edge show on television. The press was outrageous. *TV Guide* and *Entertainment Weekly* raved. *Newsweek* wrote, "*Action* breaks the rules like movers break china." I thought *Action* would be on the air for years and cleared a shelf for the Emmys we were sure to win.

We were canceled after thirteen episodes. I'm often asked, "Why did they cancel *Action*?" We could spin and spin and spin on that one and still not get an answer. That's just the roulette wheel of insanity.

CHAPTER FIFTEEN

Easy to Assemble

Putting it all together. Of all the
roles I have played, this has been the
best: writer and producer of my
IKEA-sponsored Web series, *Easy to
Assemble*. Here I am staging a dance
scene in the self-serve warehouse.

Almost ten years after premiering *The Perfect Woman* at the
Sundance Film Festival, I returned to the event in 2003,
this time with a comedy short I had written and directed called
Devil Talk. Standing in the back of the theater, laughing—luckily
for me—was the president of the Sundance Channel, Larry
Aidem. We got to talking, and he said maybe they could put

together some sort of retrospective of my short films for the channel. This became the genesis of *Illeanarama*—a collection of shorts I wrote, produced, and directed, including *The Perfect Woman, Boy Crazy, Girl Crazier, Devil Talk*, and one I had just shot, called *Supermarket*. It was based on an actual incident with an ardent fan at a Ralphs market in L.A. I was shopping with a friend and fellow actor when this incredibly nice male fan approached me in the aisle. He was overwhelmed and could not believe that I was at *his* supermarket. "I can't believe this is happening," he said. "You are my favorite actress! All my life, I wanted to meet you!"

"Thank you," I said. "That's very sweet."

He then began literally quoting every film and television performance he'd ever seen me in. Quizzing me, "Are you coming back on *Six Feet Under*?"

"I don't know," I said.

"Why did they cancel *Action*?"

"I'm not sure," I said.

"Wait," he said, "I have to show you this."

He took his wallet out, and showed me a movie ticket of *Grace of My Heart* that he carried with him. His hands were shaking as he showed it to me. I was starting to get uncomfortable at this point and wanted to move on, but he started to cry. He said, "I want to thank you from the bottom of my heart for all the joy your work has given me. It's the inspiration you have provided that makes life seem like a wonderful adventure, and God bless you. And thank you."

Oh, my God! My mother has never said anything that nice to me!

He was so sincere, and so sweet, that when he turned and

walked away I said to my friend, "Wouldn't it be funny if it turned out I was actually *working* at the supermarket instead of *shopping* here? I'd be his humiliated checker, asking him if he needed 'paper or plastic?,' and he would still be asking me, 'What's the name of the movie you did with Kevin Bacon?'"

Well, the friend and fellow actor was Gary Oldman. Not only is he a genius actor; he's a genius, period. So he stopped dead in his tracks and said, "You *have* to make a movie about that."

So I did. I wrote, directed, produced, and starred in *Supermarket* along with Daryl Hannah and Jeff Goldblum. It was the first time I played a fictionalized version of Illeana Douglas, the comic alter ego and beleaguered persona named Illeanarama. Who knew the best role I ever played would turn out to be myself?

I showed the footage to Larry Aidem, and Sundance liked the idea of *Supermarket* so much that they gave me a small budget to shoot some supplemental material—also to be shot in a supermarket—linking the shorts together in a cohesive narrative, now called *Illeanarama*. We filmed at Bel Air Foods market, in Bel Air, California. It was a kind of supermarket to the stars, because a lot of the famous folks who lived in the small and exclusive community, such as Elizabeth Taylor or Clint Eastwood, would often be seen shopping there. I myself had a chance encounter with a shopper that was pretty memorable.

It was the first day of shooting *Illeanarama*. We had started at four in the morning and wrapped around noon so that the supermarket could open to the public. The day had gone great, and Jeff's scenes were in the can. I was feeling pretty good about everything when the sound guy came up and said he needed to speak to me. We sat down at the picnic tables outside, and he basically explained he wasn't coming back the next day unless he got more money. I was shocked, because we had worked together before and he was being paid a pretty decent wage, but he meant business, and he held all of the day's sound in his hand, so I listened carefully to what he had to say.

I tried to reason with him that this was a low-budget shoot and that his salary was in line with that of a typical soundman, but he hissed, "Well, I'm sure you and Jeff Goldblum are getting thousands of dollars." I assured him that was not the case, that I was practically working for free, and after all, weren't we friends? How could he do this?

In the background I could hear Danny Ferrington—a close friend who had a cameo in the film and who happened to have a distinct Louisiana accent—calling my name. I was just trying to ignore him, but Danny came up to us mid-argument and started tugging my arm, trying to get me to turn around.

I said, "Danny, please, I'm in the middle of something." And Danny, with his Louisiana drawl, starts laughing and says, "I really think you should turn around, because you're really going to want to meet this guy."

I said, "Danny, please! I have a problem! I'll be with you in a minute!"

Peripherally I saw Danny sort of throw up his hands to the person he was talking to. Meanwhile, the soundman was unyielding. Worse, he seemed to be getting satisfaction from sticking it to me, because he knew he had me over a barrel: No sound coming from Jeff Goldblum meant no show. So I had no choice but to write the soundman a personal check for double what he was paid so that he would come back the next day. People ask me what a producer does. They solve problems. I just don't take it personally anymore. The situation now under control, Danny came and sat down next to me. I was shaking my head, saying, "You know how much money that guy just cost me?"

And Danny was grinning. "You're not going to be mad in a minute, I.D.," he said.

He was by himself, so I said, "Who was this *important* person I was supposed to be so excited to meet?

And Danny started cackling, "He's inside getting his lunch!"

Let me explain a little about Danny Ferrington. He is one of those guys who knows everyone. He was Linda Ronstadt's roommate in the '70s and '80s. He's a famous guitar-maker who's made guitars for people like George Harrison and Donovan, but he is also an excitable guy—he'd be thrilled if he ran into a session guitarist who once backed up Glen Campbell, so I wasn't expecting much and I was still steaming about the money the sound guy had cost me. Danny started to wave someone over, and I look up to see who this nobody was, and there, coming out of the Bel Air Foods market, supermarket to the stars, and walking toward our table was Albert Brooks.

Let me try to describe coherently what that name, Albert Brooks, means to me. Brilliantly funny short films I saw on *Saturday Night Live*. Comedy albums I was still listening to up until the day I met him. Anything I did or tried to do as a filmmaker—including *Illeanarama*—was inspired by films he had made. Albert Brooks describes the comic foibles of the human condition in a way no other comedian has been able to. His films are neither too slapstick nor too sentimental but fall in the sweet spot that put them in the pantheon. *Real Life, Modern Romance, Lost in America, Defending Your Life.* His work in those movies is akin to Edvard Munch's painting *The Scream:* You don't have to divine the meaning; it's right there. The films have become reference points in our consciousness. Trying to describe a feeling or situation, we can say, It's like that scene in *Lost in America* when Albert says, "I've seen the future! And it's a bald-headed man from New York." Or, It's like the scene in *Modern Romance* in which the bored sound guy says, "I think you saved the picture." Or, It's like the scene in *Defending Your Life* in which Lee Grant gets him to admit, "I was afraid."

I recently called Danny Ferrington and asked him, "Danny, what did I look like when Albert Brooks came walking out of the supermarket?" and Danny said, "You looked like you were going to pass out." Yes. That's accurate. The only thing that would have been more impressive would have been if Danny had managed to bring Peter Sellers back from the dead. I hadn't even changed out of my checker costume, and we're outside the supermarket where we have filmed and he has just gone shopping. It's like I was punished, in a bath of irony, because now I had to sit across from Albert Brooks while he was eating his spare ribs and drinking his Arizona Iced Tea, and try not to be the same fan who met *me* at the supermarket, quoting every single film and performance he'd ever been in, crying, and personally thanking him for all the joy his work had given me!

For an hour (and to put that in perspective, on the *Tonight Show* he never did more than fifteen minutes) I got pure Albert Brooks—hysterical, top of his game, commenting on everything from the new digital medium to the advent of reality TV, which he humbly acknowledged he may have had a hand in inventing with *Real Life*. To be in a profession where you meet an artist whose work you admire in the context of working was a pretty special moment. Danny sums it up more like this, "I knew what was going on inside your head, and I was impressed that you were able to keep it together, but you cried like a baby after he left."

Illeanarama played at the Aspen Comedy Festival, the New York Film Festival, and the Tribeca Film Festival. It caught the notice of some television networks and of producer Barry Katz, who I knew from the television series *Action*. We began pitching it as a series. In 2005, we made a pilot with New Line Television also called *Illeanarama* for the Oxygen network. I wrote the script with Teresa O'Neill and also executive-produced. The premise had changed a bit and was now about an actress who, having gone through a bad Hollywood divorce, is broke and has to take a job in a supermarket. I disagreed slightly with the premise. There were many stories about actresses leaving show business simply in search of happiness. Kristy McNichol, probably one of the most talented child actresses, said she left show business because she wanted to "see what else was out there." Grace Kelly became a princess. Kim Novak moved to Big Sur and found happiness working with animals. Gene Tierney struggled with depression after a female fan with the measles hugged her, infecting Tierney's unborn child and eventually causing birth defects. She suffered a nervous breakdown from the possibility that her fame had caused this to happen. Doctors thought that being in a "normal" setting around "normal" people would make *her* normal, so she began quietly working at a dress shop in Kansas. So many people came in to ogle her that she wasn't able to continue working there. Eventually she ended up back in Hollywood trying to make a comeback but her heart was no longer in it.

Illeanarama became the story of an actress who desperately wants to get out of show business but can't, because the only way she can make a living is by pawning her fame at the "Supermarket to the Stars." The issue we all agreed upon is that we wanted to satirize reality TV. As I would later say in my Web series for IKEA, *Easy to Assemble,* "It was fun to be famous when no one was famous but now everyone is famous, and I'm obsolete." What I meant by that is that I went into acting because I loved acting, not because I wanted to be "a celebrity."

Toward the end of my grandfather's life, when I asked him how he thought current films compared with those of the past, he said that—leaving Billy Wilder and Ernst Lubitsch out of it— there were more interesting directors working today. There was a through line connecting my grandfather's career, in which he worked with Robert Redford on *The Candidate,* to my working with Robert Redford on *Quiz Show* and Redford's talking to *me* about working with my grandfather. Having been through the studio system in a career that spanned more than sixty years, my grandfather always had something to teach me. When I told him that my favorite movies were "screwball comedies," he scoffed, "That is a name made up by intellectuals." Knowing film history was important to him, I learned the difference between Chaplin and the Marx brothers, Capra and Cukor. When that skill— that knowledge, which was ingrained in me—became less important, I found show business to be less fun.

Look, I will always be like the guy cleaning up after the elephant and saying, "What, me give up show business?" But it was an adjustment to see where and how I fit into this new landscape. In this celebrity culture, we were all famous, or just about to be. The idea that fame was the result of a craft that went back to the first guy who made a caveman laugh was thrown out of the mix, and "real folks" were in; in my opinion, art has never been the same. Here was my sea change: I was asked to be a "celebrity judge" on a reality show about "real folks" trying to become starlets. Ten girls would live in the former house of Marilyn Monroe while they followed their dreams to make it in Hollywood. The fact that a very unhappy Marilyn Monroe did not live past thirty-six was not included in the subplot. Faye Dunaway took the job I turned down. That's what's called a sea change with a twist of regret. Like come on in, the water is fine, and by the way there's Faye Dunaway swimming in it!

We were shooting the *Illeanarama* pilot back at the supermarket to the stars when, as if on cue, another one of my comedy idols showed up. We were blocking the produce aisle. There, waiting patiently for us to finish, was Gene Wilder!

Let me try to describe coherently what the name Gene Wilder means to me. (I know, here we go again.) Let's just say *Young Frankenstein*: funniest film of all time and call it a day. OK, I also owned the poster, the record, and still have the T-shirt. I'm finished.

Mr. Wilder was kind and adorable and kept saying, "Scoozi" every time he needed to get past us.

He agreed to cross the frame for me with his shopping cart, so I can *sort of* say I worked with him. The irony of this was one of the hardest parts of pitching the show to the executives was that they didn't believe celebrities ever did their own shopping!

I was really proud of *Illeanarama*. We had an all-star cast: Justine Bateman, Jane Lynch, Jeff Goldblum, Ed Begley, Greg Proops, John Heard, and The Beaver—Jerry Mathers. Jerry had my favorite line in the show. He asks me—referring, of course, to his beloved show, *Leave it to Beaver*—"Is that like starring in a television show, where everybody loves you, and then you grow up, and nobody wants you anymore?" and I shudder and say, "No. Nothing is as bad as that."

I had to turn down Margot Kidder, which broke my heart. Margot was basically living out the plot, having moved to Montana. We had a long talk about how much she related to the material and that meant a lot to me. I figured that once we were on the air, I could have her on. For whatever reason (see my "Roulette Wheel of Insanity" chapter), *Illeanarama* did not get picked up. Here's what did: *Mr. Romance,* about a group of "real guys" who are mentored by Fabio to learn to become more romantic, and *The Janice Dickinson Modeling Agency,* about a group of "real girls" who are mentored by Janice Dickinson to become what she used to be, a model.

I was back living in Hollywood, wondering what my next movie would be. For *Illeanarama,* I had written the lines "My life is like a movie. At first it was like a Busby Berkeley musical with everybody happy and dancing, and then it was like a French film that I didn't understand, but I looked really good, and now it's like a seventies disaster movie where I'm screaming, but no one can hear me." People don't understand that even to get a show on the air, you write out a year's worth of story lines showing where this character is going. I loved writing where this character was going, because I had no idea where I was going myself.

When the pilot got picked up, I had given up my New York apartment and moved back to L.A. How many times would I have to move my gigantic *Breakfast at Tiffany's* movie poster back and forth across the country? I had this horrible hip little '60s shotgun house in the Hollywood Hills, off Woodrow Wilson

Drive. It was one of those typical glass houses on stilts that make you think, One good earthquake, and that thing is going to fall off a cliff and take that insufferable actress and her pilot with it!

Right before I had left for L.A., I had run into Brian De Palma near Washington Square in New York City. I had known Brian ever since I had done publicity for *The Untouchables* and throughout my relationship with Marty, but I hadn't seen him in years. We exchanged numbers, and I said, "Hey, if you're ever in L.A., give me a call." He assured me that that would *never* happen, and I laughed. Good old Brian.

Months later, I got an unexpected call that he had moved to L.A., and did I want to hang out? Post-pilot slump, it was the best offer I'd received in a long time. Although, you don't exactly just "hang out" with Brian De Palma, you hang on! Brian is not the most inconspicuous person on the planet, but he was game to accompany me to some pretty artsy events. I remember he was editing *The Black Dahlia*, and he called and asked me what I was doing that night, and I told him, "I'm doing one of these story-telling evenings at a place called Sit 'n Spin."

He roared, "Oh, my God, that sounds dreadful! I want to watch!"

I said, "Brian I really don't think this is your scene—"

And he bellowed, "Are you *embarrassed*? Is it that *awful*? Are you *so afraid* of being *humiliated* by me?"

You don't argue with Brian. You just shake your head and laugh, knowing that he always tells it like it is. Shut up, listen, and try to get a word in here or there, because what he has to offer is pretty brilliant.

His movies like *Dressed to Kill* and *The Untouchables* are all known for their unusual camera angles, compositions, and choreographed long takes. They are stylized, and the images are thrilling. He's whip-smart, so sharp and intuitive, and although he might not want to admit it, deeply sensitive—but he does tend to bellow. He has never lost his curiosity about life, and it has always impressed me, because it means he has never lost touch. Sure enough, he came to Sit 'n Spin that night, sat on cushions on the floor with a bunch of hipsters, and watched me perform for the first time in public a story I was working on. That story became the first chapter in this book: *I Blame Dennis Hopper*. I looked out, and there was Brian, sitting on the ground, cross-legged in his ever-present safari jacket, just roaring, laughing his head off.

Afterward, the subject of my failed pilot came up. I really didn't want him to see it, because I figured the work was just bad, but he insisted, and as I said, you don't argue with Brian, so I invited him over to my groovy '60s house for dinner and a viewing of the show. I made roast chicken—because I knew that at least *that* would be good. Typical Brian, as soon as he walked in he started to make fun of my house. "I'm having a '60s flashback!" he shouted. "I should have worn beads!"

He scolded me, "That driveway is a deterrent to all men! *No one* will ever visit you here."

He cursed me, of course, because Brian and my friend Danny Ferrington were the only other two people who ever saw the house. Brian had scraped the bottom of his car pulling in. Danny hit the fence while trying to park his truck, and I almost backed my car off a cliff before I finally had enough of life in the Hollywood Hills!

I was in a self-help phase—you know, livin' in L.A. and all—and Brian spotted a large sheet of affirmations that I had taped on the refrigerator. He started to read them aloud with asides.

"GET WHAT YOU WANT."

"Of course."

"DON'T TAKE NO FOR AN ANSWER."

"Always."

"LET YOUR AURA SHINE."

"What the hell does that mean?"

Brian wanted to see the *Illeanarama* pilot, and I was making excuses. I said, "Brian, it's awful; it's amateurish. It doesn't work." And he shouted, "Listen, if it's shit, I'll tell you it's shit, and then we can have dinner!" That became my next affirmation, by the way. "IF IT'S SHIT, I'LL TELL YOU IT'S SHIT, AND THEN WE CAN HAVE DINNER." Works for a lot of things.

After some hemming and hawing I put the tape in the player and just left the room, waiting for Brian's inevitable skewering. The show ended, and Brian proceeded to give me a detailed and helpful critique that went beyond just mentioning the line that referenced him: "There's a ketchup spill in aisle four. It looks like something out of a Brian De Palma movie." He said thoughtfully, "There is something to this idea. Stick with it. It's good."

It was those words of encouragement from Brian that made me keep trying. I pulled myself up by my bootstraps and continued. I figured if someone of his stature took the time to encourage me, who was I to let him down? Once again, the movies had rescued me, from Dennis Hopper helping me understand and appreciate my *Easy Rider* childhood, to singing in the key of Liza, to Rudy Vallée's playing me the tape of his applause backstage at the Camelot, to Lee Marvin's wishing me good luck on Madison Avenue, to getting words of wisdom from Marlon Brando, to meeting Albert Brooks when I was directing *Supermarket*—the right person, at the right time, has always stepped off the screen and been there for me because I couldn't be there for myself.

Brian brought up the idea of putting the show on the Internet, because he said that was the future of entertainment. He was saying this in 2005! At the same time, I started to call supermarkets such as Vons, Ralphs, and Whole Foods. I met with the supply chain Office Depot. I tried to explain the premise of the show, but in the end, the idea of financing a comedy show that took place in a supermarket aisle, or in an Office Depot, seemed too far-out for everyone. Two years went by, and as Brian said, the Internet was beginning to explode. I put *Illeanarama* on YouTube, cutting it into sections that could be played as episodes, hoping to gain some interest there.

A very lucky thing happened. In addition to our getting a lot of views and winning an online-video award from the TV Guide Network, a man named Fred Dubin who worked for a media company called MEC saw it. MEC's client was IKEA, and he brought *Illeanarama* to their attention. The next thing I knew, I was meeting at MEC in New York with Fred and IKEA's marketing executive, Magnus Gustafsson, to discuss writing comic interstitials for them. IKEA and Magnus had launched a successful campaign in which the comedian Mark Malkoff lived at an IKEA for a week, but they wanted to follow it up with something a little more high-profile. I was tasked with changing the image of IKEA as a brand that only college kids used and making it seem a little more hip. The more we spoke about how to accomplish this goal, the more the idea of creating a kind of *Illeanarama* at IKEA came up. I actually used the IKEA products, so I was a consumer being given an opportunity to promote a brand that I believed in. That was good for the marketers.

On the creative side for me, there was something intrinsically funnier about my working in an IKEA rather than in a supermarket. The bright primary colors and the little home within IKEA's home displays were ideal for situation comedy. Part of IKEA's philosophy was to give me free rein to come up with any story line I wanted—as long as Jeff Goldblum was in it, that is. I remember that when I told them I was pretty sure I *could* get Jeff to make a cameo, Magnus leaned across the table and with a thick Swedish accent said, "U cud haf Yeff Guldblume at IKEA?" Thank God it happened, or we would have never moved forward, apparently. Jeff had never set foot in an IKEA, but he came through for me, appearing in the first season as himself and shooting a fake IKEA training video called *Helpful Swedish Phrases*. There was a wormhole feeling at IKEA that lent itself to having any number of guest stars. You could walk down an aisle, get lost trying to find something, and see me and Tom Arnold trying to shoot a sex video, or Jeff Goldblum discussing personal grooming with IKEA coworkers. We had Craig Bierko secretly living in one of the bedrooms after his real-life television show had been canceled. "Do you work here, too?" I ask him.

No, he says, "I live here. Don't tell IKEA."

No one likes to hear this part. The first season I wrote the script, turned it in, and waited for my notes. First note: "We don't sell ice cream; it's frozen yogurt." I got my pen ready for more. "OK, what's next?"

That was it. One note!

Magnus said, "Good stuff," and we were shooting by the summer of 2008. We filmed on the floors of a working store in Burbank with Jeff Goldblum, Justine Bateman, Jane Lynch, Greg Proops, Ed Begley—all of the folks from the original

Illeanarama—plus Robert Patrick, Tom Arnold, Kevin Pollak, Alan Havey, and Craig Bierko. Shooting *Easy to Assemble* was like live theater. Because we filmed in a working store, we had shoppers, so we used them as extras, and they were thrilled to be part of the action. They watched our fictional Justine Bateman talk show, *40 and Bitter,* and thought that it was a real talk show. Justine was so wonderfully deadpan. "In my twenties I was self-deprecating. In my thirties, I was ironic; now that I'm forty I'm just plain bitter." Then we had an actor "pretend" to be a shopper and start measuring her desk, trying to walk off with it while Justine yells at him that he can order it online. This blend of fact and fiction was exciting to all of us.

The idea of *Easy to Assemble* was to confuse the audience as to which scene was real and which was staged, but I can tell you, everything was carefully planned and written—but in the natural style of Albert Brooks. I loved writing the "frenemy" story line between me and Justine. Two actresses trying to one-up each other to avoid coworker downsizing became the subject of our second season, *Coworker of the Year.*

Magnus made sure I was given complete access to the Burbank store. We would shoot scenes with actor managers such as Jane Lynch and Eric Lange alongside real IKEA managers working at their desks. IKEA thought it was important that I be treated as a real coworker, so I was given a handbook about coming to work at IKEA. I kept explaining, "You realize I'm an actress, right, and that this is all fake?"

But a funny thing started to happen. Working for IKEA started to really affect me. I began to feel like part of the IKEA family. It went beyond loyalty. They trusted me, and I trusted them. I made IKEA seem like a fun place to work because *I* was having fun. They were letting me stage musical numbers in the self-serve warehouse. Coworkers were asking if *their* IKEA shirts could be retrofitted the way our costumer had retrofitted mine, turning them into minidresses. We once made a dress out of a 36-cent IKEA bag for actress Kate Micucci, and it was the envy of all the real employees. IKEA was a character in the show. We highlighted the yellow shirts, the meatballs, the relentless cheerfulness—even the name *Easy to Assemble* poked some not-so-subtle fun at furniture that was notorious for being *not* easy to assemble. I created fake IKEA training films introduced by celebrities and a fictional Swedish band called Sparhusen that only IKEA coworkers knew about.

We had a character, Coworker Lance Krapp, played by Michael Irpino, who desperately wants to be Swedish, so he wears this crazy synthetic blond wig. Well, "Lance" was so beloved by IKEA that he became an ambassador when we were shooting, greeting shoppers as they entered the store. No one found it at all unusual that this IKEA coworker was wearing a crazy blond wig. His name tag said COWORKER OF THE YEAR, and people just assumed that he was. Normally on a set you have what's called lock off, which means that the only people allowed are actors and crew. There's no talking; there's no moving when shooting a scene. However, we were working in a *live store* and were all wearing our IKEA outfits, so shoppers would watch us film, tell me they loved me in *Stir of Echoes*, and then, in the middle of shooting, ask, "Could you tell me where the towels are?" I once ran into a very high-profile casting director, and I had to convince him that I was not *really* working at IKEA! And I was pulling story lines from IKEA managers and coworkers. Magnus told me about a "team-building event" that was designed for coworkers to share ideas about work but turned into a singles mixer. It became an episode. All the while, I was being given more and more responsibility, and bigger budgets. We were the first Web series to go fully union. I was dealing with complex issues involving crews and budgets. We were releasing soundtracks with the band Sparhusen and working with Swedish bands, such as Marching Band. We set up distribution with companies such as Blip, My Damn Channel, and Dailymotion. I oversaw our Facebook and Twitter pages, and interacted with the IKEA fan sites. I learned all about social and transmedia strategies. It was like being paid to learn how to become a successful producer. I was finding skills I never knew I had, and I loved it.

Over the years we attracted a cornucopia of stars including Keanu Reeves, Tim Meadows, Cheri Oteri, David Henrie, Fred Willard, Patricia Heaton, Laraine Newman, Ricki Lake, Roger Bart, and Kate Micucci. We ran the production out of my little bungalow house in West Hollywood, sometimes shooting there as well. I was an actress playing a role of an IKEA Coworker of the Year who started being treated like an IKEA coworker. I was shooting a film in Scottsdale, Arizona, and my season four executive, Raymond Simanavicius, who took over when Magnus left, said to me, "Are you going to find time to visit the IKEA in Tempe?" I said, "Well, Raymond, I'm making a movie; I don't think so," and there was dead silence at the other end. It was the same joke. "You realize I'm an actress, right? I don't actually work for IKEA?"

We were getting ready to shoot the fourth season, and I was invited to IKEA's U.S. headquarters, in Conshohocken, Pennsylvania, to take part in an all-day think tank and work session with the heads of marketing. I really wanted to have an IKEA bike, because that was something all of the IKEA coworkers got, and for season four Raymond Simanavicius personally brought one to my house. Yes. It was in a box in fifty pieces, and yes, I had to put it together. We parodied the entire experience on *This Side Up*, which was our last season. This was the story line: An actress goes to work at IKEA because she wants to get out of show business but starts doing an Internet talk show called *This Side Is Up* on the floor of IKEA that becomes a big hit and forces her to go back into show business. We ended with Tom Arnold's staging an intervention to get me to leave IKEA. The hardest part for me was walking away from the safety and creative freedom. After five years, they had given me all the tools and the confidence I needed to be a filmmaker. The metaphor "easy to assemble" had also applied to me. As I worked on the show, the "life improvement" store and the "life improvement actress" meshed into a real-life story line of triumph, artistically, economically, and professionally.

I asked Fred Dubin recently, "Why on earth did you guys move forward with me?"

And he said, "I once watched you up at Sundance sing a Cat Stevens song and thought you might be a fun person to do business with." Thank you, "Wild World."

Then he said more seriously, "You thought like a marketer. My job was finding the right person to do something for the client that hadn't been done before." I think we did that, Fred. We did indeed.

Easy to Assemble was voted the number-two most influential idea created at MEC that year. *Advertising Age* awarded it one of the top five Best Branded Deals of 2010. We were featured in large profiles in the business section of *The New York Times* and in *The Wall Street Journal* as something now called branded entertainment. Featured in textbooks and case studies. We were nominated for seven Streamy Awards and won two, for Best Product Integration and Best Ensemble Cast. We won six Webby awards. I received an ITV Fest Innovator Award, the award for Best Online Performance from the Banff World TV Fest, and a 2010 NATPE Digital Luminary Award. By season four we had averaged more than 50 million views on sites such as Dailymotion, YouTube, My Damn Channel, KoldCast, Hulu, Blip, and many more. *Ad Age* called *Easy to Assemble* "the most successful branded show of all time." We even branched out, working with other brands such as Trident, JetBlue, Hasbro, and Nabisco, all of whom were featured or cross-promoted through the show.

You can't do a show about Sweden and not make reference to Ingmar Bergman. The truth is, I had never seen a Bergman movie except for *Fanny and Alexander*. I had seen Woody Allen's movies and knew he worshiped Bergman, but I didn't know why. I always felt his films would be intellectually over my head. Death plays a game of chess with a knight. What? I decided to immerse myself in Bergman, and his films became a revelation for me. You can think you've seen every film out there, and then you discover someone, and it changes you forever. I had always had ideas in my head that I thought were too far-out to actually ever write about. Bergman gave me the courage to express what I was feeling inside. He did not shy away from absolute, gut-wrenching grief, which is at the core of all comedy, anyway. *Through a Glass Darkly, Wild Strawberries,* and *The Seventh Seal* were about as close to the pain and joy of life as any other films I'd seen. Like Albert Brooks, he made films about the human condition, but he made them from deep inside. He went to the bone. He captured the living, breathing soul of a character. Watching Bergman movies dramatically changed my writing. I moved away from just jokes and funny situations to the inner life of *Illeanarama and* Illeana, who happened to be playing her. I had a vocabulary now. Simple and honest writing that felt more like I was sharing my intimate thoughts. The show took on a different tone, and it caught the notice of Robert Lloyd of the *Los Angeles Times* when he wrote, "*Easy to Assemble* is not a perfect thing . . . But I love it. It's honest and sweet and original and, especially this year, it's shot through with a feeling of ripening possibility that defines equally its main character and the person who made her."

Season three, *Finding North*, was a road trip through Sweden, so I reached out to a Swedish agency in Stockholm to see if they had any Swedish-speaking actors living in California. I got an email back from an agent there named Aleksandra Mandic. It turned out that she had represented Harriet Andersson–who had been the star of many Bergman films. She sent some wonderful Swedish actors my way, all of whom made it into *Easy to Assemble*. We were trying to work something out with a wonderful actress named Josephine Bornebusch, who was starring in a huge comedy series called *Solsidan*. A visa was too expensive and we couldn't make it work, but I stayed in touch with Aleksandra, telling her, you know, if anything ever comes up in Sweden please let me know, because I would love the opportunity of working there. That was in 2011. In 2013 I got an email from Aleksandra that Josephine Bornebusch was writing and starring in a show called *Welcome to Sweden* along with Greg Poehler, brother of Amy Poehler and a talented comedian. My dream came true when that summer I flew to Stockholm to shoot. Aside from working with Josephine and Greg, I would be acting opposite the great

Swedish actress Lena Olin. I felt like I was returning to my fictional homeland. All along the way there were these strange coincidences. I had filmed a season of *Easy to Assemble* called *Flying Solo*, in which all the IKEA coworkers were flying to Sweden for Midsummer and now I was really flying to Sweden. I arrived as if staged on the eve of Midsummer. I had written about being in the forests of Sweden, and now we were shooting *Welcome to Sweden* in the forest with Lena Olin. I felt that a trip to the mother ship—the original IKEA in Uppsala—was in order. My friend and *Welcome to Sweden* coworker Johan, who also strangely bore a resemblance to Coworker Lance, drove me. I wore my IKEA shirt, because I thought it would be fun to take pictures of me in it, and a shopper immediately came over to me and started asking me questions in Swedish! Johan began to explain to her that I did not actually work at the store and the customer didn't believe him.

During some time off, Aleksandra arranged for me to visit the Swedish Film Institute and tour its archives. To my delight, they showed me that I was in the Swedish archives—a part of Swedish film history. When *Cape Fear* came out, my scene with Robert De Niro was considered too violent to be shown in Sweden, so my scenes had been trimmed. They had the only uncensored print of *Cape Fear* along with some scathing letters from someone named Martin Scorsese denouncing censorship. I was told the debate over the movie led to the end of censorship of all films in Sweden. The other absolutely crazy coincidence was that in *Easy to Assemble* I had written the joke "I'm very big in Sweden . . . I played an ice-skater in *To Die For*." Well, it turns out what I wrote was actually true. *To Die For was* a big hit in Sweden, and everywhere I went I was complimented on my ice-skating skills and invited to come back in winter and go sea-skating.

They had a bigger surprise for me. They brought out Ingmar Bergman's private notebooks and journals and handwritten scripts for me to look at. I put on white cotton gloves to hold the script of *Fanny och Alexander*, and they told me, "We've only let one other actress do this, and that was Catherine Deneuve." Pretty good company, I thought. His journals were filled with drawings and photographs and personal stories. They reminded me of my own journals, which I began because of Roddy McDowall and which were filled with my own recollections and observations. We sat in the room while page after page was translated for me. It was as if Bergman himself were with us.

Season two of *Easy to Assemble* had a scene in which Illeana finds the long-lost journal of a fictional IKEA designer S. Erland Hussen, played by Ed Begley Jr. (Erland was named after Bergman's friend and collaborator Erland Josephson.) Hussen comes to her as a ghost, giving her words of inspiration, and they become the key to her journey of self-discovery. I was holding Ingmar Bergman's journal, holding his thoughts in my hands, and I couldn't help thinking of the line I had written, which he had inspired: "I made something with my hands that came from my heart." Ingmar Bergman wrote in his autobiography, *The Magic Lantern*, "As a child when I was shut in, I hunted out my torch, directed the beam of light at the wall and pretended I was at the cinema." I took his journal and held it to my heart, and said a silent thank you.

Epilogue

The 2014 TCM Classic Film Festival. I am about to introduce Richard Dreyfuss. He made me wear his hat. I am doing what I love—talking about movies with the folks who made me love them, like Richard.

In 2012 I began working with the Turner Classic Movies network. TCM and its prime-time host, Robert Osborne, have been a constant in my life since they first went on the air, in 1994. TCM has helped expand my knowledge of films and filmmakers, and it has kept me up all night with obscure Bette Davis movies. While I was going to school in New York City, there were many great revival houses where we'd go see classic movies. The Thalia, seen in Woody Allen's *Annie Hall*; the Metro, at Broadway and 99th Street; the Hollywood Twin, where I saw a double bill of *Mean Streets* and *Taxi Driver*; the Regency, where I saw *The Guardsman*—the only film in which Broadway greats Alfred Lunt and Lynn Fontanne starred together. When I saw *The Guardsman*, I was sitting in the fourth row with my roommate Steven and there was only one other person in the theater. When the lights came up, we saw that it was Kevin Kline. Those theaters are gone now, so the opportunity to learn from film legends has slipped away.

TCM does incredible work to fill that void. Robert's contributions as a film historian have been essential to the channel's success. His familiarity makes you feel as if you know him. Ben Mankiewicz, TCM's second host, with his own knowledge and wry sensibility, is equally adept at introducing films and interviewing legends. TCM remains a beacon, uplifting us when we are down, making us laugh, and reminding us of the commonality of movies.

The first time I was on TCM was to highlight the work of my grandfather. My role soon expanded into introducing films at the TCM Classic Film Festival. That relationship grew further, and I am proud to say that I am now part of the TCM family. In my work with TCM, I still have that same gee-whiz excitement I had as a kid doing movie reviews in high school. I get to talk about movies, write about movies, interview folks about movies. But there's more to it than that. I introduced a show on the *Friday Night Spotlight* segment called *Second Looks*, which focuses on overlooked films such as Elaine May's *A New Leaf* and Billy Wilder's *Ace in the Hole*. I like shining a light on overlooked films and undiscovered classics. The movies are an art form that I hold in high regard. Movie history is important to me, and because I also work in movies, I want to see them stay around for a while.

My work with TCM also gives me the opportunity to talk to actors I know professionally and personally whose work has inspired me. This combination of being both an insider and an outsider offers a unique perspective. It's like being in front of the camera and behind it at the same time, which is something I could have only dreamed about back in my black-and-white bedroom.

Not long after I started working for TCM, I was cast in a movie called *Max Rose*. All I knew about it was that it was going to star Jerry Lewis. When Daniel Noah, the writer-director, called me about it, I just said yes, I didn't even read the script. Of course, I had heard so many great stories about Jerry from Marty, and I knew about all the contributions he had made to *The King of Comedy*. I had seen all of Jerry's films, from the Dean Martin and Lewis comedies to the Lewis solo films. I saw many of those films for the first time on TCM back in the '90s. There was a musicality in Jerry's work that I loved—I'm thinking of *The Ladies Man* and *Cinderfella*. He also has a unique ability to combine total control and total lack of control, as he did in *The Bellboy*. And Jerry exemplifies the physical comedy of Chaplin in *The Nutty Professor*, but there is something else in Jerry's performance in that film, something I couldn't quite place.

Before filming started for *Max Rose*, Daniel Noah and Hadrian Belove hosted an evening for Jerry at everyone's favorite revival movie theater in L.A., Cinefamily, where I have spent many wonderful hours getting lost in the dark. There had been a lively Q&A session, and I threw out a question or two. Afterward, in the back garden of Cinefamily, I met Jerry. We posed for pictures, and I told him how excited I was to be in *Max Rose*. We began talking about *The King of Comedy*. He said some very nice things about Marty and Bob. Jerry treated me as if I were a peer more than an admiring fan, sharing insights about his films. He took my hand as we continued to speak. I felt as if I were meeting someone I had been searching for all my life. Someone who was so at ease with himself that he was giving me permission to do the same. We were in a roomful of people, but suddenly it felt like it was just the two of us. Jerry was holding my hand, and he said, "You must do everything with truth and love."

"My work," he said, "is an outpouring of love." I understood immediately what he meant. And that was it. That was that secret ingredient—*pathos*, my favorite word—underneath the broad comedy. It was an outpouring of love that I had felt.

I related that story when I introduced Jerry at the 2014 TCM Classic Film Festival. Being a part of TCM's tribute to him was one of the highlights of my career. Interviewing Jerry at the El Capitan Theatre before *The Nutty Professor* played to a packed house and being a part of his handprint-footprint ceremony in front of the world-famous Grauman's Chinese Theatre were thrilling events for me. It seemed unthinkable that Jerry Lewis's handprints and footprints were not *already* cast in cement in Hollywood for all to see. To know that I helped be a part of making it happen is quite a humbling experience for a movie-lover like me.

Through our conversations about films, Jerry and I became friends. I guess it was natural that he became a mentor to me. Who wouldn't take advice from Jerry Lewis? He's a genius. And I mean that sincerely. I was going to be shooting some introductions for an upcoming TCM *Second Looks* program, and Jerry helped me out with a story about Jack Benny and another one about Billy Wilder that I used in my intros. More and more he became involved with my relationship at TCM. I appreciated his guidance, because I was finally feeling like I was ready to come into my own. Jerry said to me, "By the time I'm done with you, you'll be confident!" He was right about that, and so many other things—for instance, that I should never wear the color green on camera! Remember, he said, "I dressed some of the great ladies of Hollywood." I did not argue with Mr. Lewis. Green was forever banished from my wardrobe.

One day out of the blue, Jerry asked me if I had a flashlight. I told him I didn't. He said, "Why don't you have a flashlight? You need to have a flashlight." So he gave me one.

It was a strangely significant present. When I was a child I used to have a recurring dream about leading a group of people through a dark forest. In the dream it was night. I was frightened, and lost, so I would cry out for help. Suddenly in the sky a large flashlight would appear. I would have to reach up and grab this gigantic flashlight, somehow holding it, guiding the people through the darkness of the forest to safety. Finally we would reach a meadow, and look up, and see the night sky full of stars.

I love my Jerry Lewis flashlight, and he's right, I did need it. Every time I use it I think of him. It's a symbol of what I do as an artist. To try to shine a light in the darkness. It's a role I am suited for. I'm like an usher in a vast movie theater using my Jerry Lewis flashlight, guiding people to their seats, talking about movies, showing them something they may not have seen. Shining a light on the importance of movies as an art form, from both sides of the camera lens. "My work," as Jerry taught me, "is an outpouring of love." Advice from the movie gods.

Acknowledgments

First and foremost, thank you to my family, especially my mom for her help with the photos, quotes, and stories. And see, I got Alan Bates in there! A special thank you to my dear friend Danny Ferrington. And a separate and equally deep thank you to John Carroll and to Michael Irpino. Thank you to my wonderful team at Flatiron. Take yourselves out to lunch! This entire experience has not only been fun; it's been a privilege. I will forever be grateful to Flatiron editorial director Colin Dickerman, whom I met over the phone, and it was love at first hearing. Thank you so much for listening and laughing. Thank you for shaping all these stories in such a cohesive way, for being an amazing cheerleader, and for always making it seem easy. Ha! I say to that. Mostly, thank you so much for believing in me. Whitney Frick, you came in at the finishing line with thoughtful and supportive comments that also happened to be great! Thank you also to James Melia, Diana Frost, Bob Ickes, publisher Bob Miller, associate publisher Liz Keenan, and publicity director Marlena Bittner.

I want to thank and give a big hug to my attorney, William Soble, for his everlasting faith in me. Thank you for your counsel, your constant composure, and your sense of humor—you need it representing me. A big thank you to Jason Allen Ashlock and Alan Goldsher, who got the ball rolling, and to Adam Chromy of Movable Type Management for having seen it through.

Thanks to Brentwood Management for their invaluable service and to the late, great Patti Dennis. I never could have accomplished what we accomplished on *Easy to Assemble* without Patti, and I miss her every day. Thank you to Julia Buchwald and Matt Luber for understanding every time I said, "I can't; I'm writing today."

Thank you to Paul Young and Maggie Haskins of Principato-Young Entertainment. Thanks to all the folks at IKEA for the opportunities you gave me.

Thanks so much to my TCM Family. We all love movies, and I love you. Robert Osborne, Ben Mankiewicz, Charles Tabesh, Jennifer Dorian, Sean Cameron, Gary Freedman, Genevieve McGillicuddy, and most of all, the doll of dolls, Darcy Heitrich. Your support has been invaluable. Thanks for the hours of talks and laughter and camaraderie. And to my special friend I.A.U.

I want to thank my #TCMParty gang for your support and friendship. Thanks for loving movies and for loving my comments about movies. Big thanks to Hadrian Belove and Cinefamily, the best revival house in L.A., home to many memorable moviegoing hours in the dark. Phil and Monica Rosenthal and the Sunday night movie gang: thanks for keeping me going with pizza and wine after long weekends of writing! Thank you to Ryan O'Neal/ Sleeping at Last, who provided the background music I listened to most days when I was writing and needed that extra cinematic fuel of inspiration. Thanks to the best listener of them all, Father Michael Cooper.

I am indebted to all of the friends and colleagues who have advised, helped, and encouraged:

Peter Avellino, Jeannie Berlin, Candi Cazau, Wayne Federman, Lee Kernis, Bryan Lourd, Ben Mankiewicz, Kliph Nesteroff, Patton Oswalt, Greg Poehler, and Carole Shashona.

Finally, a deep bow and tip of the hat to those who have given me opportunities to learn:

Allison Anders, Hal Ashby, Ingmar Bergman, Peter Bogdanovich, Marlon Brando, Albert Brooks, Glenn Gordon Caron, Robert De Niro, Brian De Palma, Matt Dillon, Richard Dreyfuss, John Frankenheimer, Jeff Goldblum, David Greene, Ethan Hawke, Buck Henry, Dennis Hopper, Olivia Hussey, Nastassja Kinski, Jerry Lewis, Joseph L. Mankiewicz, Frank Marshall, Lee Marvin, Elaine May, Paul Mazursky, Liza Minnelli, Roddy McDowall, Mike Nichols, Richard Pinter, Vanessa Redgrave, Steven Rogers, Martin Scorsese, Peter Sellers, Garry Shandling, John Patrick Shanley, Peggy Siegal, Sharon Stone, Jennifer Tilly, Gus Van Sant, Rudy Vallée, and James Woods.

If I have failed to remember everyone or give proper credit, it is not intentional and is based only on the author's growing forgetfulness. I'm sure I will wake up in six months and hurt myself.

Find me at @Illeanarama on Twitter

Colin . . . Can I rest now?

About the Author

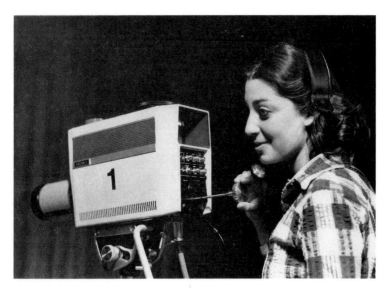

But what I really want to do is direct.